Listen to Leaders in
LAW

Listen to Leaders SERIES:

Listen to Leaders in BUSINESS
Listen to Leaders in LAW

IN PREPARATION:

Listen to Leaders in MEDICINE

Listen to Leaders in

LAW

Edited by

ALBERT LOVE and

JAMES SAXON CHILDERS

TUPPER AND LOVE / *Atlanta*

HOLT, RINEHART AND WINSTON / *New York · Chicago · San Francisco*

Designer: Ernst Reichl
85336–0213
Printed in the United States of America

Contents

Listen to Leaders in
LAW

How This Series of Books
Came About

ONE SUNDAY AFTERNOON, a group of college students were sitting around talking and the talk drifted to what they wanted to do with their lives, the careers they wanted. Some wanted to be lawyers, but admitted they didn't know much about the law. Some were interested in medicine. Others spoke of business. They kept saying they wished they could talk with the "big men" in law, in business, medicine, and other professions.

We two older men—who have turned out to be the editors of this series of books—happened to be hearing all this and we decided that here was where we came in. The students wanted to be in touch with the top men (and hundreds of thousands of other young people want this same privilege), and so we decided we would see what could be done about it.

Since they had asked for top men, and since we were already planning the whole series, we thought of top men to write for each volume—law, business, medicine, and all the other books that are to come later—and we began by one of us going to see Mr. Justice Felix Frankfurter. He thought it a great idea, wonderful for the young people of the nation to have these men tell their experiences, answer questions, and give the advice and guidance that is so much wanted. Here was *really* something worth while. But a book! He was continuously busy on the Supreme Court— for this was before his retirement—and he had no possible time to write a book or any part of a book.

This was the way it was with everyone. None of the men or women we visited for any of these books could take time from work as a Justice of the Supreme Court, or a lawyer with a demanding practice; as Chairman of the Board, or president, of some huge corporation; as a surgeon, a psychiatrist, or a doctor directing the work of some great hospital staff. Yet, each did take the time to write for young people, telling about business and the professions, telling how to make a career in whatever direction a young person wants to go.

In doing what they set out to do—to write their experiences and to advise and teach young people—these men and women have done a great deal more than that. As they related facts, both of the past and of the present, they unintentionally, unknowingly perhaps, disclosed their own philosophies of law, of medicine, business, and so on. They not only shared their experiences but also their beliefs in an open and uncommon way. The books, therefore, are far more than books for young people only. They are of professional use to lawyers, to businessmen, doctors; they are of personal use and value to anyone.

To thank these writers is impossible. What they have done puts them beyond the province of thanks and establishes only the obligation of the editors and of the readers.

Each of the writers has written his chapter in his own way, in his own style, and they have not all exchanged chapters to compare them. For this reason there are some diversities of thinking and writing; actually, at times, there are disagreements, some of them sharp and important, and this is because each writer is talking solely for himself, telling what he himself has learned, what he believes. Yet one will notice that a few basic beliefs are repeated—some of them repeated again and again—and this is because these beliefs are common to the various writers, fundamentals in the study and practice of law. It is finally true, however, that as one reads the book he recognizes that what they all say, when it is put together, can suggest to a person how to make a career, or to improve a career, and to build a worthwhile life for himself.

—A.L. and J.S.C.

_1_ The Law:

AN INTRODUCTION

BY FELIX FRANKFURTER

ASSOCIATE JUSTICE RETIRED

Supreme Court of the United States

FELIX FRANKFURTER

Born: 1882, Vienna, Austria

College of the City of New York: A.B., 1902
Harvard Law School: LL.B., 1906
University of Oxford: D.C.L., 1939
LL.D.: Amherst College, College of the City of New York, University of Chicago, Brandeis University, Harvard University

US Army: Major and Judge Advocate: ORC

Assistant District Attorney, Southern District of New York: 1906–1910
Law Officer, Bureau of Insular Affairs, War Department: 1911–14
Professor, Harvard Law School: 1914–39
Declined Governor Ely's nomination to Supreme Judicial Court of Massachusetts: 1932
Nominated Associate Justice of Supreme Court of the United States by President Roosevelt: January 5, 1939
    Confirmed by the Senate: January 17, 1939
    Took office: January 30, 1939
    Retired: August 28, 1962

1917–1918: Assistant to the Secretary of War, Secretary and Counsel to the President's Mediation Commission, Assistant to the Secretary of Labor
Chairman War Labor Policies Board: 1918
George Eastman Visiting Professor, Oxford University: 1933–34
Honorary Master of the Bench, Gray's Inn, London

Author: *The Case of Sacco and Vanzetti*
    The Business of the Supreme Court (With James M. Landis)
    The Labor Injunction (With Nathan Greene)
    The Public and Its Government
    The Commerce Clause under Marshall, Taney and Waite
    Mr. Justice Holmes and the Supreme Court
    Law and Politics
    Of Law and Men
Editor: *Cases Under the Interstate Commerce Act*
    Criminal Justice in Cleveland (With Roscoe Pound)
    Mr. Justice Holmes
    Cases on Federal Jurisdiction (With Wilber G. Katz)
    Cases on Administration Law (With J. Forrester Davison)
    Mr. Justice Brandeis
    Cases on Federal Jurisdiction (With Harry Shulman)

SOMETIME after I came to the Supreme Court, back in 1939, I noticed that even in formal conference the Chief Justice, Charles Evans Hughes, more than once addressed me as "Professor Frankfurter." So I knew that the aura—and, possibly, something of the manner, too—of my twenty-five years at the Harvard Law School, my quarter of a century as a teacher, still clung to me. In some kind of way, a pleasant way, I hoped, I was still a professor, and I was willing to be.

Even now, after almost a quarter of a century has passed, after all my years on the Supreme Court, I am not displeased to be reminded of my time as a teacher. When I was told of the plan of this book and of the older men talking to younger men—sharing experiences and reflections with them in the ways of the professions they might want to follow, in the ways of their working and living—I considered that a lot was being asked of me. I was being asked to be a teacher again; this time, a teacher to the young men of the nation.

This was a clear and a sure request, this talking to the young men who might intend embarking upon the practice of the law,

NOTE: Mr. Justice Frankfurter, before his retirement from the Supreme Court, spent some time in his study at his home talking to young people who are considering the law as a career. He talked as if they were actually in the room with him, answering their questions, teaching them, drawing on his years of experience to advise them. He took into account, too, those men and women who are already practicing law, and he spoke to them about its meaning and about their profession. His talk was tape-recorded and this chapter embodies substantially what he said.

3

and it charged my conscience as it seldom has been charged; but there was always the Court and the demands of the job. On more than one occasion I have said that even the greatest men who have sat on the Court—men like Holmes and Brandeis— could not fully meet the requirements of all the litigation that came before them. Therefore, if one is true to his job, he really has to give all that is in him to the work of the Court, for the Court is the comprehensive and all-absorbing responsibility of every Justice so long as he is a member of it.

This was my reasoning and my initial doubt about being a part of this book; but the idea, and the potential value of the idea, not only for those becoming lawyers, but for every other major calling that attracts the young, could not be put aside so easily; and so I was drawn into the orchestral scheme of the volume. Now that I am to play what part I can, it is a pleasure to take my place among the others, all so eminently qualified, as we begin our talking about the law and the possible place of young men in it.

The subject I have agreed to discuss is "The Law: An Introduction." My assignment is, of course, completely impossible to fulfill; but it is one of those things that one says "yes" to because he would like to accomplish it, because he wishes that he could. No man has a pen precise enough, and discriminating enough, to write a satisfying introduction to the law; but I can say something about the law, and tell, too, something to you young men who stand at the door of the law and look in, wondering, urged and yet hesitant about entering so demanding, so disciplined, a world.

The other day a young fellow said to me that he wanted a law degree because it had more uses than any other degree he could get. Furthermore, it was the shortest way to the top.

He was talking crudely, of course, but there is an important core of truth in what he said. He is approaching the end of his time in college. He is leaving that uncritical, loose, and what I call the dream-period of the young, and he has begun to feel the impact of imminent responsibility. He is on the edge of choosing his life work, determining whether to be a lawyer, doctor, go into business, into public relations—what shall he do? He is confronted not only with this compelling sense of responsibility but with the more exacting question of decision about himself: What shall I do with my life?

This brings us to the whole problem that confronts a young fellow—and I suspect that there are many of them—who does not have a clear, specific drive for anything. If a man has done nothing for years but study Gothic architecture and is enamored of it, if he is wrapped up completely in the uses of modern materials in building, he has clear sailing; he knows that he wants to be an architect. He is not debating with himself—he wants to be an architect. Some "inner light," as Socrates called it, something inside himself, guides him and makes him sure: I am going to be an architect.

I have known young men who had this same fierce drive for medicine. For them, it did not come into the realm, into the arena, of debate. Shall I become a journalist? Shall I be a soldier? No, they were doctors to begin with, and doubt and indecision never came into it.

Of course, now and then men do drift, and drift even after they are well along in life; but they are white crows. There is a famous case, Mr. Justice Miller, who went on the Supreme Court—he was named by Lincoln—after he had been practicing medicine for eighteen years. But he was always a debater, was concerned with public questions, was usually in the middle of things where he lived, and he quit medicine and studied law and became a Justice of the Supreme Court. He, though, and men like him are so rare that they do not furnish much basis for reflection or generalization.

Instead of these rarities, what of the young men who have only a vague idea of what they want to do, who are not sure and are probing? So often they turn to the law, and for the very reason that my young friend gave, that the law degree has more uses than any other. I have talked with young men who were in this dubious state of mind, this worrisome state of uncertainty, and they believed that going to law school might not be exactly what they wanted, but it could not possibly do any harm. Not only that, but affirmatively they knew that a training in law is related to anything else they might thereafter decide to do. Become a businessman? A journalist? A professional politician? Go into government? The opportunities for the use of the law are more versatile, provided one later decides to give up the direct practice of the law itself, than one could find in medicine, or architecture, or the priesthood, for example.

So that when the young man said that he wanted a law degree because it has more uses than any other, I think that he is rightly reflecting the position of the lawyer in American life. As a matter of fact, I have said the same thing, from time to time, and I believe it is true. Some young fellow graduates from law school and when next you hear of him he has become an important businessman, or he is in government and has become a public character. This is what I believe the young fellow, for all the crudeness of his phrasing, was thinking about; he was evaluating the training of the law not only for the law itself, but where else it might lead him. I suspect that he is only one of many young men who have looked at the law in this way, judging it for all its possibilities, and any young man who is dubious about his future course might take this into account.

Since the opportunities of life are shutting in, in a number of aspects—though they are opening up in others—and since these young men have to think about sustaining themselves and maintaining a family, I believe that they are thinking more concretely about what will give them a footing. They are thinking about themselves not in a sordid sense, not in any immediately material sense, but they are wondering—and one cannot blame them—about how they are going to get along, how they are going to make it.

This matter of shutting in is a tremendously important part of what confronts them and surrounds them. When I came out of the law school, back in 1906, one took a stable world for granted. Not only the global world, but his own world. One assumed that things were going to continue pretty much as they were, almost indefinitely; you did not question their continuance and you took them for granted, just as you take the air for granted until a room becomes fetid. So one assumed that if he went to law school and was reasonably competent, he came out and he could make a living; he could sustain himself with dignity and some comfort.

That was true half a century ago and it continued true until the Great Depression gave it a jolt, a serious jolt. The depression was survived, in a way; but the shutting in has continued until now it is intensified enormously by the overhanging threat of war, and the consequences of war in our time and under our conditions. Not only that, but owing to the general drawing in of opportunities, the expectancy of making a decent living and gaining enough material comforts of life for some beauty in it, the civilized benefits of monetary success, are now not taken for granted by the youth whom I see.

Money-making, certainly, is now more and more constricted—taxes take so much of it away—so that today the boys who go to college, and those who are about to come out of college, those who used to be the elite, as it were, meaning a small fraction of the whole, no longer can look forward, as their grandfathers did, with the belief that if all goes well they will be comfortable.

I was thinking one morning sometime ago, apropos of an editorial in the New York *Times*, about the judgeships to be filled. The editorial said that about a hundred names had been submitted by the various Congressmen and Senators. Now one hundred names is a lot of names for the difficult position of judge, and most of the names submitted probably did not indicate men who were adequately qualified. I am sure they were not.

Why, then, are there so many people going after federal judgeships today, as compared with the age, let us say, that brought forth men like Judge Learned Hand and his distinguished cousin Judge Augustus Hand? One reason is that there is security for a lifetime in such a judgeship; then, too, the salary may be a monetary magnet for many lawyers.

So this closing in—the economic environment, the social pressures, the uncertainties of the future—these are the things I have in mind when I say that, in some aspects, circumstances are shutting in upon the young as compared with the unthinking ways of my generation of young men, and for a good stretch thereafter.

The other thing, the opening up, and particularly the opening

up for the young lawyer, is partly due to these same circumstances, partly because of the uncertainties of our times, the
transforming aspects of our society; and partly because our society
now, more than ever, is a legal state in the sense that almost everything that takes place will sooner or later raise legal questions.
Government today so interpenetrates our lives that the need for
the lawyer is felt by everyone who is engaged in anything,
whether he owns a mine or has shipping interests; whether he is a
person who needs a license, or wishes to sell securities or sell apples, or is a businessman who is subject to the wide range of governmental controls. Whatever any man may be doing now, this
permeation of government into his affairs increases the need for
the kind of services that the lawyer fulfills in society.

But even though the need for the lawyer may be growing, and
the way opening up for him, one still hears the young fellows, in
their uncertainty, ask: How am I to know that the law is for me
and that I should school myself, and train myself, to be a lawyer?
How am I to be sure that this path is for me?

Well, this may be a little difficult for me to answer because I
do not remember when there was any doubt that I was to be a
lawyer. I can give no reason for this early certainty. Some of
my young friends, puzzled as they search themselves for their future, have asked if there were no moment of decision for me to
point to, no particular happening that influenced me, no nudge
that set me on my way as a lawyer.

There may have been, but by temperament I am a happy nature and I find a lot in a day to keep me busy; I do not take time
out to brood about why things have come about as they are or
why they are not otherwise. I have no idea what it was that made
me decide to be a lawyer, even though there was no tradition of
law in my family. It may have been some very shallow consideration that influenced me. Perhaps it was because I like to discuss.
Possibly because I was naturally drawn to public affairs. I can
give no exact reason and I am not disturbed by this; nor do I
think that young men should be disturbed by their wondering
about reasons and causes. I suspect that many a man, now highly

and comfortably placed in the law, could give no clear explanation for his having become a lawyer.

When I was teaching at Cambridge, I used to give the editors of the *Law Review* a dinner, year after year. On those occasions I made a point of asking them each year: Why did you come into the law? Why did you want to be a lawyer?

About half of them—and you must understand that the men on the *Law Review* are the top men at the Harvard Law School, having won that honor by their records—about half of these top men had come to the law school because they did not know what else to do next. They did not want to be morticians. They did not want to be agriculturists. They did not want to go to business school, though some of them had debated it. On the whole, they came by default. A number of them had come to the law school because their fathers were lawyers, and they had been pushed that way. Just about as many had come because their fathers were *not* lawyers. But what struck me, and what has left an abiding memory, is how few of them had that inner harmony of choice which took me to the law school.

Some men have a compulsion that molds them and determines all that they do, until they say: "I have blinders on." Such a man sees only one goal, has one idea, one purpose, and he is concerned with nothing else. He is implacable in pursuit of his one purpose. Few men, however, have this singleness of purpose, this complete shutting out of all else, and the young men whom I am addressing should not be troubled if this surety of direction, this total determination, is lacking in them. After all, they should realize that a man's life has a way of becoming clear.

Perhaps, though, as a kind of reassurance, they would like to know that some of the great men of the law have been uncertain about their course. Holmes, for instance, had a great struggle over this. He was drawn another way and it was not until seven or eight years after he had left the law school that he finally realized that a man could live greatly in the law as well as elsewhere. Before that he had thought of becoming—and this was also true of Learned Hand—a professional philosopher.

The young men who finally decide that their general direction
in life shall be in the law will find that entering the law school,
when their time comes, is a very serious matter. I found it so; in
fact, I was scared stiff. I was small and there were two huge fellows, one of them a football player, in my first class at the Harvard
Law School and they just shot their mouths off and talked glibly;
a question was hardly put before they had an answer, and I assumed that they would not have answered if they had not known.
This quick display of what I supposed was knowledge terrified
me and I began to feel fear and say to myself that this is too much
for me, I have to get out of here. My teachers, too, were so superlative that they added to my sense of awe and intensified my
feelings of inadequacy.

But somehow, after a while, this fear wore off, as fear has a way
of doing, and there at Harvard, amidst all the diversity and proliferation of talent and opportunity in the University apart from
the Law School, I lost my sense of awe and lived in excitement
and desire. I said that I would drink at all these various fountains
of stimulation. And so I went to all sorts of lectures, and I went to
hear music, and I looked at paintings, and I did this and that.

And then along came a test, an optional test given in the middle of the year, and I did not fail but I got a B instead of an A. I
had a roommate who was a year ahead of me and while he was
the most fertile-minded lawyer I ever knew, he did not have
my diversity of interests. He thought that I was going to get ship-
wrecked, disgrace him, disgrace the college from which we had
come, the College of the City of New York, and disgrace myself. He would preach at me, but I would say, "Well, I don't believe that the study of the law requires that I grub at it from
eight o'clock in the morning until midnight."

So I indulged myself. Then came this test and that was a jolt,
a frightening jolt, and I said to myself, "Maybe this demands
more attention than I have been giving it." So I worked harder
and at the end of my first year I was back at my home in New
York and the mail brought a letter. It came in August and I knew
that this was the report of my examinations and I remember how,
in a cowardly way—a passing streak of yellow—I dallied with the

letter. I did not dare open it because I had no sense of how I had done on the examinations and I feared the worst.

I just stood there holding it until finally I did open it and there were the marks—A in everything. I did not then know that I was first in the class. I was asked to join the *Law Review*, so I knew that I had done well; but it was not until after I graduated that I learned I was first for all three years at the Law School. I suspect it was just as well that I did not know at the time.

What happened to me, the way I stood there holding that envelope, leads to consideration of what I think is very important. What about the boy who holds the envelope, then slits it open and there are some B's on the record, and maybe a C or two? What about him, with a record that is unsatisfactory to him and no chance to get on the *Law Review?*

There are men who never get over the fact that they did not, as the phrase runs, "make the *Law Review.*" It is a disappointment that they carry with them, a blight on their lives. Strangely enough, this is true of some men even after they have had distinguished careers. Somehow or other they cannot absorb the fact that this one thing was denied them.

The law does not require intellectual eminence of everyone. It could not, in the nature of things. If it were demanded of all functionaries of the law to be intellectually powerful or distinguished, there would not be people enough to satisfy that requirement— there just would not be enough people to go around for law's needs.

The law is a sprawling network of means, habits, traditions, and practices, pursued by a large number of people, for dealing with the affairs of mankind within the areas in which those affairs call for peaceful arbitration according to rules and processes grounded on reason and justice. To fulfill all the requirements of the law, a good many more men than just those of the highest intellectual distinction are necessary. It is true, and it is fortunate, that a lot of people have the many kinds of qualities that the law requires. Most men who go to law school have these qualities.

I should place first—reliability. You as a lawyer will be dealing with other people's affairs, their most intimate, delicate and difficult affairs. The first requirement of a lawyer is reliability in the most extensive content of that word.

Discretion is necessary—the limitless capacity to keep your mouth shut, and not even by indirection or by mumbling to open it. I came across a sentence the other day in a book by Thomas Carlyle, and he says this so well: "Men are very porous, weighty secrets oozing out of them like quicksilver through clay jars." This tendency to loose talk is not the quality of a good lawyer.

Control of your mind is sharply needed. There must be the ability to maintain strict adherence to the subject immediately concerning you, an unwavering persistence in the continuity of your thinking.

Power of disinterested analysis will be required of you, the ability, in complete detachment, to understand a problem before reaching a result. Most people, when they are in trouble, or when they have a problem, are confused in stating it. It is like a ball of wool that is all ensnarled, and you will have to unsnarl it, laying it straight and plain before those who need the guidance of your analysis and advice.

No doubt certain sympathies will be needed, certain basic human qualities; but along with these must go a sure and careful detachment. A lawyer who gets mixed up with his client's affairs, who gets as hot as his client about somebody who had "done him wrong," will not be a good counselor.

All these qualities are needed in the law and the men who get B's, even those who get C's, may have them in as ample measure as the straight A men. Most of these men know, and are sensible and honest enough to say, "I cannot think as fast as John Smith. I cannot be as brilliant as John Jones. Nevertheless I have qualities that will serve me well as a lawyer, and that even in the narrowest professional sense will find a market, and possibly a very good market."

Some of these men, who have not great intellectual power, may have one quality that mankind is particularly seeking, and will gladly pay for—namely, judgment. Many a fellow who has not taken honors in "book larnin'" may still be a wise and useful man.

This whole matter of academic grades, and academic records,

the worship at the shrine of academic honors, has led me repeatedly to point to the B men, and even the C men, who have attained eminence in this country, and rightly so, at the bar, and certainly in public life. They show up the foolishness in thinking that one has to be a brilliant fellow in order to be a successful, a useful and esteemed lawyer. Just because a man is not intellectually very gifted is no reason to suppose that he is not very good.

Proper regard, just respect, for men of lesser grades does not, even in the slightest, lessen the significance of the academic A. The man who achieves high academic record has shown that in a fair contest, in the unyielding competition of the law school, he is more gifted, or perhaps his gifts have developed earlier, than another. What is true about marks and rank at law school can be put in the same way that somebody said about philosophy: "All philosophies are true insofar as they assert, and false insofar as they deny." The fellow who gets an A *proves* something. The fellow who gets a C does not *disprove* anything except that in the examinations he did not get a high mark. But the man who sinks his mind and his soul into his tasks at the law school and receives an A proves that at this time of his development he is making himself a master of his craft. It is not farfetched to consider this at least as a possible indication of the future.

But making himself a master of his craft is not enough. A young man going into the law needs to broaden his interests beyond those of the immediate demands of the law. I have spoken of reading books, of listening to music, of looking at paintings, and I have been asked, by a surprising number of people: What has this to do with the law?

Holmes said that "the law is not the place for the artist or the poet. The law is the calling of thinkers." Men who go into the law are not likely to be poets or artists. They do not see with the mind's eye the things in nature which they then put on canvas. The imaginative faculty is not the predominant force in most men who are drawn to the law. They reason and deal with the logical process—from A, B follows, etc.

But lawyers are counselors, advising and dealing with human beings, their trials and tribulations, the vicissitudes and complexities in the lives of Tom, Dick, and Harry. They deal with the problems of businessmen, of labor unions, fraternal organizations and churches. All this involves an understanding of the other fellow, the ability to get people out of the snarls into which people get. To do this, a lawyer must have a capacity to realize the needs, desires, and best interests of others. This ability to get in under the other fellow's skin is also a faculty of the imagination.

But imagination, as I have said, is not natively a quality of lawyers. They do not live a fantasy life or think up fictional things, and, for them, there is need for a vicarious way to stimulate their imaginative faculties. A judge who reads Yeats with pleasure, or who goes to the National Gallery once a month and takes himself out of the groove of the world in which he is living, is likely to be less wooden than if he just walks the treadmill of the law. What I am saying is not directed to the man himself, but to his development, experience and enrichment as a human being— what I am saying relates directly to the lawyer equipping himself to be a better lawyer.

How does this equip him? The way in which it plays a part in his life as a lawyer, how it bears on professionally counseling other men, I have already indicated. Its influence in court should also be understood. Any judge worthy of his place has disciplined himself to his task, and, by his own disinterestedness and detachment, safeguards himself against personal considerations. But judges are human beings, and I can assure you that to hear a man of learning and breadth of culture argue a case is a very different thing from listening to some other man dully recite the facts and dully expound the law. Art in exposition, law woven into the tapestry of culture, may not decide a case, but is bound to have impact.

Some time ago a twelve-year-old boy wrote to me that he was "interested in going into law as a career" and asked my advice about "some ways to start preparing himself while still a junior in high school." I wrote him a letter which I will quote here, letting it stand not only for this very young boy but also for his elders:

"My dear Paul: No one can be a truly competent lawyer unless he is a cultivated man. If I were you, I would forget all about any technical preparation for the law. The best way to prepare for the law is to come to the study of the law as a well-read person. Thus alone can one acquire the capacity to use the English language on paper and in speech and with the habits of clear thinking which only a truly liberal education can give.

"No less important for a lawyer is the cultivation of the imaginative faculties by reading poetry, seeing great paintings, in the original or in easily available reproductions, and listening to great music. Stock your mind with the deposit of much good reading, and widen and deepen your feelings by experiencing vicariously as much as possible the wonderful mysteries of the universe, and forget all about your future career."

What, now, of the law itself that awaits all the young men who may be considering it as their future? What of the meaning of the law?

The law, I would say, is not fixed, is not a system, closed within itself forever and forever, world without end. The law is an instrument of reason and justice; morality infuses the law to no small degree, and morals are not static. What we think and deeply feel today is not what we thought and felt fifty years ago or what men will think and feel fifty years hence. No human brain has ever been equal to imagining all the situations that would rise in the unending future and that could be taken care of by *lex scripta*, by the law written down, or evolved by the judicial process, immutable and forever. There is the changing conscience of society, the changing consensus of opinion, that must be taken into account, and that *is* taken into account in the exciting and lively unfolding of law.

The thumbscrew has been outlawed for some three hundred years. Just so, the third degree, the extortion of a confession by violence, is now being forced out of use. The law has become more and more sensitive to the kind of pressure that can be put on a person before he caves in, and the courts, acting as the instrument of the increasing public moral consciousness, are increasingly ruling against it, putting it with the thumbscrew as a thing unworthy of man. The courts in this, as in so much else, represent and reflect a deep and endless stream of history.

And what of the Constitution? Well, the Constitution is a vessel out of which meaning is drawn and into which meaning is poured. The Constitution says, "No state shall deprive any person of life, liberty, or property without due process of law." But it does not tell us what "due process of law" is. Indeed, the framers of the Constitution purposefully used these big and undefined terms—terms that are largely indefinable—in order not to fetter the future but to give scope for the future. This, I think, is in many ways the greatest thing that the framers of the Constitution did. They left room for the future.

It is clear and certain that the future includes not only the law and the courts, but the young men who shall come into the law, these young men to whom I have been talking and who, in their time, will be called upon to interpret the stream of history and to contribute to it. May they see it clearly and speak it well!

_2_ *Law School–*

AND YOUR STUDY
OF LAW

BY ERWIN N. GRISWOLD

DEAN OF THE LAW SCHOOL

Harvard University

ERWIN N. GRISWOLD

Born: 1904, East Cleveland, Ohio

Oberlin college: A.B., 1925
   A. M., 1925
Harvard Law School: LL.B., 1928
   S.J.D., 1929
LL.D.: University of British Columbia, Brown University, University of Sidney, Dalhousie University, Harvard University, University of Melbourne, Amherst College, Columbia University, University of Richmond, Brandeis University, Northwestern University, University of Michigan, Notre Dame University, Allegheny College, University of Toronto
L.H.D.: Case Institute of Technology, Tufts College
D.C.L.: University of Western Ontario

Admitted to Ohio Bar: 1929
Admitted to Massachusetts Bar: 1935
Practiced with Griswold, Green, Palmer & Hadden, Cleveland: 1929
Attorney in office of Solicitor General and Special Assistant to the Attorney General, Washington: 1929–34
Harvard University Law School:
   Assistant Professor of Law: 1934–35
   Professor of Law: 1935–46
   Dean and Charles Stebbins Fairchild Professor of Law: 1946–50
   Dean and Langdell Professor of Law: 1950—

Alien Enemy Hearing Board for Massachusetts: 1941–45
Consulting Expert United States Treasury Department: 1942
Harvard Law Review Association
President, Association of American Law Schools: 1957–58
American Law Institute
American Philosophical Society
Vice-president, American Academy Arts and Sciences: 1946–48
Trustee: Oberlin College
   Bradford Junior College: 1942–1948
   Teachers Insurance and Annuity Association: 1942–46

Author:
   Spendthrift Trusts
   Cases on Federal Taxation
   Cases on Conflict of Law (with others)
   The Fifth Amendment Today
General editor: American Case Book Series

THE LAW is an ancient profession, with a long history and high traditions. In the United States, our legal system is largely derived from that of England, and is known as "the common law." As long ago as the fourteenth century, the legal profession began to appear in England as a specially trained and organized group of persons prepared to represent suitors before the courts and to give legal advice. In the course of time the legal profession in England became rather highly organized and stratified. One group of lawyers there does what we would call office work; they are known as solicitors. Another group obtained the sole right of audience in the superior courts. These are known as barristers. One becomes a barrister by becoming a member of one of the Inns of Court (Gray's Inn, Inner Temple, Lincoln's Inn, and Middle Temple). When an applicant becomes a member of an Inn, he is called by the senior barristers to a barrier or bar in the great hall of his Inn. This is known as being "called to the bar." This is the origin of the phrase "member of the bar," which is applied generally to lawyers in the United States.

The division of function is not followed anywhere in the United States, though some lawyers specialize by choice, being office lawyers or counselors, on the one hand, or trial lawyers on the other. But most lawyers perform at least some of the functions in both fields. Admission of lawyers to practice in the United States is under the control of the Supreme Courts of the several states. A person is admitted in the state in which he lives, but this does not ordinarily serve to qualify him to practice in any other states. Within his own state, however, he is free to perform any of the functions of a lawyer. The wide variety of opportunities available is one of the attractions of the legal profession.

The lawyer's work is varied. Whether he is in or out of court, he is a principal factor in the operation of our social and economic system and in the administration of justice. Much that he does is for the purpose of helping people, individually and collectively. Although the more dramatic aspect of the work done by lawyers is that done in the courtroom—and many lawyers have won fame and fortune and satisfaction as trial lawyers—much of the work done by lawyers today is less spectacular, but may be equally useful. Lawyers are the negotiators, the adjusters, the advisers, the draftsmen, the organizers, the planners, the peacemakers, in many business and personal transactions. Much of the work of lawyers is in preventing controversy.

Both by tradition and in fact the lawyer is a minister of justice. When a lawyer is admitted to the bar, he becomes an "officer of the court." This means that he remains subject to the control of the courts, and can be disciplined or disbarred if he misbehaves in any aspect of his practice. But the lawyer's license also carries with it an affirmative responsibility to aid in the administration of justice. Lawyers vindicate the rights of their clients. They protect the rights of their clients when they are wrongfully assailed. Every defendant against whom a criminal charge is made is entitled to proper legal representation. The protection of civil liberties owes much to the courageous conduct of lawyers and judges. Lawyers have a great responsibility to make our legal system work effectively. They play a large part in the development and protection of free institutions. In a very real sense, it may be said that one of the reasons democracy has flourished in England and America is that these countries have had a strong and independent bar.

The law is a public profession. The lawyer holds himself out to the public as especially qualified to advise on legal matters; and he has a special responsibility not only to his clients and the courts, but to the public generally. The lawyer must devote himself to his clients' interests, but he should also maintain his independence, his impartiality, and his perspective. He should never forget the public interest in formulating his advice to his clients. No loyalty to a client requires a lawyer to engage in unethical practices; and the ethics of the bar are a proud part of its heritage. Lawyers as a class have a great public influence; they must constantly strive to see that this is deserved.

One more thing may well be said at the beginning. The life of the lawyer is not likely to be an easy one. The demands on him are great and are likely to be rather constant, and it can almost never be said that he has done all that can be done on the matters which are entrusted to his responsibility. Lawyers as a group work very hard, and put in long hours. The work is often exciting and satisfying, but a lawyer frequently carries heavy responsibility and can claim little of the day's time as his own. If you are looking for a quiet, easy life, you should probably stay away from the law. If you are willing to work long and hard, at tasks which require much of mind and energy, a legal career may be a very rewarding and satisfying one.

The law is a learned profession. Ability of a high order is required if one is to meet his responsibilities in this profession. This road should not be entered upon lightly, and entry into the legal profession can be attained only by persons of substantial qualifications, and after a long period of thorough study.

It is clear, though, that there is no one particular type of person who should study law, to the exclusion of all others. There are many types of lawyer, and many sorts of opportunity in the legal field. In some areas it may be an advantage to be something of an extrovert. But there are, too, opportunities in many relatively quiet areas of the law. If a person craves a completely placid career, he probably should not think of being a lawyer, for any lawyer is bound to be confronted with problems, and to be looked to for advice and guidance, often in times of personal or business stress. Indeed, the lawyer is one of the chief problem solvers in our society. He is also a negotiator and an advocate; that is, in either case, a persuader. He is the man who stands up for people's rights and seeks to have them vindicated, often against vigorous opposition. Day in and day out, a lawyer is a man who deals with people. If you do not enjoy working with people, and with their problems, if you do not like working with situations and ideas, it seems very likely that you would not be happy in spending a lifetime with the law. On the other hand, if you do like working with people, even difficult people, with sympathy and understanding, if you are interested in social and economic and business problems, if you enjoy "working things out," finding ways to bring conflicting factions into harmony and working agreement, then the law offers manifold opportunities for interesting work and for service to society.

There was a time in our history when it was thought that anyone could be a lawyer, and when people more or less gravitated into the law because it was thought to be a field where almost anyone could "live by his wits." This is sometimes referred to as the "Abraham Lincoln" view of the lawyer. There are, however, very few Abraham Lincolns; and the law has become vastly more complex since his time. It is doubtful whether even Abraham Lincoln could have made his way in the law today with the almost complete lack of training available to him. At the present time legal training requires a long period of sustained hard work, and should not be undertaken except by those who are willing to make the substantial investment of time and energy which is required. A man who is to become a lawyer should have a certain amount of iron in his soul. He need not by any means be hard, or hard driving; and he should not be cold or indifferent to his fellow men. But he must be willing to work. Indeed, he should like to work, and to work with things of the mind and spirit, in the realm of words and of ideas. It will help if he has a certain amount of fire in his soul, too. It is doubtless not necessary that one have a "call" to the law, as to the priesthood or ministry. But it is desirable that he should have a measurable amount of zeal for his fellow men, and a genuine desire to be a part of the process by which society lives and operates.

Having said this, it should be said again that there is no one type which is especially qualified for the practice of the law. There is room in the law for the quiet person, as well as for the more flamboyant one. There is room for the scholar and the thoughtful user of words. There is room for the person who is quick on his feet or with his tongue. There is room, too, for the person who works best in his office or in the library. All aspects of the law today, though, require both training and ability. If a person is a poor student, if he is unable to meet deadlines, if he fades out in a crisis, if he is unhappy in any sort of a competitive situation, he should probably stay away from the law as a career.

It may be helpful if this is put in more academic terms. Thus, it may be suggested that if you are a student who is going to have trouble getting into a good law school, and trouble maintaining your standing there as a student, you should not start down this road. Similarly, even though you may be able to get through a law school, if you are going to have difficulty in passing the bar examination, it seems doubtful that you should begin legal studies, except possibly as a deliberately chosen means of training for a business or other career. If you can get through law school and pass the bar examination without difficulty, if you are intellectually and emotionally qualified for a probably strenuous career in a learned profession, then there is every reason why you should study law, and the opportunities available to you through the legal profession may well be considerable.

This is all very well, you say, but how can I tell in advance whether I will be able to do all right in law school, and then pass the bar examination? Of course, there is no clear answer. Your record in college is one basis for decision. This will depend, in appreciable part, on the standards of the college which you attend. If the college is one which is hard to get into, and which exercises a considerable degree of selectivity in admitting its students, you may well give serious thought to the study of law if you get through your college course, perhaps not at the very bottom of the class, but with at least a reasonable margin. On the other hand, if your college is one which has less stringent requirements for admission, and perhaps lower standards for staying in the class, then you should probably not think of studying law unless you are fairly well up in the class, at least close to the middle, or above. There is also another guide, through the Law School Admission Test, a special aptitude test devised for the law schools, and administered by the Educational Testing Service of Princeton, New Jersey. If your score on that test is rather low, say, below 400, it can probably be said that it would be wise for you not to study law. With such a background, the chance of your having a successful and satisfying legal career may not be sufficient to warrant your embarking on the long route through law school.

There is one more point which should be mentioned, on the affirmative side of the picture. It is often hard for young people to know and understand the nature of a lawyer's work; and thus many students necessarily come to law school without a clear picture of where the road leads. Many students have embarked on the study of law who were far from sure that they wanted to be lawyers when they went to law school. Yet, this has worked out well in a high proportion of cases. This suggests that one need not be *convinced* that law is for him before deciding to try it. It may also be said that many students decide to study law late in their college careers, rather than early. Indeed, many students make the decision even after their graduation from college. This, too, works out well when the student has the proper intellectual equipment and a good background. Thus, it is clear that law need not be part of a long-range career plan, formulated before college. It is often a field which shows its attraction late, rather than early in the college years. It is a field where real enthusiasm sometimes develops only after the student has experienced a considerable period of actual law study.

The law is a field which should not be undertaken on a permanent basis unless you like it. But, in many cases, the only way to find out whether you like it is to try it in law school. Many people find this a successful adventure.

How, then, does one prepare to study law?

Requirements for admission to practice law—under control of the Supreme Courts of the various states, as I have said—vary from state to state, but there is considerable uniformity. Almost without exception, they require at least three years of college education; and in a great many states the requirement now is a college degree after four years of college education before entering on the study of law.

Thus the first answer to the question: "How does one prepare to study law?" is that one first goes to college.

What college? This does not make much difference, except that it should be a good college, and a full-time day course if that is at all possible. There are hundreds of colleges in this country, and practically all of them have prepared one or more persons for law study. Some colleges are better than others, but there is no pattern about this. Some of the bigger universities, private and state, can be counted on as good places for pre-legal education. But sound pre-legal education can also be obtained at a liberal arts college, or at a local or municipal college or university, if the course there is a thorough one with high standards, and is conscientiously and earnestly followed. Some institutions are better than others, and it is desirable to make careful inquiry from persons who know about educational institutions—from high-school principals or guidance officers, for example, or from friends who are themselves lawyers, or who have general acquaintance with educational standards.

Going to a "big name" college is not necessary. The prestige of the college attended usually has little bearing on gaining admission to a law school. The important matter is the caliber of the work offered by the college or university, and especially the quality of the work done by the student there.

Law schools want their graduates to become educated and learned lawyers in the best tradition of their learned profession. It is clear that the foundation of liberal culture must usually be laid in college and before. Law schools quite generally take into account the nature of the student's college work as well as the grades achieved.

It is ordinarily undesirable to recommend particular courses as preparatory for work in law school, and most law schools do not undertake to prescribe any specific courses as prerequisites for law training. There is a large variation in both the quality and the content of courses that go under similar titles in various colleges. Moreover, in college it is often more important to take work with outstanding faculty members, no matter what their field may be.

One thing on which law schools are agreed is the importance of acquiring an ability to use the English language. Over and over again, law schools have complained that many of their students are unable to think accurately because they cannot express themselves accurately. In giving up classical education, our colleges have sacrificed some of the discipline that made for precision in the choice of words and a resulting precision in the handling of ideas. Some work in college to meet those ends is most desirable. This means something more than the basic freshman English composition course. A course in essay writing may be offered in the junior or senior year, which may be very useful for this purpose. And other courses involving the writing of a number of papers may give useful experience and training in the writing of effective English. Courses in English literature, when well taught, can also be valuable in showing the variety and richness of language, and the possibilities in the effective use of words.

It is also important that the student who is thinking of coming to law school should learn something about the history of our civilization. This can hardly be done merely by taking courses in history, because a knowledge of the progress of our thought and our ideas is as important as a knowledge of events of the past. Here, too, English literature can play an important part in training; and philosophy has an equal claim with literature and with history in this field. Some colleges have good courses in English constitutional history, and these can provide excellent background for legal training.

The student in college should also obtain some real facility to deal with abstract ideas. Courses in mathematics tend to develop this. They have the qualities of being precise, of being closely articulated, and of being an entering wedge to techniques which are, in their essence, symbolical logic, whether or not they go under that name. Similar benefits may be derived from courses, particularly from advanced courses, in the exact sciences, such as chemistry and physics.

We stand at the edge of an era during which there will be

great scientific and technological advances. Tomorrow's lawyers will need an understanding of the possibilities and limitations of science and scientific methods. More than just an elementary course is needed. It is well to pursue some field of science far enough to see the point where it ceases to be purely scientific. Similarly, it is desirable for a student to know something of methods in the field of social science by way of contrast to those employed in the natural sciences. It is also desirable that the student should have some training which leads him back to the original sources in some field, so that by the time he reaches the professional school he will have lost complete reverence for the printed page. The lawyer should always have an inquiring mind. He should always ask: "Why?" "Is this the complete answer?" "Are there no other materials bearing on this matter?" "Is there anything else that can be done?" A substantial and thorough piece of original research, such as is sometimes done in connection with an advanced college seminar or required in an honors program, can be an excellent vehicle for training and developing the qualities of probing and persistence which are useful to a law student and to a lawyer.

Generally speaking, law schools are agreed that students in college should avoid courses in "law" which are offered in some colleges to anticipate or supplement their later training. Such college courses in law may be very valuable for college students who do not go to law school. But the prospective law student will usually do better to take some other work. He will have plenty of opportunity to immerse himself in law when he reaches law school. The important thing for him to do in his undergraduate training is to take courses and develop interests that he will not normally take or acquire in his professional training.

Many law schools prefer a broadly liberal college education to one which is narrowly specialized. They recognize with favor a showing of thorough learning in some wide cultural field of a student's choice, such as history, economics, government, philosophy, mathematics, science, literature, or the classics. Many law schools do not favor concentration on courses given as vocational training, such as business administration, accounting, engineering, speech, drama, music, and journalism. Undergraduate studies of this type are not regarded generally as being of themselves the best preparatory training for the legal profession. It is recognized, however, that some schools of business administration and engineering plan their programs with attention to educational breadth, and well-planned courses at such schools may have enough general educational content to provide appropriate background for legal training.

In many colleges, faculty members act as advisers in helping the student plan his course of study. These advisers can be very helpful, both because of their general background, and because of their knowledge of the offerings available in the particular college. Nevertheless, the prospective law student should always be sure that his adviser is fully qualified to advise with respect to pre-legal studies. The adviser need not be himself a lawyer to have such qualification, but he should have real familiarity with the essential nature of law study, and with the standards and expectations of law schools. More than one young man has entered a large university, and, at the very start of his academic career, has gone to his adviser. The adviser asks him what he thinks he wants to do, and he replies, "Well, I sort of thought I might like to be a lawyer." The adviser has then told him, "The best way to get ready for law school, is to start by taking the business course."

Before the young man knows it, he is registered in the College of Business Administration, where he takes a succession of specialized courses, mostly with small intellectual content. These courses may be useful for business training, but, with few exceptions, they fail to meet the basic needs of pre-legal education. By the time the student finds out that this is so, he is already knocking on the door of a law school. Even if he obtains admission to law school, he is likely to carry with him a handicap in background that will add to the difficulty of his law study, and may limit his effectiveness in law practice. The time to plan a sound pre-legal course, of adequate breadth and true depth, is at the beginning of the college program.

College should be a time for broadening and deepening and

stretching the student's mind. His work there should not be diffuse and scattered. There should be a reasonable amount of specialization in it, even some rather intense specialization, if that can be worked out. But the student in college should learn about society and mankind, in some of their many aspects. He should have a truly humane and liberal education, as a background for highly specialized professional studies. He is entering upon a learned profession, and the process of learning should be carried out during the college years, as well as at the professional school.

In short, there are no required courses to be taken in college as a prerequisite for a legal education. Few, if any, law schools make such requirements. But most law schools are concerned that their applicants should be truly educated men, who have had a substantial opportunity to glimpse the world of learning, and who are ready, on the basis of that experience, to undertake the professional portion of their training.

As to where one should study law, there are in the United States about 150 law schools. Of these, more than 130 have been approved by the American Bar Association; and about 110 meet the slightly higher standards of the Association of American Law Schools. It can fairly and reasonably be said, it would seem, that a person should not, if it is at all possible to do otherwise, undertake to study law except at one of the schools which is a member of the Association of American Law Schools. This leaves a large choice, both as to geography and as to type of school.

In the United States, law may be studied on a "full-time" basis, in which case the law course extends over a period of three years; or it may be studied on a "part-time" basis, in which case the course requires at least four years. Part-time law study is usually done in the evening, so that the student may engage in other employment in the daytime. Some schools have both day and evening divisions. A few schools operate in the evening only. Many other schools have day divisions only, and operate on a "full-time" basis.

Many able and successful lawyers are graduates of part-time courses, and there are a number of schools where a person can get a good legal education on a part-time basis. Furthermore, this much can be clearly said: a part-time legal education at a good school, with high standards, is better than full-time legal education at a school which operates with low standards. Some so-called full-time law schools actually have classes only in the morning hours for five days a week, and the great majority of their students have outside employment in the afternoon and often in the evening. Such a school is "full-time" in name only, and should be avoided. It is not likely to provide a sound and adequate legal education.

A student who believes he must go to a part-time school might well make some inquiries and investigations before he makes his final decision. The number and variety of law schools today is such that a high proportion of students can attend an excellent full-time law school on a full-time basis, if they are determined to do so. Many law schools are attached to state universities, others to city universities, and at these schools the tuition charge is low, providing what, in effect, amounts to a general scholarship for all students. Still other schools are connected with "private" institutions, which receive little or no public support; but they, too, have been able to provide increasing amounts of aid for students, in part through scholarships, and in part through loans.

A student who is sure that he wants to study law should not hesitate to take loans for the purpose of financing his legal education. These loans may come from family sources, from banks, or from the school which the student decides to attend. Such loans should, of course, be taken seriously; but they can be regarded as a capital investment. The student's education will provide him with the means of making a livelihood over many years to come, and long experience shows that the loans incurred can almost always be paid off in a reasonable time after graduation, without undue burden on the young lawyer or his family.

Assuming then that through savings, family support, scholarships, or loans, the student is able to finance his legal education, he has a wide choice of schools where he may study. Some people feel that it is desirable to study law in the community where one expects to practice. It is felt that the acquaintances made at law school will be useful in later practice; it is also felt that there may be an advantage in close study of the peculiarities of the local law of the state where the student thinks he will be practicing. Although such advice is often given, the importance of these points can easily be exaggerated. A considerable proportion of the lawyers in any community have studied their law elsewhere, and have not suffered any handicap from that fact. Indeed, there may be an appreciable advantage from making acquaintances among students from other areas; and there may, too, be considerable educational advantage in studying with a group of students, with varying educational backgrounds, who come from many different parts of the country. In many cases a good legal education can be obtained locally; but the argument that one *should* study law in his own community will not stand the test of analysis or of experience.

What kind of law school, then, should the student go to? This will depend upon a number of factors: the student himself, his background, his ability, his estimate of his own prospects—and on this he should be realistic, and not unduly modest. Should it be a large school or a small one? The larger school is likely to have greater resources, a larger and more varied faculty, a more diversified curriculum, and a possibly more stimulating student body. The smaller school may provide more contact between faculty and students, and more personal attention to the student and his needs. The importance of these qualities, though, may easily be overemphasized. The student in law school is just one stage removed from his active career, where he will be acting considerably on his own responsibility. If the law school he attends is one which expects him to accept responsibility for obtaining his legal education, this itself may be an important element in the soundness of his legal training.

It is clear that it is not necessary to go to a "name" law school in order to get a good legal education. On the other hand, if a student is qualified to obtain admission to one of the better-known schools—which usually have many more applicants than they can admit—he should think very seriously about going there. In such a school, he will meet a highly qualified and well-diversified student body, which will help to set the tone for a high standard of legal education. He will find an excellent faculty and fine library facilities. He will find a long tradition of excellence, which will provide a stimulating setting for his work.

There are at least twenty law schools in the United States which provide what may fairly be called a first-class legal education; and there are perhaps thirty more which are very close to the first category. Thus, the prospective law student has a wide range of choice, enabling him to take into account such personal, financial, geographical, and other factors, as he may think desirable and appropriate, and still go to an excellent school where he can get a sound legal education. But the student should not settle for anything less than the best he thinks he can attain.

A few students may have the opportunity to study law in another country, and may wonder whether this can be adequate preparation for admission to the bar in the United States. Generally speaking, it is clear that study of law in a country which does not follow the "common law" derived from England will not take the place, in any part, of an American legal education. Thus, study in France, Germany, Italy, Spain, Mexico, Japan, or other countries outside the common-law tradition, while valuable in itself, will not minimize the time required for an American legal education. On the other hand, study in Canada will usually be recognized to some extent by American law schools, and by American bar-examination authorities.

The question most frequently arises with respect to study in England, particularly by students who have been awarded Rhodes scholarships, or similar scholarships providing opportunity for study at an English university. Such a scholarship opportunity should be carefully considered. It may well be, though, that it should be utilized for study in some other field, even if the student does expect eventually to become a lawyer. English legal education is, in many respects, quite different from American legal education. In the first place, legal education in England is at the undergraduate level; while legal education in the United States is essentially graduate study. In the second place, legal education in England is highly theoretical, being based largely on such subjects as Roman law, legal history, and jurisprudence. These are fine subjects for background in an American law school, but they are rather different from the subject matter of most of the courses in American law schools.

As a result, many American law schools will give one year's credit for two years of law study at an English university. This does not express any disapproval of the work done at the English universities, but is merely the result of an effort to evaluate the work done there in terms of the type of instruction at the American law school. In this situation, the American student would be well advised to consider carefully whether, even though he attends the English university, he should not study there some other subject than law—literature, science, philosophy, economics, for example—and then return to the United States and take here the regular three-year course in an American law school. This requires a substantial period of time, but it may also provide a truly superlative education.

Something of the flavor of legal education at most law schools can be had from a story which is told about a famous professor of a generation ago. At his opening first year class, he said, in his rasping voice, "Young gentlemen, if your *moral* character has not been nourished by your parents, the kindergarten, public school, and college, there is little the law school can do for it this late in the day. What this law school is concerned with is your *mental* character, training a mind that refuses to do a sloppy piece of work."

Law schools have always emphasized qualities of the mind. Studying law is largely an intellectual experience. With this in mind, it is helpful, in understanding the methods and objectives of American legal education today, to have some background.

In England, legal education was long apprentice education, and still is, to a very considerable extent. A young man who wanted to become a solicitor, "articled" himself to a solicitor's firm. Or, if he wanted to become a barrister, he "devilled" with a practicing barrister. Instruction was also offered at the Inns of Court, but this was more or less incidental to the work which was done in the chambers of a barrister. The first university lectures in law were those given by William Blackstone at Oxford in 1768. These were later published, and this work, called Blackstone's *Commentaries on the Law of England,* had profound influence on legal education both in England and in America over the next hundred years. During the eighteenth century, some hundreds of young Americans went to England and studied at the Inns of Court and with English barristers, and were called to the bar in England.

Late in the eighteenth century, law lectures were given at the College of William and Mary, in Virginia, by George Wythe. Later, law lectures were given at the University of Pennsylvania by James Wilson, and by Chancellor James Kent at Columbia University in New York. These lectures were modeled to some extent, with appropriate revision for the American scene, on Blackstone's *Commentaries.* Kent's lectures were published as Kent's *Commentaries,* and these, too, were widely read and studied in America during the first half of the nineteenth century.

These several series of lectures, though important, could not be regarded as a "school." They were lectures, given at a university, but incidental to other instruction, and mostly to undergraduates. They were simply part of the general intellectual fare made available through the university.

At the end of the eighteenth century, several private law schools were founded by individual lawyers. The most important of these was known as the Litchfield Law School. It was founded and conducted for many years by Judge Tapping Reeve, in Litchfield, Connecticut. Judge Reeve had his law office in Litchfield, and in a small one-story wooden building, adjacent, conducted his law school. This began in 1784 and continued until about 1833. During this period, several hundred young Americans, from nearly every state, received legal instruction from Judge Reeve and his successors. Many of these Litchfield graduates achieved high distinction in the subsequent practice of their profession. It may fairly be said that it was the Litchfield Law School and its success which started the pattern under which American legal education has come to be conducted primarily in schools set up and devoted to that particular purpose.

In 1817, the Harvard Law School was founded in Cambridge, Massachusetts. At that time, and for the rest of the century, the prevailing method of law study was, and continued to be, through "reading law" in a law office. Even when students went to a law school, and stayed for a year or so, they often then continued their studies in a law office. During its first thirteen years, the Harvard Law School had only a few students and there was doubt, in 1828–29, whether it could successfully continue.

At this point, the authorities of Harvard University elicited the interest of Nathan Dane, the draftsman of the Ordinance of 1787 which established the Northwest Territory. He was also the author of a legal work known as Dane's *Abridgement,* from which he had received a financial return which was substantial for that time. Mr. Dane gave his library to the Harvard Law School, and also a fund to establish a professorship which was known as the Dane Professorship. Indeed, the school was from that time, for the next fifty years or so, known as the Dane Law School.

The next step taken was to persuade Joseph Story to become the Dane Professor at the Harvard Law School. This was probably the most important and significant single step taken in the history of American legal education. Joseph Story was at the time a Justice of the Supreme Court of the United States. He was also the author of a number of scholarly and significant treatises on various branches of the law. He sat in Washington during the then relatively short Terms of the Supreme Court, and also journeyed to Cambridge where he, and one or two other professors, conducted the Harvard Law School.

Almost immediately, gentlemen from all over the country began to send their sons to Harvard to study law under Justice Story. Story continued to fill the Dane Professorship until the time of his death in 1845. By that time, and almost entirely through his influence, a new pattern in American legal education had become firmly started. In truly significant changes, American legal education was now well on its way to becoming

(a) academic, rather than apprentice, and (b) national in out-look, rather than essentially local.

These tendencies have continued into the present century and apprentice education has almost entirely disappeared in the legal field. It is still possible to "read law" in a law office in a few states, and then take the bar examination, but it is seldom done success-fully. In the second example set by Story, there are now numer-ous "national" law schools that draw students from all parts of the country. In fact, nearly all law schools are now "national" in their outlook, paying only incidental attention to the peculiarities of the law of their own jurisdiction.

In the early times, legal instruction was based on the lecture system, although students from the beginning engaged in moot court work where they had an opportunity to develop their skill and capacity to uncover and to use legal materials. But a major change was introduced in 1870 when the "case method" was in-vented and used as a basis of instruction by Christopher Colum-bus Langdell, then newly appointed as first Dean of the Harvard Law School.

In the course of time the case method came to revolutionize American legal education, and it has had considerable impact on education generally. The essence of the case method is its teach-ing through the careful study and analysis of specific, concrete situations. For centuries it has been the tradition and practice of English and American appellate courts to express their decisions in writing, in opinions written by the judges. These opinions are published, and are thus available to the public and to all mem-bers of the legal profession. In them, there is available a complete and comprehensive review of all of the ways in which human beings have, over a period of many years, come into contro-versy, either with other persons or with governmental authority. There is also a record of the careful thought, after hearing argu-ment, of judges, often of great learning and experience, as to the proper resolution of these controversies.

Under the case method, a selection of these opinions is care-fully gathered, edited and organized into a "case book," and this is used as the basis of law study. Thus the student comes to learn not only the history of the law and its development, but also the way lawyers and judges think and express themselves. Through examination and comparison of cases presenting similar facts, he learns the importance of precise statement and evaluation of the facts; he learns, too, that slight variations in them may lead to a difference in conclusion, and he analyzes and considers why this should be. He learns that the law is not simple and clear and that two judges, both of great ability, may come to different conclusions on the same question. From the decisions on a number of fact situations, he may endeavor to generalize and to develop a more comprehensive rule applicable to the area. But his thinking is largely inductive. He does not start with a large generalization, and seek to deduce specific results from it. Instead, he follows carefully the course of reasoning of the courts in coming to specific conclusions, and considers whether the aggregate of the specific conclusions is such that he can, by inductive reasoning, formulate a more general principle which will serve as a guide in the decision of other concrete cases.

Over the years the case method has been greatly modified and developed. It has been well said that there are as many "case methods" as there are law teachers. It is, indeed, sometimes said that the case method is now outmoded, and that it is being abandoned by many law schools. But this is simply a confusion of terms. It may be, especially in the second and third years in law school, that cases, as such, are not as much studied and analyzed and dissected as they were two generations ago. But legal instruction in American law schools still remains specific and concrete. The student still considers decisions in actual cases, and analyzes and builds on these decisions to gain a conception of the over-all structure of the law.

Of course there is much more to the materials of the law than the decisions of courts. There are statutes passed by Congress and state legislatures, treaties, ordinances of cities and towns, administrative decisions, and rules and regulations made by governmental bodies and officers. The volume of materials with which the law student must become familiar has greatly increased in recent years, and some modifications in legal education have resulted. It is no longer possible for the student to be brought into contact with all of the law, and it has become increasingly clear that that is not necessary, or even desirable, since much of the law with which the student will be concerned in practice ten years, or even five years, hence is not now in existence.

What the students should learn in law school is what has been called "the art of the lawyer's craft." He should learn to talk and think like a lawyer. He should learn the materials of the law, and how to find them and use them. He should learn the importance of careful and accurate thinking, the importance of facts, and the necessity of expending great care and effort to be sure that the facts are fully and accurately ascertained and presented. He should learn the standards of the profession for honesty and candor in dealing with fellow lawyers and the courts and other governmental officers. With the basic background of his legal education, he will not know all the law, but he will be able to undertake any legal task, even if he has not studied about it in law school. He will know how to go about learning what he needs to know about any particular area of the law, no matter how new it may be to him. It has been said that the responsibility of the lawyer is to learn more about his case and the law applicable to it than any other person in the world. This is not an impossible task, even in a wholly novel field, if he has a sound legal education.

In law school the student will attend classes on a regular schedule. In many law schools these classes, especially in the first year, will be quite large. The classes will generally be conducted on a "discussion" basis, sometimes based largely on questions by the instructor, and thus known as the Socratic method. The instructor, through questions or comment, will lead and guide the discussion, but he will seek to get students involved in it, and often in discussions with each other. Experience shows that such discussions may be more effective in relatively large classes, under the guidance of a gifted teacher, than in smaller classes. Even though the individual student may not take part in the discussions very often, he profits from following closely the discussion of others, and the questions and comments of the teacher. For a great many students, the study of law, including the class discussions, is an exciting experience. Each day brings new elements to light in the systematic process of reviewing the situations in which human beings may come into controversy, and the way the courts have dealt with such controversies. As the student learns more and more of the details of the law, he comes to have a far greater grasp of the society in which he lives, how it operates, its problems, and the function of the lawyer in avoiding those problems through careful planning, and in alleviating or resolving them when they do in fact arise.

Lawyers are the planners and the organizers and the adjusters in society. It has been said that their function is to serve as a lubricator so that the machinery of society will work smoothly, without grinding to a halt. The popular conception of the lawyer is the advocate engaging in controversy; and that is an important function of a lawyer. But far more of the time of most lawyers is spent in preventing controversy, in planning business and family matters so that disputes will not arise, and in counseling and guidance which will, so far as possible, enable people with varying interests to get along in relative harmony. The lawyer also aids his client to comply with the law so as to minimize development of controversy with the government. Often his advice goes beyond the law. The lawyer may, for example, advise a client to give up rights which are plainly his, legally, if, for ethical or practical reasons, he feels that the client would be wise to take less than everything to which he is legally entitled.

In the first year in law school, the student will concentrate rather heavily on the technique of the lawyer. In the second and third years, his study may have a more general purpose. Within some limits, he may be able to specialize somewhat, though it still remains true that the best specialist in the law is the man who is the best lawyer; and law schools, for this reason, are much more interested in training lawyers than in training specialists. Some of the work in law school, especially in the third year, may involve rather intensive work in a relatively narrow field of the law, including the writing of a fairly substantial paper. This may be a highly educational experience, both because of the thoroughness of the work which is required and because of the opportunity it gives the student to develop his capacity to express himself effectively in writing.

In addition to class work, most law schools also provide opportunities for moot court work, that is, for the preparation of briefs, and the presentation of oral argument in cases which simulate those considered by the actual courts outside the law schools. In addition to this, there are often other activities in which some of the students may participate. Most law schools now have a *Law Review*, which publishes articles on legal topics, usually written by judges, lawyers, or law professors. These Reviews also contain Notes and Comments on current problems or on recent cases which are written and edited by student members of the *Law Review* Board. It is an interesting development in the legal field that most of the periodical publications are under law school auspices, and are generally student edited. The student, usually one of those in the top-ranking part of the class, who can become a member of the *Law Review* Board has an unusual opportunity to enhance his own legal education.

Indeed, it has well been said that most legal education is self-education. This was put by President A. Lawrence Lowell of Harvard University, himself a lawyer as well as an educational leader, in these words:

You may aid the man, you may guide him, and above all, you may inspire him; but the only thing that is worth having is what he gets by his own exertions, and what he gets is proportionate to the effort he puts into it.

The law school and the professors can make the materials available, in case books and in the library, in class presentation and discussion. They can lead and encourage the student in the use of the materials. But it is only the student himself who can learn. In this process, though the student's own effort is imperative, he may be aided greatly in the development of his learning and understanding by his fellow students. Sometimes complaint is made by outsiders that law students will do nothing but "talk law." On the whole, though this can be overdone, it seems generally desirable. It is by talking law with his fellows that the student can best learn the law. In these discussions, with their opportunity for careful criticism and the evaluation of other views, students can almost see their own minds work as they grasp more clearly the inter-relationships with which the law is concerned. It is in consider-able part because of this opportunity for mutual discussion and effective self-criticism that work on a *Law Review* Board may be so valuable a part of legal education.

There are other opportunities available in most law schools for those who do not become eligible for law-review work. There is often a Legal Aid Bureau, where valuable experience may be obtained in the handling of actual cases. There may be a student newspaper, on which writing experience may be obtained. There may be opportunities to do research for a professor, or for some public agency. In recent years it is becoming more and more the practice for law students to find employment in a law office dur-ing the period between their first and second, or their second and third years. All of these things may provide valuable experience, not only in seeing the law in action, but in utilizing the materials with which the student has been working in the classroom. Nev-ertheless, the basic element in any legal education is the day-to-day work in the classroom, and the consideration and discussion outside the law school which results from the classroom work. It is traditional in most law schools that this day-to-day work is done on the student's own responsibility. Indeed, one of the things that makes most law schools exciting places, and memorable in-tellectual experiences, is the fact that students are treated as adults. No one looks over their shoulders; they are expected to do their work themselves; and almost without exception they do.

It is especially true of law students that their work, and their joy in their work, will be governed largely by their own standards and expectations. If a law student looks for a vigorous and stimu-lating, and often exciting, intellectual experience, he should cer-tainly find it. There will be many challenges to meet, fine friend-ships to form, and countless opportunities for growth and professional development. On the other hand, if a student goes to law school expecting a miserable year, a time of tension and pressure, a period of unremitting work and no pleasure, he will probably have just that.

A law student should go about his work with zest and enthusiasm. He should work hard, and enjoy it. If the law is to be his career, he should find satisfaction in doing his work well; if he does not, he has made the wrong choice. Law schools think of their students as lawyers, as adults, as mature and responsible men and women, and they have great confidence in the students' ability to work independently and to solve their own problems and to conduct their own affairs. The school and its faculty members stand ready to help the student when he feels that help is needed. But the basic task is largely one for him himself. He will be successful if he works hard and thoroughly, and finds that he likes the work.

A student's desire to go to law school, and his motivation while in law school will, understandably enough, be affected by the opportunities which will be available to him when he graduates. At the present time it may be said that the opportunities are considerable, and good. But this statement should also be put in a larger setting, which can perhaps be summarized in the statement that *there are too many lawyers in the United States today,* but *there are not nearly enough good lawyers.* Thus the prospects for the young lawyer depend a great deal on how capable and qualified he is. This was the basis for the statement made earlier in this discussion that a man should not undertake to study law today unless he really feels himself to be well qualified for the practice of the legal profession.

It was pointed out earlier that there was a time when it was thought that almost anyone was qualified to practice law. For many years standards for admission to the profession were relatively low, and standards for admission to many law schools were very low indeed. One consequence of this was that a very considerable proportion of those who finished law school, and came to take the bar examination, were unable to pass that examination, even after several tries. This represented a great and unfortunate wastage of time in the study of law. It also meant that a number of persons were being admitted to practice, after several tries and final success in the bar examinations, although their qualifications for law practice were what might be called minimal.

There has been a substantial change in this in recent years, although the change has not yet gone as far as it probably should go. Requirements for admission to law school have been increased over the past thirty years, so that—as I have said previously in this chapter—at least three years of college education are required in every state; and four college years are required in a considerable number of states. In addition to the basic education requirement, a number of law schools have increased their general requirements, and are quite selective in their admission of students. However, the over-all number of law schools in the country is such that it still remains true that any student who has the requisite three years of college can still get into some law school. It is true, also, that a considerable number of students who undertake the study of law, when meeting minimal requirements only, are ill advised to do so. They will probably have great trouble in passing the bar examinations, and will be, in all likelihood, marginal lawyers at best even if they are successful in gaining admission to the bar.

In the United States at present there are somewhat more than 40,000 law students in approved schools. This number is almost exactly the same number as the number of law students in 1930, although the population of the country has increased 40 per cent to 50 per cent in that time. This might be cited as evidence that the number of law students is too small now, so that there is an unusually good opportunity for the law graduate.

It is true that this statistical evidence must be taken into account, but there are also other facts to be considered. Students who are now in law school are, on the average, better qualified than they were thirty years ago. A much higher proportion of them will graduate and take the bar examinations. Though failures on the bar examination are still rather high, the number of persons who are successful has increased somewhat over the past thirty years.

However, despite this increase in the number of graduates from law schools and the increased number passing bar examinations, the volume and complexity of legal work has increased so substantially that opportunities for the really qualified law-school graduate today are undoubtedly considerable, and probably greater than at any previous period in our history.

After you graduate from law school, and pass the bar examination, what are the kinds of opportunities that may be available to you? There is considerable variety.

First, historically, and in the number of participants, is the private practice of law, the backbone and pride of the legal profession. The private practitioner is one of the last outposts of individual enterprise in our society. He makes his living through his inherent and developed mental ability; and he has a constructive career, for he uses his brains and judgment and training to help his fellow men in their business and personal affairs. In a very real sense, he is the man who keeps the wheels of business and government turning. Our modern government could not exist without him, for his attention and advice are essential in enabling businessmen and other citizens to meet the necessarily complex and multitudinous requirements of government. He also aids companies and individuals in getting along with each other, and he is constantly at work seeking to prevent controversies, and striving to resolve them satisfactorily when they do occur.

This important function may be performed by the lawyer in many diverse settings. He may go to a big city, to a smaller city, or to a country town. The big city is where most of the "big business" is centered. Here there is work of great importance, with the possibility of earning substantial remuneration. Such work, however, is ordinarily available only to the most highly qualified lawyers. There is, however, a substantial amount of what might be called ordinary law work, simply because in a big city there are a lot of people who get involved in legal matters. In big cities, too, there are many small businesses whose legal affairs must be handled.

In the small city, it may be said that the lawyer does much the same sort of thing that the big-city lawyer does, the difference being that ordinarily smaller amounts are involved. It may be easier for a lawyer of less spectacular ability to make his way in the smaller city, and, whatever his ability, if he prefers not to work under heavy pressure, he may find the life in the smaller city more congenial. If he likes to be at the very center of things, the big city may be the place for him; but if he is content to work with smaller matters, in a close personal relation to his client, and with an awareness that what he does affects the lives and interests of many people whom he sees from day to day, he may find work in the smaller city more satisfying.

Finally, the lawyer may work in the country town. Here he is less likely to be concerned with business matters. He will deal more directly with people and their personal problems. He will be family guide and counselor. He will advise about wills and trusts and estates. He will help people when they become involved in marital troubles, including property adjustments and getting a divorce when that is called for. He will deal with the many disputes which arise between individuals, ranging from automobile accidents to controversies about land boundaries, and possibly bitter affairs in the area of libel and slander. It is not suggested that these matters do not arise in the big city or the small city, for, of course, they do. But they are more likely to be an important part of the daily work of the lawyer in the small town. Handling these matters effectively and smoothly can be very important and satisfying work. The good and wise lawyer in a small community is one of its most important citizens, and is widely respected and relied on for counsel and advice, not only by his clients but by all elements of the community.

Apart from the type of community where one goes—big city, small city, or country town—there is considerable variation in the type of office which one may enter. Many lawyers practice law in partnership, or firms, that is, in close association with one or more other lawyers, with a sharing of income and responsibility. In some of the big cities a few of these firms are very large. They may have over a hundred lawyers, and as many more other employees. Such firms are sometimes referred to as "law factories," and, indeed, they are often a very efficient instrument for turning out large quantities of legal services of the highest order. Most firms, however, even in the big cities, tend to be smaller. Some have twelve to twenty partners, for example; while many others are even smaller. Firms with five or six partners are frequent, especially in the small cities; and firms of two or three partners are perhaps most numerous of all.

Generally speaking, it can be said that the most successful lawyers practice in firms, though this is not always true. More than half of all lawyers, however, practice alone. Sometimes they share offices with other lawyers, on a divide-the-expense basis, though not in partnership. It can surely be said that the "solo practitioner" is the last great stand of individual enterprise in the legal profession. Some individual practitioners are extremely successful, and many who practice alone would not care to do it any other way.

The young man who leaves law school and wants to start into practice by himself does it by "hanging out his shingle." This means simply that he finds himself some sort of an office, makes his name known by a sign—called his "shingle"—and waits for clients to come to him. He cannot advertise, consistent with the ethical standards of the profession, so that his shingle is the only public way that his availability can be known. He may have to wait a long time for any clients, and this may be very discouraging, as well as a severe financial strain. In many cases, however, he has family connections, or friends, who can recommend him, and see that perhaps some small bits of legal work come his way. If he handles these well, he may begin to develop a reputation, with the result that more and more clients come to him, and he thus develops a clientele and standing at the bar. This can be a long and difficult course; but many thousands have done it successfully, and the man who has started out from scratch and built up a legal practice can take real satisfaction in the work he has done and the contacts he has made and the services he has performed.

If a young man does not want to hang out his shingle, how does he proceed? If he is well qualified, that is, if he has had a good record in law school, and has successfully passed the bar examination, he can ordinarily obtain employment in a law office. In the old days, he had to be content with "desk space" at no salary. Sometimes he got a small salary, and many venerable lawyers of today proudly tell of their first legal employment at a salary of $5 a week. But times have changed, and many current law-school graduates can obtain immediate legal employment at substantial salaries. Such employment may be with a large firm in a large city, with a smaller firm in a large city, with a firm in a small city, or, occasionally, with an individual practitioner in a country town. The student should make his choice carefully, depending on the kind of opportunities open to him, for the place he starts may have a great effect on his whole legal career.

If the student goes into a law firm, he will be what is called an "associate"—that is, he is not a partner. He does not share in the profits of the firm, or take the risk of the firm's business. He works on a salary, though he may also receive a share of the firm's receipts from work which he brings in. For the most part he will work on the problems of other people's clients. He will assist partners and senior associates of the firm in handling the matters in which they are engaged. At the beginning, his work may be mostly library work. He will prepare memoranda on law points which arise in the firm's cases; and he may do much "leg work" in hunting up witnesses, interviewing them, and in making other investigations and reports which pertain to the problems being handled by the firm.

As time goes on, and as he develops and demonstrates his abilities, he may take over various matters "on his own." As he shows that he can handle these, he may be given more and more responsibility. With this may come some increase in his pay, which will, of course, be very satisfying, as well as useful. After a period of some years, he may be asked to become a partner. In that event, he is "taken into the firm," and this may be a very real sign that he has made his mark, and is now regarded as a full-fledged member of the practicing legal profession.

In a very real sense the work which a young man just out of law school does in a law office is apprentice work. There is much for him to learn after leaving law school, and the law office is one of the places where he can learn it. The American law student is very fortunate that he is often paid, and sometimes quite well, for his apprentice work. In many other countries, the law student is required to do his apprentice work *before* he can be admitted to practice, and he is either not paid at all for his services, or he is paid a mere pittance. In the United States the typical well-qualified law-school graduate now commands a relatively substantial salary. Of course, it is incumbent on him to show that he is worth it. If he is not, he will in due course lose his law-office employment, and will have to search out some other form of work, legal if possible. On the other hand, if he does make good, then he can look forward to a partnership.

This, however, is not a bed of roses, for the partners have the responsibility for making the whole operation go, including earning enough to pay the salaries of the associates and the other staff. But the partners in American law firms ordinarily do reasonably well, and almost always have very busy and satisfying lives. The successful American lawyer makes a good living, but usually does not get rich. He can live well, but even if he should have an extraordinarily good year, he will not have too much left after taxes. All of his earnings are taxable as ordinary income. He does not have the benefit of stock options or of pension plans. He is a truly individual entrepreneur. There is no other life quite like it, and, many lawyers would say, no other life as good. But it involves long hours, hard work, great responsibility, and a very considerable amount of constant tension and pressure. No one should enter upon this road if he is looking for a life of leisure and luxury, with great rewards available for a minimum of work. There are great rewards, but, for the most part, they are not financial, and almost without exception they come only after long hard hours of intensive intellectual work.

There are many other sorts of opportunities for the lawyer. For example, the law is one of the many avenues to public employment. The young lawyer, just out of law school, may enter into public employment, either for the experience, or as a means of starting his career as a public officer. For experience, he may obtain an appointment as an assistant district attorney; or he may obtain employment in the Internal Revenue Service or in the Department of Justice, or in a corresponding legal office in the state or local government. In such work, he will almost immediately be put in charge of cases, and he will have a great grist of experience, probably greater than he could hope to find available in a private law office. He will also have some supervision, through the older lawyers in the office, but he can ordinarily expect to be "on his own" at an earlier period than would be the case in a private office. Such experience in a public office can be not only an important and useful public service but also a fine opportunity to see government operations from the inside, to get and develop an understanding of what "makes the wheels go round," and to learn the organization of the government offices, the people in them, and the way they operate. All of this can be of great value in a later period of private practice.

Of course, the young lawyer may also enter the government with the expectation of making government legal service his career. Many lawyers have had very satisfying legal lives in government service. In such employment they find security, though often at a relatively modest salary, and freedom from the importunities of clients. They also have the satisfaction of engaging in important public service.

Other lawyers enter public legal service later in their careers. They may do it through elective office, as a means of seeking political advancement. Thus, a lawyer may run for the office of district attorney or attorney general in his community or state. Or he may accept appointment to a relatively senior governmental legal post, both for the public service he can render, and because this may be a means of developing further a political career. One of the important things about qualification in the legal profession is the fact that it always gives a man something to fall back on. A lawyer is particularly free in moving from private practice, into public office, and then back into private practice, should he tire of the public position, or if political fortunes should change so that the public post was no longer available to him, or was no longer attractive. Thus, a man may be Attorney General or Vice President of the United States, or Governor of New York, or candidate for President of the United States, and then return to law practice. And the same is true of many lesser offices. A very high proportion of lawyers engages in some sort of public service during the course of their legal lifetimes, and this is, indeed, one of the attractions of a legal career.

There are still other sorts of legal employment. Perhaps the most important that has not been mentioned is that of legal work in the employment of a business or financial company. Many companies now have a "legal department," headed by a "general counsel" of the company. Sometimes these legal departments are quite small. In a few cases, they may be very large, as large or larger than the biggest of the big-city law offices. Lawyers who are in the employ of companies are sometimes called "house counsel." They handle all of the general or routine legal matters of the company. In effect, the lawyer who is a house counsel may be engaged in general law practice, but for one client only, his employing company. Such lawyers work on salary, and do not have to worry about whether clients will seek their services. They may also come within company pension plans, and may even be eligible for such things as profit-sharing plans or stock options. Thus company employment can be quite attractive. Often, though, there is not a great variety of work, and some lawyers chafe at working all the time for a single client. Nevertheless, many lawyers have found great opportunities to use their legal talents while working in company employment.

Some times a young man just out of law school can find an opening in a company legal department. More often, though, such posts are found by a lawyer who has had four or five years' experience in law practice. This may be a lawyer who has started as an associate in a law firm, and who feels that he is not going to be made a partner in the firm, or that he does not want to become a partner. Often in his work for the law office, he may have had contact with company lawyers, and the opportunity to obtain company employment may develop out of this. It should be said, too, that many persons who have gone into company legal departments have gone on into general company management. Many of the presidents of great companies in the country today entered the employment of the company in the legal department. In many ways, a legal training, and experience in a company's legal department can be an extraordinarily fine training and background for a position of importance in the general management of the company.

Finally, there are two other types of legal work, to which reference should be made:

1. *The bench.* One of the most honored and most important assignments available to a lawyer is a position as a judge. In most of the states in this country, judges are elected, and this may represent, in fact, an obstacle to the self-respecting lawyer who wants to be a judge, for he may find anything like campaigning to be distasteful to him. Even in such states, however, many fine lawyers go to the bench. In other states, judges are appointed; and all of the federal judges are appointed.

It need not be pointed out that a position on the bench is one of great responsibility, and an important public service. The judge not merely decides the cases that come before him, but, especially if he is on an appellate court, he helps to formulate and develop the law of the jurisdiction where he sits. The judicial post is one of great responsibility and respect, of great potentiality for public service, and should always be highly regarded by all lawyers. Some lawyers may not want to be judges; others may not have the opportunity. But for the law student, and for all young lawyers, the bench remains one of the opportunities of the profession. The chance to go on the bench should never be lightly declined; and it may well be one of the greatest of the attractions of the legal profession.

2. *Law teaching.* Another possible road for the young lawyer to follow is that of law teaching. There are only a relatively small number of full-time law teachers in the country, something less than fifteen hundred all told, or about ¾ of 1 per cent of the whole legal profession. Ordinarily a young man will not think of full-time law teaching unless he has had extraordinarily high marks in law school. If he has been an outstanding student in school, though, and if he thinks he would like the scholarly life, he may well want to consider a position in law teaching. Law teachers are likely to receive salaries which are relatively high on the academic scale, but they are even less likely than other lawyers to become rich. They have full, satisfying lives, if they really like to work with the intellectual problems of the law. They also have a good deal of routine, and even of drudgery—for careful class preparation is required, and American law teachers customarily mark all of their own examination papers, contrary to the practice in many other parts of American education.

Of course the law teacher teaches. That may be said to be the basic part of his task. But he is also expected to make contributions to the better understanding and the improvement of the law. In order to do this, he writes. He may write articles, book reviews, and lesser pieces. Or he may, if he is rugged and able, write great treatises which help to stabilize or remake the law. In addition, he may be called on for many speeches; and he may have frequent opportunities—even demands—for public service. He may advise public bodies on pending public questions. He may in some cases advise private clients. Altogether, the modern American law teacher can have an extraordinarily active and interesting time, and may fairly feel that he has considerable influence not only on his students but also on the development of the law.

Some persons enter law teaching right out of law school. Others engage in a period of practice first, and this is ordinarily the desirable way, provided that they do not stay in practice too long. Experience seems to show that the man who practices too long does not ordinarily make a thoroughly satisfactory law teacher, perhaps because his extended devotion to practice tends to show that he does not really have all the qualities which are desirable in making the truly successful law teacher. A period of practice, perhaps up to five years, however, is often very helpful in giving the law teacher an insight into the actual operation of the law. In the older days, there may have been some tendency to employ as law teachers persons who, though scholarly, could not have been successful in practice. In modern times, however, the typical law teacher is a man who has the qualities for success in practice, but who also has the special intellectual abilities, and the scholarly bent, as well as a zeal for the law and an interest in teaching, which, added together, make him a good law teacher. It can be said with some confidence, though, that a man should not think in terms of law teaching unless he has had very high marks in law school, or has some other quality which makes him particularly qualified for a teaching position.

From this recounting of the opportunities available to the young lawyer, and the variety of work which he may undertake, it should not be concluded that the life of the young practitioner is always easy. It has been emphasized throughout this discussion that the lawyer must work, and work hard. Moreover, it should be recognized that the law is inevitably a competitive profession. Some lawyers are more able than others, and are thus more likely to find better openings in the profession. Lawyers of lesser ability may encounter real difficulties, both in finding a good place in which to start their legal work, and in maintaining themselves, and advancing, as their legal careers progress.

It is for this reason that there has been much emphasis in this article on the ability of the prospective law student. Once again it may be said that though there are not enough good lawyers in the country, there are too many lawyers. Many persons who go through law school, and gain admission to the bar, have great difficulty in finding the opportunities which the law may provide for others. If one is a marginal practitioner, the road may be very hard and discouraging, and the results disappointing, both in usefulness and in reward. At its best, a legal career offers great opportunities. At its worst, it can be very slim. The factor which is likely to lead to one result rather than the other can often be put in terms of ability, though it should be clearly recognized that there are many types of abilities which are recognized in the legal profession.

Now we come to the end of our discussion of law study. It is a great road for those who are really qualified to enter upon it. Many have followed that road in the past, with great service to their fellow men, and real satisfaction to themselves. A student who has confidence in himself, and is fairly sure that he has the rather considerable intellectual equipment required, should not hesitate to enter upon that road. If he feels that there are financial or other obstacles to his doing so, he should not give up until he has really exhausted all of the considerable opportunities which are available for obtaining help.

If he undertakes the study of law, he should do it with high purpose. A lawyer is not a mere money grubber, and anyone who thinks of law practice as merely a means of making a living has picked the wrong profession. A lawyer is a man who helps people, and the opportunities available to the lawyer for service, great and small, are constant and unlimited. The law student should have his eyes fixed on the stars. He is entering a great profession, with long and honorable traditions. It should be his endeavour to add to the greatness of the profession, and to lengthen its honorable traditions. He can do this if he enters on his task with enthusiasm and with high expectations. There will be times of discouragement, of course. But let him always remember the words of a very great lawyer, Henry L. Stimson. In the conclusion to his book entitled *On Active Service in Peace and War,* he wrote:

Let them have hope, and virtue, and let them believe in mankind and its future, for there is good as well as evil, and the man who tries to work for the good, believing in its eventual victory, while he may suffer setback and even disaster, will never know defeat. The only deadly sin I know is cynicism.

BIBLIOGRAPHY

You may be interested in further reading about the law, and law study. Here are some suggestions:

Catherine Drinker Bowen, *The Lion and the Throne:* The Life and Times of Sir Edward Coke (Little, Brown & Co., 1957). A detailed and well-written biography of a man who played an important role in the shaping and recording of decisions which are embodied in the common law. Coke (pronounced Cook) lived in 1552–1634.

Benjamin N. Cardozo, *Selected Writings of Benjamin Nathan Cardozo* (Fallon Publications, 1947.) This is a compilation of a number of the writings of one of our most famous and articulate judges. Probably the best for pre-law reading is "The Nature of the Judicial Process," which is also available in other editions.

Frank E. Cooper, *Living the Law* (Bobbs, Merrill, 1958).

James G. Cozzens, *The Just and the Unjust* (Harcourt, Brace & Co., 1942). The best account in fiction of the daily life of the ordinary lawyer.

Karl N. Llewellyn, *The Bramblebush* (Oceana Publications, 1951). A brilliant survey for students and lawyers of what law is and what legal education does and can do to make a man a lawyer.

Alpheus T. Mason, *Brandeis: A Free Man's Life* (The Viking Press, 1946). An interesting and well-written account of a great career at the bar and as a justice of our highest Court. A reviewer has said that for law students, the book might well have been entitled: "A Case History of a Successful Legal Career."

William B. Nourse, *So You Want to Be a Lawyer* (Harper & Bros., 1959).

David W. Peck, *Decision at Law* (Dodd, Mead & Co., 1961). An interestingly written discussion, for laymen, of some of the leading decisions in the law and the factors that led the judges to the conclusions they reached.

Ferdinand F. Stone, *Handbook of Law Study* (Prentice-Hall, 1952).

Arthur Train, *Yankee Lawyer,* The Autobiography of Ephraim Tutt (Charles Scribner's Sons, 1943). A fictional account of an imaginary but well-known lawyer. Another book by Mr. Train is *Mr. Tutt's Casebook* (Charles Scribner's Sons, 1936).

_3_ A Law Firm–

AND WHAT IT EXPECTS
FROM YOU

BY DILLON ANDERSON

Houston, Texas

DILLON ANDERSON

Born: 1906, McKinney, Texas

University of Oklahoma: B.S., 1928
Yale: LL.B., 1929
Texas Christian University: LL.D., 1954
Allegheny College: LL.D., 1956

Colonel, US Army: 1942–45

Admitted Texas Bar: 1929
With Baker, Botts, Shepherd & Coates (formerly Baker, Botts, Parker &
   Garwood), Houston: 1929—Partner: 1940—

Special Assistant to President for National Security Affairs: 1955–56
Member, U.S. Delegation to Summit Conference at Geneva: 1955
Consultant National Security Council: 1953–54; 1957–60
Member, The President's Committee To Study the United States Military
   Assistance Program: 1958–59
Director: Monsanto Chemical Company
   Westinghouse Electric Corporation
   Federal Department Stores, Inc.
   Foreign Policy Association
Chairman of the Board: Texas National Bank
Trustee: Schlumberger Foundation
   Foley Foundation
   Carnegie Endowment For International Peace
   The Brookings Institute
Fellow, American Academy Arts and Sciences
Member, Council Foreign Relations, Inc.
Houston Committee Foreign Relations (President: 1950–51)
Texas Institute of Letters

Author: *I and Claudie*
   Claudie's Kinfolks
   The Billingsley Papers

LET US assume that you are twenty-three years of age and you are sitting alone in your room, contemplating your new diploma from law school and wondering what you are going to do about it. And where. Your meditations are interrupted, let us say, by a knock on the door and your visitor is Mr. Michael Anthony, a complete stranger, who comes in with a solemn face and a startling announcement. Mr. Anthony says that an enormously rich benefactor in a distant city, John Beresford Tipton by name, has decided to give you, tax free, a cool million dollars.

A rather sunny daydream, I think you would agree. But it happens only in fantasy on a television program entitled "The Millionaire."

So let's wake up before this fatuous idea of something for nothing spoils our perspective. Let's take a look at a much better deal which actually awaits you if you are up to it. And this time it is no fantasy. This time you have bestirred yourself from your room and traveled to the place where you would like to live. *You* have knocked on a door. You are calling on a real Mr. Jones, or Smith, or Brown, a lawyer. You are there to talk to him about a place for yourself in his law firm. You don't have to conjure up this interview out of thin air; this need not be a daydream, for there are many lawyers like him in every city.

If his is a typical city firm, it will be made up of lawyers at various stages of their careers—all engaged in rendering varied legal services to sundry clients. Perhaps you are wondering, as the interview begins, about the attitude of lawyers in the firm toward law graduates. I can tell you. In nine cases out of ten they have a very keen interest. In the first place, they are mindful of the day when they sat where you sit, and they would like to help you. More importantly, though, *they* need help; your kind of help, if your record in law school discloses good aptitude. Their recruiting activities are as important to their firm as the childbearing activities are to a family, since in the way of life their successors must be found and trained if the firm is to function with the vitally important aspect of continuity for the group and for the never-to-be-overlooked beneficiaries of its activities—the clients.

If you can go and make your place in that firm, emerging in due course as a senior participant in its affairs, then the lawyer in it who signs you up will have a more meaningful contact for you than Mr. Michael Anthony with that million-dollar check. Moreover, if you live out the actuarial estimate of your adult years, you probably will have received for your participation something in the neighborhood of the million dollars * after taxes, and it will doubtless mean a lot more to you than it would have in one lump when you were twenty-three. Also, by the time you have received the monetary fruits of your professional endeavors, you doubtless will have concluded that the money was of lesser lasting significance than the other rewards. You will have built a career in the learned and congenial company of like-minded professional men, and you will have gained the enduring satisfaction of steering the affairs of many clients along the paths of law and order prescribed by our state and federal constitutions and statutes, as construed and interpreted by our courts. Thus, though you will not have become rich (for lawyers scarcely ever do), you will have been financially comfortable while filling your years with values that all but eclipse the purely pecuniary aspects.

Too rosy a picture? Perhaps, but perhaps only in the event you don't have the ability and the will to practice law as a member of a team. And if you don't, the sooner you can find this out, the better it will be for you. Right here probably is as good a place as any to clarify the role of the lone wolf or prima donna in such organizations as we are considering. If you are going to bring these tendencies to the bar, spare your brethren in the firms. Better to bring a ball of barbed wire to a bridal shower.

As a matter of fact, the team spirit can, and often does, overcome such deficiencies as less than complete fascination with each

---

* See "A New Look: The Economics of the Profession," Segal, September, 1957, issue of *American Bar Association Journal*, wherein the author concluded: "Net earnings for lawyers in firms with nine or more members average $36,102.00, or almost five times the average income received by lawyers in solo practice."

and every task which befalls one. It's like the case of the weary paratrooper General Maxwell Taylor used to tell about. At an inspection, the General asked him if he really liked to jump.

"No, sir," he said stiffly.

"Then what are you doing in this outfit?" the General asked.

"Sir," the paratrooper replied, "it's because I like to be with people who like to jump."

So, I suppose we must make another assumption: You feel you are a team player at heart (otherwise there isn't much point in reading further). But you would like to get now a better feel as to how you might make out in a firm. What is the outlook? What other qualities do you need to be successful in a firm? Will you be likely to live up to all that is expected of you?

Generally speaking, you can be sure that a law firm will expect a great deal of you—so much, in fact, that if you don't have a real liking for the law and an abiding zest for work in that field, the performance expected of you will almost surely seem to be too much for your taste and you probably should not go into a law firm—or, for that matter I would say, into the profession at all. As someone once put it, "If you'd rather be doing something else, then whatever you are doing is too hard."

On the other hand, if you bring to the profession good legal aptitude coupled with a love of the law (and you can tell a lot about these matters before you are graduated from law school), the chances are great that your services will naturally tend to meet all that the firm expects of you and probably exceed your own expectations.

Perhaps it is in order, before going further, to clarify my concept of a law firm, as distinguished from a group of lawyers who share a suite of offices, a library, and other common facilities simply as a matter of convenience and economy. A true law firm is an entity. Again, it has many of the features of a family circle, wherein the older members are responsible for the more important decisions, the major undertakings, the plans for the future, the delegation of tasks where practicable, and the training of the younger members of the group. It is this entity which undertakes the representation of clients, though the service in any particular matter may be rendered principally by one of the members. At

the same time, the delegation or sharing of part of the undertaking with others in the firm, whose expertise in some facets of
the client's problems will doubtless improve the quality of the
total service, redounds to the benefit of the firm as well as the
client. For in a well-organized firm, client D can get the benefit
of "know-how" developed by any one of the members in work he
has done for clients A, B and C; and the lawyer to whom client D
carries his problem does not have to be educated at the client's
expense on special aspects of his problem as to which other members of the organization are already experts.

Thus, whether the organization consists of half a dozen lawyers
or a hundred, the legal product of the firm tends to become an
amalgam of the efforts, experience, and judgment of several lawyers. Some of them may be elders in the firm, some may be
juniors, but the needs of the elders in such fields as pin-point research, factual investigation and preparing "first-draft" of documents, complement the needs of the juniors for experience and
seasoning. But don't forget, when you start, your need will be
greater than theirs. They have clients' problems, and, despite all
the high-sounding things you heard during your commencement
exercises, your three years in law school have given you little more
than the vocabulary of the lawyer and an understanding of some
general principles in the fields of law where you are going to
work. You will be an apprentice for a while yet, and the lawyer
who does not have to go through this apprenticeship to reach the
full use of his talents simply has not come down the pike.

The elements of performance expected of you in a law firm will
be, happily for you, the very ones which will nurture your growth
in stature as a lawyer, broaden the horizons of your practice, and
build your natural place with the firm's clientele. For the fact of
the matter is that those who are senior to you in the organization
will be educating you in the rendition of legal services and will, at
the same time, be educating the clients in accepting your services.
Though the timing is never a precise thing, the general course toward succession to the clientele of the firm is an inevitable one,
since, normally, the men in the firm who are at the top of the profession when you begin will be moving out and needing successors as you, in turn, move toward the top. In this natural proc-

ess, you, as a young lawyer on your way up in a firm, will soon have a much greater stake in the organization than the most senior of partners. For you will have many more remaining years than they in which to cultivate your talents in the service to old clients of the firm and to new ones who will be attracted by you in the process and, by the same token, many more years to receive compensation accruing to the firm in fees and retainers.

What, then, are some of the specific elements of performance expected of the young lawyer? At the risk of giving this chapter a *Poor Richard's Almanac* flavor, I should like to name the ones which occur to me and elaborate on them in a few respects where they seem to have peculiar applicability to life in a law firm.

In the first place, you will naturally be expected to develop a sense of loyalty to the organization and to the clients.

Frequently I have heard law graduates say, "I want to go with a good law firm where I can get some experience before going out for myself." Certainly the first half of this program is sound, because, undeniably, legal apprenticeship in the presence of active practitioners is a prime way to gain valuable experience. And if the young lawyer finds, after a few years in a firm, that he will be happier in another group or by himself, he is always free to make such a move. But I think it is a serious mistake to enter upon a career with a tentative attitude toward the firm with which one begins his practice.

The span of adult life allocated to us by Providence affords little or no time for false starts or frequent changes in a legal career. The building blocks of experience are essential; yet they are hardly more important to you than those of continuing performance in the presence of the clientele where you would build your career. No Madison Avenue techniques are available to the lawyer; his one "advertisement" is the excellence of his professional services, and it takes time for these services to become excellent and to become *known as excellent* by existing and prospective clients. Much of your investment of effort as an apprentice will be forfeited the day you decide to pull out. And if this is to be your plan, the longer you wait to make the change, the greater will be the forfeiture. True, you can take with you the experience and the expertise gained in serving the firm's clients, but you will be leaving forever your hard-won acceptance by the firm's clients of your competence to handle increasingly important legal affairs for them—unless, indeed, your plan is to work for the firm awhile and then take some of these clients out with you. Here I think you might agree with me that this would hardly be a wholesome approach to bring into a new affiliation.

The foregoing considerations seem to emphasize the importance of your doing all that you can to satisfy yourself that the firm where you would begin your practice is one to which you can give your wholehearted professional allegiance. For, even though you might contemplate gaining experience and then leaving, you would be wise to seek a firm congenial to your tastes, just in case you might change your mind later and want to stay on.

During your initial interviews you can do a better job than you think in finding out about a firm and its clientele. You will find that the partners will welcome your questions about the firm and its field of practice, and respect you more for asking them. Don't hesitate to ask them to name some representative clients. They will be glad to do so and to tell you, as well, about some of the types of services they are called on to render these clients. If the lawyers who populate the firm want you and are willing to make the rather considerable investment in you that employing you implies, it will be important to them to know that you will be happy as a part of their group. For this reason I have always felt that the courtship between the young lawyer and the law firm should be very much a two-way street. It is like contracting a marriage in one sense of the word; and, indeed, if your law-firm affiliation and your marriage both work out well for you, you will doubtless spend about as many of your wakeful hours with your associates as you do with the little woman.

Now a word about loyalty to the clients. After you go with a firm, there may be, and doubtless will be, some lag in time before you come, full-swing, into the attorney-and-client relationship; and it may be just as well for you that the clients do not come too closely into contact with you in the "green" stage of your career. Though you will be meeting clients and participating with your elders in conferences with them fairly soon, you can afford to wait awhile before you are carrying the ball. Likewise, the client can afford to wait until you have learned some more than you did in law school, and perhaps *unlearned* some things that you felt pretty sure of the day you got your diploma. But, in time, the attorney-and-client relationship will develop naturally, and it is vital to your career that it become one of mutual trust and confidence.

I once knew a lawyer who consistently looked down on his clients. He seemed to feel that they were stupid, inept in handling their affairs, and hardly deserving of the services he would confer on them. In their presence he tried to assume a more tolerant view toward their manifold weaknesses, but his real attitude had a way of showing through and, in time, he gave up the law to become a drama critic. And even in that incarnation he remained quite hard to please.

Actually, a lawyer's loyalty to clients implies no servility; the relationship is neither one of the master-and-servant nor employer-employee. Loyalty to a client does not mean that you have to believe that in every attitude or controversy he is always in the right. But, right or wrong, every lawyer's client is entitled to the best professional efforts that can be mustered to serve that client's legitimate best interests. In a sense, the lawyer's role is like that of an independent contractor who, with all the dignity that becomes a learned profession, shares the most intimate and confidential affairs of his client. The client's confidences must be respected and are, indeed, cloaked with a traditional protection in our jurisprudence. The client needs you, you need him, and your unswerving dedication to his cause is essential. He will be calling on you because he has problems in the area of your proficiency. Let him see that his problems are yours, too. Try to see them as he does. Get right in there with him.

The firm will expect your willingness to work quite diligently on its clients' affairs and, at times, without too much regard to regular working hours. Thomas A. Edison once said that, if he had worked the forty-hour week all his life, he doubted that he could have finished anything. And if you have been wondering about the hours in a law office, I am tempted to suggest the relevance of John Pierpoint Morgan's advice to a friend who contemplated buying a yacht and asked the great financier about the cost of maintaining one. "If you are wondering about that," Mr. Morgan observed, "you should not buy a yacht."

I believe with all my heart that if you are determined to succeed in a legal career, you will never find the hours oppressive. Your only problem about hours may be with your wife who may not understand why you don't come home from the office a little earlier. Inevitably there will be times when the exigency of some clients' affairs will call for you to stay on the job until the problems are in hand. Commensurately with the firm's expectation that you will do what is needed in such cases, there will undoubtedly be a recognition that, when your work will permit, you will be free (and even expected) to take part in leisure, recreational or other non-office activities. Fortunately, lawyers do not punch time clocks. They are neither piece workers nor mass-production workers. You will find—and be glad to find, I predict—that, in the lawyer's career, the quality and the quantity of what he accomplishes become more important than his slavish adherence to any particular office routine.

The firm will expect you to conduct yourself with dignity and to show sincerity in your work, to take your duties seriously and yourself seriously in your role—but not too seriously, I hope, for this is a deadly tendency with many lawyers. Downright stuffiness can repel customers and patients and patrons, but I truly believe that in a lawyer it is a sure-fire client repellent. It is also hard on your friends and the members of your family.

You will be expected to learn at an early stage to be orderly in the organization of your time in the office and to develop the habit of thoroughness in all that you do. One of the most successful lawyers I know keeps a current check list on matters in his charge, together with priorities and deadline dates assigned to each. Your meticulous attention to details is essential in forming your habits and methods of practice, for often an omitted detail can become a major blunder and be quite costly to the client where matters of timing or statutory requirements are involved. But aside from these instances, the importance of thoroughness in making your work the best you can produce can hardly be overestimated.

A case in point here is the simple matter of draftsmanship. I venture to suggest that you have not encountered, either in college or law school, standards of excellence in English composition comparable to those which will be required for success in a good law firm. The difference between a sloppy letter, pleading, or other legal document and one that is letter perfect may represent quite a bit of effort. But the time required to make each document the best one you can write will not simply be hours expended. These hours will be among the best investments you can make in your career.

You will be expected—and rightly—to bring to your performance the quality of pertinacity in serving the firm's clients. A merely acceptable solution of a client's problem is not good enough if his lawyer can find, by digging a little harder, a better answer. Or, if you go the trial route, your client should be entitled to your most determined, vigorous and persistent fight in court for the vindication of his rights. Even when settlements of litigation are made, as they often are for the benefit of both sides, the client whose lawyer has shown that spirit of pertinacity in preparing his case is always better served. Unless this spirit characterizes your service to the client, you should—and probably will —lose him to a better fighter.

There is more to be said about pertinacity; there is its relationship to resourcefulness, another quality which, in my judgment, is one of the greatest assets which a lawyer can bring to a firm— or to the profession in any connection. And resourcefulness surely grows with experience. While a part of this rare quality is doubtless born in some more than in others, and while an imaginative approach becomes easier to some than it does to others, I believe resourcefulness is a trait which can be cultivated and that the plow is pertinacity.

The client wants and will pay handsomely for these qualities in your service. One of the highest compliments I heard paid to my late partner, Jesse Andrews, was that he had the knack of "telling his clients what they could do instead of what they couldn't do." Granted, the client may sometimes have to be told that what he wants to do is illegal. But aside from things which are illegal, the client is entitled to your expert help in doing what he wants to do. He should be able to find, with his lawyer's dedicated help, the best legal avenue to accomplishing his valid business objectives.

The above point was perhaps never better illustrated than it was in the early days of World War II in Washington. Statutes altogether inappropriate and inadequate for the scale and speed of procurement required were still on the books. The capital was alive with bureaucrats who could cite chapter and verse on why many needed things could not be done. Judge Robert Patterson, then Under Secretary of War, brought into the service a group of civilian lawyers whose task was to deal with the pressing needs of mobilizing our resources for waging war. Their task was to find ways, within the law, of doing things *that had to be done.* Their experience in representing civilian clients provided the resourcefulness required, and, indeed, their service in the vital procurement program became an unsung, but significant, chapter in the early months following Pearl Harbor.

The firm will expect you to develop a spirit of give and take as one of the group, evidenced perhaps by a willingness to see one of your colleagues receive an assignment that you might have liked; evidenced perhaps by patience with your progress toward the competence that will gain for you a partnership. Some people mature in the profession faster than others, but the slower maturers sometimes mature more in the full course of the legal career. And remember this: When you attain sufficient professional stature and competence to become a partner, it becomes good business *for the firm* to make you a partner.

Will a firm expect you to specialize? This question is a bugaboo that often haunts the prospective lawyer's thinking. He has heard about the cog in a gigantic big-city law firm who does nothing day after day but draft admiralty pleadings, or the one who fills out SEC forms from dawn to dusk, or the one who became such a specialist in *second* mortgages that he died before he ever got to work on a *first* mortgage. While these are overdrawn examples, I think it must be said that some degree of specialization is inevitable within a law firm or out. In the firm where I practice we strive to give our younger lawyers as broad an experience as we can in the several fields of civil law. We encourage them to resist early specialization and invite them to diversify their work and interests in the office, in order to develop a well-rounded foundation for the practice. At the same time, I think it must be said that some of our most productive practitioners gradually and gracefully lose the struggle against specialization in the process of their success.

The legal system in America today, growing in tandem with our rapid industrialization under increasing governmental regulation, has become so complex and diverse that no one can be an expert in everything. A client's problem or proposed transaction may have a dozen legal facets, and the lawyer would be a rare one who could bring knowledge in depth to all of them and acquaintance with all the current decisions, rulings, and regulations which apply. This is one explanation of the phenomenon in this century of the growth of large firms with teams of lawyers equipped to deal with every aspect of a matter.

The lawyer who loves trial work (and greater love hath no man than this) is not likely to be an expert in the field of corporate finance, taxation, or patents. But be it said on his behalf, when litigation arises in those fields, the good trial lawyer will astonish his office-lawyer colleagues by the ease with which he absorbs the lexicon of their expertness and the facility with which he espouses in court the principles which are the ingredients of their specialty.

The question of what you will do in a firm about bar associations, bar committee work, and bar conventions is relevant to our title, but the course you are likely to follow will doubtless depend more on your own taste and convictions about such activities than upon the firm's expectations.

Some lawyers build quite successful careers without ever holding more than the minimum required or acceptable number of memberships in organized bar groups and without attending any bar conventions whatever. Others seem to have no resistance at all to the lure of such organizations. There are city, county, district, state, national, and specialists' associations, and each has its own committees, sections, conventions, and programs. Some of these organizations, committees, etc., are difficult for the lawyer to join, but mostly this is not the case; and all of us who have been practicing long have seen some of our fellow lawyers who have gone hog wild in the organization field. We have seen some really eager ones go so far that their multifarious bar activities proliferated and threatened to interfere with their law practice, if not, indeed, with their ability in some cases to make both ends meet. In other words, unless one uses restraint, this sort of thing can get out of hand in the lawyer's life.

Certainly your firm would not expect you to go overboard on bar activities. But as you develop your areas of special interest, knowledge, and proficiency, it will be a natural and probably a profitable thing to associate yourself in the appropriate bar organization with others who, in other firms, cities, and states, have the same areas of interest. The exchange and cross-fertilization of ideas in such sub-groups can, and undoubtedly does, contribute much to the clarification and improvement of the art in which we lawyers deal. Moreover, if the thought interests you, leadership in the various committees or sections of bar groups usually is earned by years of membership and service. And your acquaintance with other practitioners in your field or fields will help you in making wise selections of lawyers to whom you may need to refer your clients' problems requiring attention in other cities. And this sort of thing, of course, can work both ways.

In bar organizations, much, if not most, of the constructive work is done in the committees, sections, and other smaller groups, and you will have a wide choice in finding the vineyard where you wish to concentrate your labors. In favor of such concentration, I can point out that the lawyers in my observation who have appeared to deal most wisely with association affairs, have done it with selectivity and moderation and a great deal of both.

Civic, educational, social, cultural, religious, and other community activities usually play their part in the life of a successful lawyer. But, again, your own sense of responsibility for participation in activities for the betterment of your community, rather than your law firm's expectations of you, would seem to indicate the likelihood that you will want to lend a hand in these activities. In this connection, it should be recognized that many law firms enjoy considerable social and professional prestige, and you will likely find that your association with the firm will be a real help in getting oriented in such community activities as interest you.

But I respectfully submit that, here again, the keynote is moderation. For by the time you become a member of the board of directors of your state bar association, a contributor to the law journal of your alma mater, and chairman of the lawyer's division of the Special Gifts branch of your local Community Chest drive, you are perhaps another kind of asset to your firm; by then you may be in a phase of expecting some things *from* the firm, namely, that your associates there will carry more of the burden until you can complete your civic and other outside commitments and get back to your legal knitting. Meantime, if you have done these civic and professional jobs well, you are going to have to develop some pretty firm answers to the Symphony Society, the Chamber of Commerce, the Art Museum, the Committee for Judicial Reform, the local Judicature Institute, the Committee on Continuing Legal Education, and the City Charter Committee of Lawyers. They all have work to do and they seek a willing hand. Unless you can learn to say *NO* to some of these extraneous demands that will surely take you more and more away from your desk, there can arise another kind of expectation on the firm's part. Your colleagues there will expect you *back*—unless, indeed, you have wandered too far afield.

No treatment of what a firm will expect of you would be complete, in my opinion, unless it included the point that other criteria will soon emerge in your practice there; your own expectations of yourself are likely to become more important to you than the firm's. Naturally your association with the firm will help you to identify your own goals of performance and enable you to formulate your own concept of the dimension of the career to which you aspire; then, if you are determined to succeed and alert to what goes on around you, you will discover that your own objectives exceed the bare minimum expected of you in the firm, and you will find ways in which your performance can exceed the routine discharge of routine responsibilities assigned to a beginner.

Do not begrudge the firm this excess! Do not withhold your energy or your talents from any assignment, however small. Do not make the mistake of trying to adjust your early efforts downward to the triviality of your first tasks or to the modesty of your beginner's salary. Give the firm the best that is in you! There is an old adage: Unless you are willing to give more than you get, you are never likely to get more than you give. I believe this to be as true in a law firm as it is in any other context in the world. I believe, too, that most lawyers receive more from their firms over the years than they put in. Again, I do not refer to money alone. For such organizations have a way of defying the laws of mathematics in the sense that the whole becomes greater by far than the mere sum of its several parts.

As you have read, I hope you have gained a clearer idea as to the nature of law firms and as to your prospects as a young lawyer in a firm. I should like to conclude by asking you to look a little further down the line toward the time when you will be a young lawyer no longer.

Let us assume that you have found the right firm for you and have brought to the group the qualifications we have considered. I venture the belief that as your career matures you will encounter rewards of a dimension more discernible to you with each passing year. For one thing, you will doubtless develop a greater interest in what you can do for the firm than in what it can do for you, and this attitude will enrich your days. You will be gratified to find that your own contributions have not been limited by what was expected of you when you began; instead, you will probably find that some of the standards of quality in the firm have been of your own making. By the excellence of your performance in important cases or transactions, you doubtless will have added to the firm's stature in the community of clients. And lastly, you will know the fulfilling role of leading young talent toward its natural fruition in the profession—repayment in a sense for the guidance you received when you were younger in the organization.

When these things can come to pass, and when you can round out your career in the sure knowledge that the firm you leave when you die or retire will be a better firm than it was when you joined it, the chances are very high that you will agree with me on this proposition: At no stage would you have traded your place in the firm for Mr. Tipton's million-dollar gift.

_4_ *Beginning Your*

LAW PRACTICE

BY JOHN V. HUNTER III
Raleigh, North Carolina

JOHN V HUNTER III

Born: 1930, Winston-Salem, North Carolina

Davidson College: B.S., 1952
University of North Carolina School of Law: J.D., 1955

U. S. Army (Private): January, 1956
Judge Advocate General's Corps (1st Lt.): April, 1956
   Various posts in the United States: 1956–57
   France: 1957–59

Institute of Government, Chapel Hill, North Carolina: 1955
Practice of law New York City: 1961
Now engaged in the general practice of law in Raleigh, North Carolina

IT HAS often appeared to me that most men, whether they are happy or unhappy in their professions, are men who selected those professions largely by chance, and without any real knowledge of the nature and amount of work which would be involved. Even after a great amount of investigation, it is difficult to know whether one is suited for a particular calling until he has had experience in it. Therefore, if this book as a whole, and this chapter in particular, can remove a part of the element of chance from the crucial task of selecting a profession, especially as it concerns the law, it will more than have served its purpose.

I believe that a man should be able to form a fairly good idea, even before he enters college, as to whether he is suited for the law and the law is suited for him. By the time one is sixteen or seventeen years of age, he should have formed an interest in working with ideas, and thinking in logical patterns, if he is going to form such an interest at all. He will also by then have had some indication as to whether he enjoys argument and likes hard work.

In my own case, I became interested in the law as a profession largely as a result of two factors which touched me entirely by chance. First, I was born and grew up in a neighborhood in which my family lived across the street from a very good lawyer who often talked with me about his profession, and secondly, I happened to take a course in public speaking during my first year in high school which led to a great interest in it and developed in me a skill in speaking in public which could be nicely worked in with the practice of law. In addition, I discovered in connection with the work I did in some of my English courses that I liked to work with words and particularly to express ideas in written or spoken language. The result was that by the time I entered college, I knew definitely that I wanted to be a lawyer, even though I had had virtually no experience that touched upon the law itself or the type of work which a lawyer does.

It would certainly be helpful for you to spend some time in the courtroom observing lawyers in action, and also to call on some lawyer in his office in an effort to get at least a basic understanding of what a lawyer does in the course of an average day's work. As you do this, you will find that the types of law practice are so varied that you will probably discover a specialty or area of concentration which suits your particular temperament, so long as you have the fundamental requirements of enjoying constant work with words and ideas, and take pleasure in the construction of logical thoughts and arguments. Since the ultimate business of law is to determine what all living human beings may and may not do and what are the consequences of their acts, the law touches upon human relationships in every imaginable form, and a person with a reasonably good mind and an interest in thinking through problems in a logical fashion can always find some aspects of human life which have consequences that interest him.

An approach which may be quite helpful to you, and one which is often overlooked, is to take some type of aptitude test designed to measure roughly your ability to deal with legal problems. Such a test requires no knowledge of law and generally involves your ability to select the correct legal principle to solve a particular fact situation, the legal principles being furnished to you as part of the questions. I took a series of such tests during my last year in high school, and although I made higher scores in some of the areas other than law, I was completely fascinated with the situations which were presented in the legal aptitude test and decided that it would be very interesting to spend the rest of my life solving just such problems. I was surprised to discover, when I eventually entered law school and started a first-year course in torts, that one of the situations presented to me on the aptitude test was based on an actual case which had caused the Court of Appeals of New York to split four to three, and I was comforted to discover that my answer on the aptitude test was the answer arrived at by the majority of the judges on the court. Such law aptitude tests are generally designed for college graduates, but I think they are equally valuable for a high-school senior, and taking the test that early will, of course, give anyone the advantage, if he decides that he does have some aptitude for law, of being able to select courses in college which will later be useful to him in law school and in practice.

Although, of course, it is very important that you reach some decision about your career as soon as you are in a position to do so intelligently, it is definitely true that an early decision is not nearly as important with regard to law as it may be in some other fields—medicine, for example. This is so because the law touches human relations at such an infinite number of points that any knowledge which a lawyer has managed to acquire in any field, at any time, on almost any subject, will probably prove to be useful to him at some point in his career. It is literally impossible for a lawyer to learn too much in any area, and any study which requires him to work to the utmost of his ability, and to develop his powers of concentration and reasoning, will eventually prove to be valuable.

It is of the utmost importance that a person entering law school have a sound basic understanding of the economic, political and cultural structure of the world in which we live, some understanding of how the world has come to be that way, and enough information about it to enable him to make at least an intelligent guess as to where it is likely to go from this point. If you can get such an understanding from your four years of college, you will have the best conceivable foundation for the study of law. Generally speaking, I believe that broad courses in the humanities, with particular emphasis on history, English, philosophy, and foreign languages will provide the most desirable foundation for the study of law. The overriding consideration is that you learn how to think and to think analytically, while at the same time learning enough about enough things to give you sufficient material to think about. It follows that you may derive more benefit from what others might consider a narrow and specialized course in an unusual or particular field, if it happens to be taught by someone who forces you to discipline your mind, than you would derive from some other course which, at first glance, would seem to be more naturally connected with the study of law.

When I was in college, I did my major work in English constitutional history, and I will have to confess that since that time, I have met only a handful of individuals who knew enough about it to carry on even an elementary conversation. But this course gave me some understanding of how the first great democracy of the modern world, England, came to develop a system of democratic government and free institutions, and this has always been of tremendous value to me in trying to understand what our own law should be designed to accomplish. In addition, the course was taught by a professor with one of the most brilliant minds I have ever had the opportunity to observe in action, and the habits and methods of thought which he tried to develop in me have since been useful in almost every problem I have approached. When I arrived at law school, I discovered that most of my classmates had majored in business or political science, and some of them had even had college courses in business law or constitutional law. It was and still is my definite impression that their preparation was not so good as mine. For one thing, they had to unlearn at great expense in time and effort most of the legal principles which they had picked up in their undergraduate law courses, because such courses are usually taught on too simplified a basis to be of any value to a lawyer. Also, they seemed to find it much more difficult to understand the real considerations which motivated a court in reaching a particular decision, particularly when some burning social or economic issue was involved. I am certain in my own mind that the study of history is the finest possible preparation for the study of law, and I would advise you to give it serious consideration if you attend a college which has a good history department.

I do not think that your choice of law schools is of the greatest importance. This statement undoubtedly comes as a surprise to you. There are many lawyers who would disagree violently with me on this point. I myself went to law school at my own state university and eventually settled down permanently to practice law in that same state. In my daily practice, I come constantly in contact with other attorneys who have attended the large, nationally known, and excellent law schools located in the Northeast. I have never been able to find the slightest connection between the ability of any lawyer I know and the institution in which he received his legal training. As a legal officer in the United States Army, I tried cases against other young officers from law schools, large and small, which were located in almost every area of the United States, and the proportion of very competent, and not so competent, lawyers from any given school always appeared to me to be about the same. I think the explanation is twofold. First, law school cannot really teach you very much in the ultimate sense. At best, it can teach you how to think as a lawyer and where to look for the law in connection with a particular problem when you don't know the answer (which will be the case about 99 per cent of the time). Second, your success as a practicing lawyer depends far more on what you do after graduation from law school than on what you do while you are there.

I believe that your choice of law schools should be determined largely by the type of practice you want to enter into, and the place where you desire to carry on that practice. I have practiced law both in New York City and in a Southern city of slightly over 100,000 population, and I can say to you without much fear of contradiction that if you intend to practice in one of the large metropolitan centers of the United States—New York, Boston, Philadelphia, or Chicago, for example—it will be definitely to your advantage to attend a law school which has a well-established national reputation, and by that I mean a school such as Harvard, Yale, Columbia, Michigan, or Chicago, although there are many other such schools. If you enter practice in a city of a population of several millions after having received your legal education at a very good but not particularly well-known law school, you will be at a definite competitive disadvantage even though you may know more law than your contemporaries from one of the bigger schools. The bars of the great cities of this country, and particularly the bar which is engaged in the practice of corporation law, are composed almost exclusively of men from the larger schools, and it will be quite helpful to you if you have many friends practicing in the same area.

It, on the other hand, you know definitely that you want to practice in the state in which you have grown up and there is a good law school located in that state, by all means go there. Such a school will emphasize the peculiar legal rules of the state in which you will be doing your work, and, what is even more important, you will have the opportunity to form friendships with many men of your own age who will be practicing in the same area throughout your working life. The chances are that the amount of pure law which you will learn in one of the good smaller institutions will be about the same as that which you would carry away from one of the larger schools.

In any case, I would advise you against attending college and law school at the same institution. I think this is unwise because it deprives you of the opportunity to make two completely different sets of acquaintances and perhaps also of the opportunity to become acquainted with people in two different parts of the country. Many lawyers have received their undergraduate and legal education at the same school, but I feel that life is too short for one to limit one's experiences in such a manner.

Before I tell you what you may expect to be faced with when you enter law school, I think it will be well for me to attempt to give you a very fundamental idea of what a court does when it determines a legal controversy, even at the risk of repeating something which is probably said better in a more detailed chapter of this book.

Life in any modern civilized country creates a staggering number of disputes between, and among, human beings and organizations. In fact, you will probably be inclined to believe, after a few months in the practice of law, that disputes are the most prominent aspect of human society. Since we have evolved past the stage at which disputes were settled by brute force (except for disputes among nations, which unfortunately are still occasionally resolved in that manner), society has had to provide some mechanism for settling these controversies, and it has done so by establishing courts which purport to settle them by applying what we call legal principles. Most of these disputes in a society such as ours concern property or property rights—the relative importance of the criminal law is decreasing with every passing year.

What, then, is a judge doing when he is presented with a case which involves, say, the right of two different individuals to inherit a particular piece of property from a common ancestor? The average layman would tell you that the court is confronted with the problem of finding "the law," and deciding the dispute in accordance with the already established principles of that law. If this oversimplification were a correct analysis of the problem, society would be able to continue to exist with a much smaller number of lawyers than it now has at its disposition.

In actual fact, in a great number of cases, there will be no exact precedent for the situation with which the judge is confronted. The judge, therefore, will proceed, with the help of the attorneys for both parties, to examine all the precedents which seem to have some relevance to the problem at hand; he will then, ordinarily, render a decision which seems the most logical in view of what those precedents say. When the court does this, it in effect *makes* law, regardless of the terminology which may be used to describe what it has done. The decision which the court hands down then becomes a precedent; that is, a case to be considered when similar cases arise in the future, and, in the fullest sense of the word, it becomes a part of the law itself. In the Anglo-American system of law, we now have hundreds of thousands of such decided cases, and those which are relevant must be considered in connection with the decision of every new case. Therefore, what your professors will try to do for you at law school will be to give you what they hope will be a good acquaintance with the more important cases; some idea of why the cases already in the books happened to be decided as they were; and some idea, too, of the direction in which the cases are developing, something of the trend of the law.

At the same time, your professors at law school will be concerned with the development of your ability to take a novel situation, study all the applicable cases, and predict what a court would say if it had to make up its mind about the situation with which you are confronted. For when a lawyer says that "the law" is thus and so, he is really doing nothing more than making an educated prediction that the court, which would have jurisdiction of the particular controversy, would decide it in such a way if it had to do so.

You will soon discover, upon entering law school, that this brief sketch of the judicial process is greatly oversimplified, and that in many areas such a judicial process is being replaced by statute law; that is, laws made by legislative bodies, and administrative regulations. Still, the case system is the real basis of Anglo-American law and probably always will be, because lawyers need decisions of the courts in order to interpret statutes and regulations.

To give you some example of what is involved, I shall tell you something of one of the first cases which I studied in torts, a basic course in civil wrongs to which you will be exposed during your first year in any law school. The particular incident occurred in England in the fifteenth century. A drunk traveler arrived at a small English country inn late at night after the proprietor and other guests had retired and violently beat on the door and made a good deal of noise in an effort to have himself admitted. This was too much for the innkeeper's wife, who opened a shutter on the second floor, stuck her head out, and told the traveler in rather colorful fifteenth-century English that he would not be admitted and had just as well go elsewhere to seek lodging. Upon this, the traveler became insistent and threw an axe at the woman, which missed her by several feet. The traveler was convicted of assault, and the conviction was affirmed even though the woman had not been physically harmed. This was the first occasion where such a result was reached at English law. We now take it for granted that it is as unlawful to threaten another with immediate violent bodily harm as it is actually to bring about such harm, but the case represented a rather startling new development in the law of assault in medieval England.

The professor who taught the course proceeded to raise a series of very interesting questions about the case. Should society in fact penalize a man for trying, without success, to do harm to another human being? Suppose the traveler had simply brandished the axe in the air without actually throwing it at the woman? What did contemporary social conditions in medieval England have to do with the decision which the judges reached? Under the law laid down in the case, what sort of conduct between merely brandishing the axe and throwing it would constitute an assault? Fortunately, such incidents seem to be more rare in modern society, but if you find yourself stimulated by the questions which are raised by the case, the chances are that you would enjoy the study of law.

The one thing which can be predicted with certainty about your experience when you enter law school is that you will find yourself working harder than you have ever previously worked in your life, and probably harder than you will work later when you are engaged in practice. Depending upon the quality of your college education, you will find yourself working at least twice and probably three or four times as hard as you were accustomed to do in undergraduate school. This is a necessity of legal education, and there is nothing which can or will be done about it. The work in all law schools is becoming steadily harder with every passing year, for the simple reason that the number and variety of human relations with which the law must deal is rapidly increasing and is building up a constantly greater body of law with which the lawyer must have at least some acquaintance. I should have said at an earlier point, but will take the opportunity of saying now, that if you are interested in making your living without expending much effort, you had better pick some field of endeavor other than the law.

It is impossible to predict what your reaction will be when you are finally exposed to the study of law, after so many years of preparation for and anticipation of its study. You may feel like a drowning man for a year or even longer. Conversely, the entire structure of the law may impress you as being a beautifully logical body of learning in which you immediately feel completely at home. The odds are that your reaction will lie somewhere in between these two extremes. I myself had the immediate feeling that the law was the most logical structure ever created by the mind of man, and I never felt any particular sense of confusion, even in the earliest stages. This was a matter of great concern to my faculty advisor, who predicted that I would probably flunk out of law school at the end of the first semester for the simple reason that I was too confident of my ability to master the work. I did not flunk out, as is evidenced by the fact that I have been asked to contribute a chapter to this book, and I believe that the law has appeared more logical to me as the years have passed.

Your first few months in law school should reveal to you whether there is any point in continuing in your aspiration to be a lawyer. You will find that there is not necessarily very much correlation between what you accomplished in college and what you can accomplish in law school. I have seen men with brilliant scholastic records in undergraduate school who were able to make only mediocre grades in the study of law, and who were thoroughly miserable during the entire time they were in law school. I have seen men who showed no exceptional promise whatsoever in undergraduate school, but who went on to finish at the top of their class at law school. This seemingly paradoxical situation exists because lawyers are born, not made. Although intelligence is a great advantage in the law as in any other activity, there are many individuals with brilliant minds who cannot succeed in the study and practice of law. If you have had a good record in college, have above average intelligence, and yet find it impossible to make respectable grades in law school, or find yourself quite unhappy with the work, bear in mind that this is no insult to your ability. It is simply an indication that your intelligence can better be put to use in some other endeavor.

If you are one of those rare individuals who was made for the law, or for whom the law was made, you will find law school, and particularly your first year there, the most exciting and stimulating intellectual adventure you will have in the course of your entire life. You will find yourself literally living, sleeping, and eating the law. During the precious little spare time that you have away from your classes and studies, you will find yourself having heated arguments with your classmates about the cases which you are studying. Most of the cases which are reprinted in the books used in law school are close ones about which reasonable men may differ, and you may frequently differ with everyone around you about a particular point.

Law school as a whole, and especially the first year of it, is a considerable test of any man's concentration and staying power. If you allow yourself the luxury of letting your mind wander very far from your work very often, you will find that you are unable to maintain the pace which is set for you. You may decide after a few weeks of working from the time you rise in the morning until the time you go to bed at night, six or seven days a week, that the satisfactions of working with the law are not enough to compensate you for the time and energy you are devoting to it, and that you would be better off in another calling. This is nothing to be ashamed of, for there are many individuals of great worth to society who are incapable of becoming passionately involved in an area of study such as the law.

The importance of hard work from the very beginning in law school can hardly be overemphasized. If you do not master the material as it is presented to you, the chances are that your confusion will eventually become hopeless and leave you in a position from which it will be impossible for you ever to catch up with your classmates.

The opportunity for specialization during the standard three-year course in law school is rather limited. Although generally you will have no required courses after your first year, the number of basic courses which you must take in order to be a competent practitioner is fairly great, and they will leave you relatively little time to concentrate on fields in which you are particularly interested. Consequently, you might, after receiving your Bachelor of Laws or the equivalent degree at your school, want to consider a year or two of graduate study in some particular field of interest. Frankly, I would not advise that you engage in such further study unless your field of interest happens to be taxation, or unless you think you may want to enter the profession of law as a teacher.

Law is an eminently practical profession, one which daily requires hard decisions based on the realities of everyday life, and it can be a serious mistake for a man to spend too many years in which his acquaintance with law is limited to what he studies in books. The shelter and insulation from the hard problems of human life, which an academic institution can provide, is for some individuals an insidious thing which may eventually lead to great reluctance to encounter the real world. Also, the brief number of years that I have practiced have convinced me that most of the techniques you will use in practicing your profession as a lawyer are techniques you will learn in the hard school of everyday work. A very successful senior partner in a very fine Wall Street law firm in New York once said to me quite seriously that if it were not for the requirements of the bar examiners in his state, his firm would be quite willing to take young men after their second year of law school. He believed that after two years, a man had gotten as sound a foundation in the theory of the law as he needed, and that any academic work thereafter was a waste of time which could be better spent learning how to apply the theory to real problems. This is perhaps an extreme point of view, and I have heard no one else put it forward, but I think there is enough truth in it to emphasize the fact that there is some danger in learning too much theory in law before one has had an opportunity to become acquainted with the practicalities.

After graduation from law school, you will probably be faced with the gruesome prospect of taking a bar examination in the state in which you desire to practice. By all means, as soon as you have some idea of where you want to establish practice, contact the board of law examiners of that state and ask what subjects you will be examined on and what the residence requirements are. The latter question is particularly important in some states, because they will not allow you to take the examination unless you are already a bona fide resident of the state or have resided there for a particular period of time.

The kindest thing I can say for bar examinations is that they do give one an opportunity, usually during the summer following graduation from law school, to review and study all the courses in the law-school curriculum and derive therefrom a picture of how the various arbitrary subdivisions of legal learning fit together to form a whole. The odds are that you will forget most of what you learned in that summer's study within a few weeks after passing the examination. In any event, the bar examination is something which you must face, and the chances are that if you have a good law school record and study hard immediately prior to the examination, you will not have any difficulty in getting over this barrier. There are "cram courses," of varying quality, offered in the various states, which may be of help to you.

If you have a military obligation which you have not fulfilled by the time of your graduation from law school, and are interested in doing something at least remotely connected with law while you are in uniform, you might want to investigate the possibility of taking a commission in the Judge Advocate General's Corps of the Army or in the legal branch of one of the other military services. This will probably entail considerable extra time in service, because the minimum tour of duty of a legal officer is ordinarily three years. I myself served for two years in the Army as a First Lieutenant in the Judge Advocate General's Corps and spent a part of those years in France as a trial observer in French courts in cases where American soldiers were tried for violations of French law. I learned a great deal about French criminal law, which was interesting, but will probably never be useful to me professionally, and a great deal more about life in general which was more interesting than French law and is quite useful to me every day. However, it was just as likely that I might have spent those years in some obscure Army post in the southern or western United States as that I would be put in a position to spend all my weekends in Paris and London. If you are still relatively young upon graduation from law school—by which I mean twenty-five or younger—and still single, you will want at least to consider spending two or three years as a military lawyer. If you happen to be one of those lucky individuals who spends his career as a legal officer trying court-martial cases, you might get as much trial experience in these years as would come your way in thirty years of ordinary practice.

Once law school and your military service are behind you and you are, at least in theory, a lawyer, you will be faced with the most important decision in your life—that is, you will have to make up your mind what sort of law you want to practice, where, and with whom. I cannot possibly exaggerate the seriousness of this decision, for relatively speaking, it is more important than any other which you will ever be called upon to make. I have heard older lawyers say in a not entirely joking manner that this decision is more important than a lawyer's choice of a wife, for the simple reason that the average lawyer spends a greater portion of his waking hours with his legal associates than he is able to spend with his family. If you are practicing with other men whom you respect, and with whom you are able to get along with a minimum of friction, this can go far to making your life in the law a happy one; if you are not so fortunate, you will undoubtedly be miserable in your practice. Most law-school graduates do not devote even a small fraction of the time and effort to the making of this decision that it deserves. The traditional oversupply of lawyers no longer exists; indeed, the situation is rapidly becoming one in which there is a serious shortage of young lawyers, and this is yet another reason why you should take your time in making up your mind and not be tempted to accept the first offer made to you upon the theory that the only alternative is starvation.

At least by the end of your second year of law school, you should be making inquiries in the part of the country where you would like to practice, and you should arrange for interviews with the individuals or firms which appear most attractive to you. If you are able to do it, I think it would not be wasted time to spend several weeks traveling around the state of your choice talking with every lawyer who will listen to you, whether he happens to be looking for a new associate or not, for what he says about those lawyers who are looking for associates may later be invaluable to you. Also, if you have the time and can afford it, you might do well to investigate opportunities in other places which you do not feel really interest you. I think that the week I spent interviewing the giant down-town law firms in New York was an experience well worth the time and money involved, even had I ultimately decided to leave that city without any time spent in law work there.

The first and most fundamental decision confronting you, of course, is whether you desire to open your own office or to enter into an association with some other lawyer or firm already well established. The statistics on the subject show beyond a shadow of a doubt that the number of those who open their own offices is decreasing with every passing year. The reasons are simple. The incredible growth in the complexity of the law within the last few decades has created a legal world in which it is virtually impossible for any man, who is not a genius in the fullest sense of the word, to be a competent practitioner in all fields of the law. Many fields, such as taxation, demand the full time and attention of very brilliant men, if they are to be competently practiced. The specialist can best exist as a part of a firm which includes other specialists and which, taken as a whole, can provide all types of legal services for its clients. Furthermore, the statistics indicate clearly that the larger the firm, the more money the individual attorney in it will make in the course of his career.

This is not to say that it would be a form of suicide for you to hang out your own shingle, even in a large and strange city. It is still quite possible for a person with real ability to practice law competently and successfully on his own, particularly in the smaller cities and towns. Although I have never practiced by myself, I can see that opening one's own office would have certain satisfactions which might be impossible ever to attain otherwise. I am sure that the feeling that you are your own boss, that you alone are responsible for the quality of every job which you turn out, may go far in compensating you for the extra hours of work and the smaller monetary rewards which would be yours as a sole practitioner. It all depends on you as an individual. If you have the slightest feeling that only in this type of work would you be happy, my suggestion would be that you try it at once. You can always enter into association with another lawyer if the danger of starvation becomes too great, and I think that the urge to open his own law office is one which a man must indulge by following it or otherwise risk being haunted for the remainder of his life by the thought that he has failed to try the one type of law practice which he might have found the most satisfying.

I personally have practiced with a law firm in New York which comprised some ninety lawyers, and with a smaller firm of about twelve lawyers in a middle-sized Southern town. Frankly, I prefer the latter type of practice. Many of my friends in New York would be extremely unhappy in a smaller firm, just as I was in a larger firm. However, I think I can say with some objectivity that a medium-sized firm of some five to twenty lawyers (what is medium-sized and what is large, of course, varies with different areas of the country) offers the maximum of opportunity for a rewarding and satisfying practice of law. Such a firm usually has clients whose problems are big enough to call for every ounce of mental ability you have, but no clients whose problems are so big that they may require you to work for a year or more on the same case. The financial rewards in such a firm, although generally not fabulous by any means, are such that you can be reasonably assured of having a comfortable existence. In some such firms, but not all, you may have the same degree of independence in your practice which you would find as a sole practitioner.

If you do join one of the great law firms in one of the larger cities, it is almost inconceivable that you will be able to avoid specializing in some area of the law at a very early stage in your career. The large law firms handle problems of a staggering importance and complexity, and, generally speaking, only those who are specialists are able to deal with them. These problems are fascinating in many ways. The outcome of many cases on which you will work in such a firm will have a profound impact on life in the United States or even in the entire world. On the other hand, the competition is grueling. Only about one out of six young lawyers who begins work with such a firm stays on to become a full partner. About three will decide that this type of work is not something for which they are suited, and they move on to work with corporations or with smaller firms in smaller cities. There then ensues a competition among the remaining three for one seat at the partners' table, and the element of chance involved in ever sitting in that seat is a great one. The odds are that you and your competitors will be of about equal ability, and simply doing your job well, or even doing it superbly, will not insure that you will become a member of the firm. If you do become a partner, your financial reward will be great, for it is not at all uncommon for senior partners in the great metropolitan firms to make $100,000 or more per year.

If you think this type of practice would be exciting and satisfying, try it. I was amazed to discover that a young lawyer with a good academic record can more easily find a position in New York City than in almost any other part of the country. It is not necessary that you have any contacts in any of the firms and you will be surprised at the consideration which will be shown you if you simply wander in off the street and tell the receptionist that you are interested in talking to some of the lawyers about working for the firm. If you have no idea at all of the type of work which such a great law firm does, by all means go to New York and find out for yourself. It is a fascinating experience even if you decide not to work there.

The general public's ideas about a young lawyer's salary are now unduly pessimistic because of certain changes which have taken place within the past few years. Although there are great variations from city to city and state to state, and from firm to firm, it is no longer necessary that someone beginning the practice of law eke out a bare existence for two or three years before he begins to be compensated adequately. In New York, in 1962, the starting salary for lawyers in the large down-town firms was $600 per month with a bonus once a year, which might bring the first year's earnings to $8,000 or more. In some other parts of the country, the starting salary was $400 per month or less. It is quite unlikely that you will make very much money in the first five or even ten years of practice, and, even if you did, you would probably not have sufficient time to spend it. If you do not, you will probably not have sufficient time to miss it either, so it would really seem to be a matter which is not so important as you might think. Your first years of practice will be so crowded with novel experiences and will so completely absorb nearly all your energy that, as long as you are making a sufficient amount of money to assure you a modest but reasonable standard of living, it is not likely that you will worry a great deal about how wealthy you are becoming. Whatever its disadvantages may be, one great advantage of a career in law is that one's earning power increases steadily with age and experience, and does not reach a peak and then decline in later life as is the case with some other occupations. The financial aspects of law as a profession can truthfully be summed up by saying that the practice of law is in no sense a business dedicated to the making of money, and that a lawyer realizes certain types of income, in satisfaction with his work, which are not strictly pecuniary but which go a long way toward compensating him for his efforts.

What may you expect when you begin actual practice, in the types of experiences you will have, and the work which you will perform? I think it is correct to say that going from law school into practice is the biggest single "jump" that you will make in your entire life. It is a much more fundamental transition, for example, than that from college to law school. Here again, as at all stages in becoming a lawyer, some men will find the change too violent and may conclude even at this late time that the practice of law is not for them. Some young lawyers say that it took them between three and five years to feel sufficiently relaxed in their practice to enjoy their everyday work, and, I assure you, that after a few months of practice you will be able to understand and to sympathize with them.

You will find quite early that the practice of law does not consist entirely of smashing and dramatic victories in the courtroom. These you will have, from time to time, but you will also have to get out of bed on many a cold and rainy Monday morning and go to your office to draw up a deed or contract in which you have not the slightest interest. Then, too, applying the neat, abstract principles you have learned in law school to the unruly realities of everyday work is not easy. You will soon realize that many of the strange cases which you read in your law-school case books, involving situations which ought not to arise more than once in a thousand years, are actually typical examples of the problems which people have in everyday life. You will further find that your clients, in addition to having talent for getting into extraordinary types of trouble, always do so in such a way that you can never find any decided case which exactly fits their situation. But if this is a source of much of the frustration of the practice of law, it is also the source of most of its satisfaction.

Except in certain specialties which you can easily avoid if you choose to do so, you will find that the great beauty of the practice of law is that it is ordinarily not monotonous. When you open your office door in the morning, you will never have the slightest idea as to what fascinating, violent, tragic, or comic problems you may be called upon to solve before you are finally able to lock your door and go home for a well-earned night's sleep. For example, on the morning of the day that I was planning to write this chapter, I came to the office with five or six fairly routine problems on my mind, which I intended to dispose of before the day was over. However, I have practiced long enough to know that such a tranquil day almost never materializes, and I thought, during the course of my drive to the office, that some unexpected, very pressing, and very interesting problem would likely appear before the morning was gone. It did, about half an hour after I sat down behind my desk. An individual had resigned as an employee of a corporation which is one of our clients, and was threatening to dispose of certain shares of stock which he was obligated by contract to sell back to the corporation upon resignation. By noon, I had drawn up all the necessary papers to begin a lawsuit against him, had filed them, and had procured a temporary restraining order from a local judge to prevent the defendant from transferring the shares of stock until the right to them was finally determined. By the middle of the afternoon, the restraining order had been served upon the defendant, and my client's interest was protected, at which point I was able again to turn my attention to the routine matters which I had on my schedule for the day. On another day, I might be visited by a woman in tears, who desires to have her marriage annulled three days after the ceremony was performed. Or, in court on a routine matter, I might be called up to the bench by the judge and appointed on the spur of the moment to represent, at a preliminary hearing, an individual charged with a capital crime, who did not have sufficient money to hire a lawyer. All this is mixed in with the more routine daily matters of searching titles to real estate, drawing contracts and leases, and trying automobile-collision cases.

In the very beginning, your problems will seem very great. You will find yourself obliged to spend five or ten times as much time on every matter you handle as would be devoted to it by a more mature and experienced lawyer. You may also be required to spend hours of research finding the answer to some simple procedural problem which thereafter will require only five minutes of your time at the most. These early years are very important in that, if you take the time which is necessary to be certain that what you are doing in every instance is correct, you will build up a competency as a legal practitioner which will eventually make you one of the respected members of the bar. Of course, in emergency situations, you will be called upon to accomplish at a moment's notice something with which you are not familiar, and on such occasions you will simply have to do your best and hope that what you do is correct. You will have many difficult days if you have not learned, before beginning your practice, how to remain calm and collected however great the pressure exerted upon you by others and by circumstances may be. If you are unable to develop this quality of remaining cool in a crisis, it is hardly likely that your life in the legal profession will be a lengthy one; for the lawyer who cannot deal with his problems coolly and methodically, and forget them until the next morning, leaving them at the office after a hard day's work, is not likely to lead a long and healthy life.

In your practice, you will see human beings in almost every role which they are capable of assuming. You will have the opportunity to laugh with them, to cry with them, to congratulate them, and to deplore them. You will see life at its finest and at its worst, although at times you will be tempted to think that you see it more often in the latter aspect because of the obvious fact that those persons who are happy will not come to see you to tell you about it, while those who are not will often come in order to see whether anything can be done about it.

In the larger firms, you will probably spend your first few years in the library, preparing memoranda of law, and preparing briefs on subject after subject, in case after case. Indeed, you may often wonder what the difference is between your existence as a researcher in the law and the life which you once led in law school. But if you survive this stage, you will have opportunity to make decisions enough, and decisions of a frightening importance. If you have an office of your own, or if you are with a smaller firm, you will probably find that your work has a tremendous variety. In my first year of practice with a firm, I searched titles to real estate (many of them), did some work in taxation, participated in a few labor-law cases, helped one of the other members of the firm with a patent case, tried some automobile-collision cases, drew countless wills and contracts, and still found time to defend a few indigent criminals. Each new task involved a great amount of study, as it was always in an unfamiliar field. Yet, within about six months, I had developed enough confidence in my ability to perform the work given me to be able to enjoy almost all of it. After two years, I could honestly say that almost nothing frightened me, and that every case I handled in a new or unfamiliar area of the law provided me with a new satisfaction once the job had been accomplished.

The working hours of the young lawyer are long. You will soon discover that the amount of time you spend at the office, beyond a certain point, depends largely on you as an individual. You may prefer to concentrate all your attention on your work for eight or nine hours a day and relax at night, or you may prefer to relax at intervals during the day and return to your office at night. Much advice has been given, in many books, to young lawyers as to whether or not they should work at night. I can only say that this is strictly a matter of individual taste and need. There are times when the most efficient and experienced lawyer will be unable to perform his work between nine and five o'clock; at other times, there may be a rare afternoon when he will be able to leave the office after lunch and play a round of golf. The work load in any law office constantly fluctuates; but whatever work there is to do has to be done and done promptly. If you are working for a firm, you will probably find that it is very liberal with respect to your taking long weekends and extra days off after you have worked night and day for many days on a particular project. To me, and to most lawyers, the fact that the working hours are not predictable is one of the attractive features of the profession.

You may decide after some years in the private practice of law that you prefer the more regular hours, and more certain existence, of the lawyer who works for a corporation or who is engaged in business. If so, you will find that the years you have spent in law school and in private practice were far from wasted. The law is an excellent springboard, regardless of the direction in which you feel inclined to jump; it would hardly be an exaggeration to say that no training is so generally useful to the average man as a training in the law.

In my own case, I feel sure that I never will be tempted to give up private practice in order to use my legal training in any other way. Ever since I began practice, Monday morning has been a point in my week which is just as glamorous as Saturday night, and I think that any man who is fortunate enough to be in such a situation would be foolish indeed to look for something better. The law is a glorious profession. If you are one of those individuals who can find happiness in it, it would be most regrettable for you to miss such an opportunity for personal fulfillment. I sincerely hope that this chapter in this book will guide into the profession some of you who can find fulfillment in the law, and, at least in some small degree, will make the road to that fulfillment a smoother one.

5 *You in*

TRIAL LAW

BY EDWARD BENNETT WILLIAMS

Washington, D. C.

EDWARD BENNETT WILLIAMS

Born: 1920, Hartford, Connecticut

Bulkeley High School
College of the Holy Cross: A.B., 1941
Georgetown University: LL.B., 1944

Admitted to District of Columbia Bar: 1944
Williams & Stein (Washington)
Professor Criminal Law and Evidence,
    Georgetown University: 1946–58
Guest Professor on American Criminal Law,
    University of Frankfurt, Germany: 1954
Lecturer, numerous universities and colleges

American Bar Association: Chairman,
    Committee on Criminal Defense Procedures, Criminal Law Section
Bar Association of District of Columbia:
    Second vice-president: 1949
    First vice-president: 1950, 1955–56
Fellow, American College of Trial Lawyers
International Academy of Trial Lawyers

Author: *One Man's Freedom*

THE BEST WAY, so it seems to me, to write about trial law for this particular book is to answer the questions that I have been most often asked at colleges and universities, especially at law schools where I have spoken. Always after a talk there has been a question-and-answer period and usually one of the first questions asked is the obvious one: What *is* trial law?

The whole trial practice breaks down into two parts. There is civil-trial practice and criminal-trial practice.

In civil-trial practice, one is concerned with the assertion or the defense of property rights.

On the criminal side of the court, one is concerned with human liberty, sometimes with human life, and always with human reputation.

The trial practice really is the art—and I think it is an art—of advocating on behalf of a client his rights to property or his rights to liberty.

The skills required in the trial of a civil case are the same skills necessary in the trial of a criminal case. There is simply a different application of rules to a different set of facts, but, unfortunately, there is now a reluctance on the part of many civil lawyers to get into the criminal field. One reason for this is that in our time there is a stigma that attaches to the lawyer who devotes himself exclusively to the trial of criminal cases. The concept of "guilt by client" has insidiously encroached until there is a tendency on the part of laymen to identify the lawyer with his client, no matter who the lawyer may be or what his character. Merely because he defends a client, particularly an unpopular one, some

99

of the client's unsavory reputation becomes associated with him.

The unreasonableness of this has come to the point where moral judgment is now passed on a lawyer because of his client, and he is even labeled with the label of his client. He is called "left wing" or Communist if he defends a Communist, when, in fact, defending a Communist no more makes a lawyer a Communist than defending a murderer makes him a murderer, or an advocate of murder.

Always a lawyer defends a client, not a crime. Nor, for that matter, does defense suggest approval of either client or crime; the lawyer is merely fulfilling his obligation, the unwritten law of his profession, that he cannot refuse defense. There should be neither honor for him, nor obloquy; there should be only recognition that, in the enduring tradition of the law, he can do nothing else. This is his responsibility, his necessity, and, in my opinion, he has no choice.

Despite this obligation, however, some men have turned away from taking the defense of an unpopular person or unpopular cause because of the critical and denunciatory attitude of the public. This same public misunderstanding, with its accompanying social and professional pressures, has also turned some young lawyers from the practice of criminal law and from the courtroom, thereby lessening the effectiveness of trial law in our country and weakening the cause of justice.

This, incidentally, is something that does not happen in any other profession. I think that we can take all forms of human troubles and break them down into roughly three classes. We have physical troubles, and the medical profession handles these. We have spiritual problems, and the clergy handles these. Then we have social problems, which are man's problems with his fellow man, and the legal profession handles these.

No doctor worthy of his name, and of his profession, would ever turn away a patient because he had some loathsome or incurable disease. No matter how horrible the disease might be, under his oath as a doctor he would treat the patient.

No clergyman, I think, worthy of his name would turn away a

man who sought his aid because his sins were too awful or too heinous.

I believe that the same rules apply with respect to the legal profession. This is a basic rule of logic, finding expression in the Sixth Amendment to the Constitution of the United States, which makes it the obligation of a lawyer, in my opinion, to afford his counsel to anyone who seeks it, so long as it is sought within the limits of integrity and decency.

I say it is an obligation for this reason: when the founding fathers wrote the Bill of Rights and it became a part of the Constitution, they gave to every accused the right to counsel, no matter what the accusation might be, and no matter who the person might be. It does not say every accused except a Communist, or every accused except a narcotics peddler, or every accused except a murderer—it says that *everyone* has the right to counsel.

This is true, and must continue true, no matter how obnoxious an individual may be personally, no matter how offensive he may be politically to many people in whatever stand he takes on whatever issue. It is true also of any person accused of violence, regardless of the nature of his crime or how strongly the evidence may point to his "guilt." It is especially true when he has already been convicted in the court of public opinion. This man, and every man, has the right to trial and it is the obligation of his lawyer to raise for him every possible defense that is authorized by the law of the land.

Now rights and duties, as I understand them, are correlative ideas. There cannot be a right for one person without a corresponding duty on the part of someone else to respect it. I am convinced that a man's right to a trial and to counsel bespeaks the duty on the part of my profession to afford that counsel whenever it is honestly sought.

You may ask: What is "honestly sought"? I mean that a lawyer is always called on to defend a man, but never called on to accept and use weapons of fraud. Suppose a man comes and says, "I am charged with bank robbery. I know that you are the best advocate in the country and I want you to represent me. I will pay you a big fee because I don't want to go to jail for thirty years. Now I did it, but I want you to get me off. I'll get a couple of witnesses who will produce an alibi for me and, of course, I'll take the stand and deny it."

These are weapons of fraud, outside the standards of honesty, and the lawyer cannot take that case. Here is a man who wants to commit perjury and suborn perjury. The lawyer can only turn him down and refuse his case; in fact, throw him out.

But there is a no reason that this same man cannot have a defense, provided it is an honest defense. He has every right to ask for the aid of a lawyer, provided he simply wants his Constitutional right of trial, and wants the Government's case tested in the crucible of cross-examination, while he himself stands silent and offers no evidence.

In such a case as this, which may very well seem to the layman to be a complete paradox of justice, we must immediately make the fundamental and essential distinction between *moral* guilt and *legal* guilt. As we use the term "guilt" in this chapter, we are concerned with it only as a legal term. It is essential that this fact be understood; that always we are talking of guilt only within the law. The making of moral judgments is beyond us, and should be, for they are within the exclusive jurisdiction of God.

But one asks, "What should a lawyer do when a man comes in and directly says, 'I did it'?"

This is a basic question, and should be asked, but first we must take it out of the abstract. He directly says he did what? That he robbed the bank. That he stole the money. That he murdered the man. That he is *guilty*.

You know, I have had people come to me who thought they were guilty of terrible crimes, but in fact they were not. I will give you an illustration of this: I had a woman come to me who had killed a man. She just shot him in cold blood early one morning in Washington, D. C. I talked with her and within a few minutes I had formed a layman's opinion that she was psychotic.

She had a great feeling of *moral* guilt, but she was subsequently examined by six doctors appointed by the Government, none of them appointed by the defense, and every doctor came to the conclusion independently that she was seriously psychotic. They concluded that the crime was the product of a diseased mind, and that, under the law, she was not guilty of murder.

This is a simple and obvious case, but there are others that are not so clear. Our criminal laws have become so complex in some fields that a layman may not be qualified to judge legal guilt, even when it concerns him. He can only go to his lawyer and lay the facts truthfully before him. It then becomes the lawyer's responsibility to apply the law to these facts and decide whether the defendant is legally guilty and should enter a plea of guilty, or should go to trial to defend himself.

If defense is decided upon, the final arbiter of the facts and of the law is the court, where the issue of legal guilt will be tested and determined.

It goes without saying that many people who are morally guilty of bad acts escape the law. Under our system of justice every man is presumed innocent until, in a court of law, he is proven guilty. It is possible that this has been said so often, and has become so familiar, that its significance has been somewhat lost in our daily thinking. But the requirement that each man be presumed innocent is basic in our whole system of Anglo-Saxon justice; for in that system we regard human liberty as so important that we would rather have twenty guilty men go free than hazard the conviction of one innocent man. And yet, if we believe in the concept of divine judgment, we have the certainty that they who are morally guilty will one day face the majestic vengeance of God. This, in a far more enduring way, rectifies the imperfections of our human system.

We have reached the day of such specialization in the practice of law that it is a mistake for a lawyer, no matter how capable he may be in other fields, to go into court and attempt to try a case unless he is experienced and skilled in such practice. We are slowly coming to a modified form of the English system where certain lawyers, called the barristers, go into court and the other lawyers, the solicitors, do the office work.

The distinction between a practicing trial lawyer and what we might call an "office lawyer" is very real, but the distinction on the surface may not be quickly apparent. I think, however, it is time for us to consider the trial lawyer himself. What kind of man is he? Must he have special qualifications?

I do not believe there are any particular physical qualifications that he requires, because if one looks back over the history of the great trial lawyers in our country one will find all manner of men physically. Among these lawyers, some were small in stature, some were big men physically. Some were handsome, some ugly. Some even had bad voices. I think that the importance of physical attributes is negligible.

As for mental qualities, a good trial lawyer must first of all be a good lawyer. He needs sound judgment and a thorough grounding in legal principles just as much as the office lawyer. He must, in addition, have a very fast mind. In the vernacular of the Westerns, he must be a "quick draw." In trial practice, a lawyer often has to shoot from the hip because in the courtroom he has no opportunity for reflection. If he is not a quick mental draw, there is always somebody across the table who is going to knock him over.

The bigger his reputation gets in trial practice, the more eager is the man across the table to bump him off. All the trial lawyers who do national work will tell you that when they go into a strange place, it is like Billy the Kid showing up in one of those old Western towns. The local boy is looking for a chance to shoot him dead. A successful trial lawyer, in any courtroom, always has to be on the watch and very fast in what he does.

He has to be eloquent, too, though his eloquence must be in a modern appraisal of eloquence, and without any suggestion of the old-time, spread-eagle oratory.

Even more than eloquent, however, he must be articulate. He must be able to express his thoughts in the simplest, the clearest, and always the most forceful way.

Most of all, he must have a real knowledge of human nature and of human behavior. He has to understand people, and this means all kinds of people. He has to learn, too, to deal with all kinds of motivations, strange desires, and conduct that cannot be explained.

Among the other needs of a successful trial lawyer is the ability in the courtroom to make people like him. This has nothing to do with trivial popularity, or with any acclaim of the moment. Instead, it is an enduring factor in the courtroom, especially in his dealings with a jury. There is no way to tell how this can be done; the lawyer can only do his best and hope that the jury will like him.

Something even more important for the lawyer, a good deal more important than causing people to like him, is his ability to make them like his client. The principal actor in every trial is the defendant himself. People often think differently about this and talk about the trial lawyer taking the center of the stage. This he does occasionally, for even in the great plays the subordinate actors sometimes take the stage. But the truly fine trial lawyer will rarely take the spotlight from the defendant, certainly not for long, since the defendant must always be the star of the show. He is the one to be built up so that people will become interested in him favorably. If the lawyer for the defense really does his job, the jurors at the end of the trial will like the defendant, or at least feel sympathy for him, no matter how unfortunate the role in which he may have been cast.

This talk of the theater, of trials and productions, leads me to say that I believe the practice of trial law is perhaps the most creative art extant. At one time I had an argument about this with a friend who is a great motion-picture director. His name is Robert Rossen. He, to the motion-picture industry, is what a triple-threat man used to be in the old days of football. He is a writer. He is a director. He is a producer. He once wrote, directed, and produced a picture which won the Academy Award in all three departments. It was called *All the King's Men,* and was adapted from Robert Penn Warren's book of that name.

One night we were sitting at my home while I was representing Rossen in a matter. We began talking of law and I said that the trial of a major criminal case required more creative talent than the production of a great motion picture. He disputed this.

The reasons I gave him, which finally convinced him, were these:

When a lawyer is in the trial of a major criminal case, he is staging a production that is designed to create an impression on the jury and he has no opportunity for retakes. One mistake and he may be through.

Secondly, he has no backdrop, no lighting, no effects to create illusions. He is working on a bare stage.

Third, he is not dealing with fiction. He has only the facts and he must always confine himself within their limits. There is no chance for fabrication, no way to extricate himself by breaking the bonds of truth.

Fourth, he is working to create an impression on an audience of twelve people, and he must create that impression not on seven out of twelve, or ten out of twelve, but *twelve* out of twelve. He must win everybody to get an acquittal, whereas a playwright, or a movie producer, who gets ten critics out of twelve on his side has done a great job.

Lastly, of course, he is working for the highest stakes for which a man can compete. He is working for human liberty, and, in some cases, for human life.

Long before the lawyer goes into the courtroom, he begins preparing for the staging of the production. He prepares his case patiently, thoroughly, with infinite care in regard to witnesses, timing, every detail—all of it is planned so that his case will have the greatest persuasive impact possible on the minds of the jurors.

For instance, in preparing for a trial, one of a lawyer's most serious responsibilities is to advise the defendant as to how he should testify. This may sound quite shocking! Do I mean that the lawyer has to tell a defendant what to say? He really does, in a sense.

A man on trial for his liberty can, in one and the same answer, create a totally different impact on the minds of the jury. I will give you an illustration of this. Suppose in the trial of a case it becomes relevant where the defendant, John Smith, was on January 6, 1958. Almost certainly he will be asked that question by the prosecutor on cross-examination.

John Smith, unprepared, goes on the stand.

PROSECUTOR: "Where were you, Mr. Smith, on the night of January 6, 1958?"

He looks at the prosecutor and he says, "I don't remember."

This answer certainly does not create any *positive* impression in the minds of the jurors. At best, it is neutral. And it may be negative.

On the other hand, dealing with the same fact, namely that Mr. Smith does not remember where he was on January 6, if the question is answered in another way it gives a totally different effect.

QUESTION: "Where were you, Mr. Smith, on the night of January 6, 1958?"

Mr. Smith says, "Mr. Prosecutor, I thought you were going to ask me that question and I have racked my brain trying to remember where I was on the night of January 6, 1958, because I want to answer all these questions. But for the life of me I just can't remember where I was on that night."

In both answers, the defendant has given, so far as actual facts are concerned, the same answer: He does not remember. But he has not ended with the same impression. The first form of his answer may have left a vague, neutral impression. The second form is not neutral; it may have made a positive impression, it may even have evoked sympathy for him because he has shown to the jury that he is trying to co-operate. He is trying to help, and yet, human frailties being what they are, he just can't remember where he was on some particular night several years ago.

This is why I say that a trial lawyer has to teach a witness how to testify. When he does, things that otherwise might not be fruitful for him, which otherwise might make a doubtful impact, can make a tremendously positive impact on the jury.

And at this point, so that there will be no possible misunderstanding about a trial lawyer's purpose, let me make it as clear and as positive as I can that his purpose, his business at all times, is to exploit every fact in the case, *within the limits of truth,* toward the idea of gaining for his client the greatest possible impact on the jury in his favor.

Now let me make an important distinction in this matter of testifying. One must unmistakably differentiate between *how* to testify—as I have just indicated—and *what* to testify. One can legitimately influence the "how," but the "what" is always determined by the facts.

In preparing a witness, one can never tamper with the facts, with the truth; but what I am trying to demonstrate is that, within the most exact demands of truth, there is a great play of impact. This variance of impact, on the minds and on the emotions, is possible in every action in the trial, every question, every answer. This is why I say that in staging a trial, a lawyer is producing a great drama, especially vivid because it is circumscribed by the limits of truth. No one who watches a major criminal trial, or even an exciting civil trial, can doubt that trial practice is a creative and powerful form of art.

This sense of the dramatic is in all the great trial lawyers I have met in this country. They all have a histrionic flair in staging their productions and, moreover, each of them has a little of the actor in him. In fact, some of the finest actors in America are trial lawyers. They are not actors on any theatrical stage, but in their own legal setting they are almost incomparable in their sense of demonstrating the emotions. Clarence Darrow made some of the most powerful pleas in the history of the American courtroom. He may also have been one of the greatest actors in the history of American drama.

The best way for any trial lawyer to gain his training is in the courtroom itself. The law schools of the country do not provide the courses in advocacy that they should; but even if they did offer these courses in the classroom, there is no final substitute for the courtroom and the actual trial itself.

There is a way, however, that courtroom experience could be provided by the law schools. Young doctors, after taking their work in medical school, go into the hospitals for further training as interns. This is the system that should be followed by law schools, sending their graduates, and even their third-year students, into the courtrooms as "interns."

Moreover, this training could be properly integrated into a very serious problem in this country, one that now shades the whole administration of criminal justice; namely, the defense of the indigent. The problem is so great that the figures at present show that about 60 per cent of all persons charged with crime across the country cannot afford a lawyer. This is a tremendous problem in the matter of justice.

I do not believe in socializing the problem. I do not think that we should create an instrument of the state to handle it. The easy way is always to take our obligations and put them into some state bureau; but I think that the obligation is on the bar itself, and that there should be a rotating system of experienced trial lawyers to afford experienced counsel to the indigent. At the same time, there should be a constant use of law students, of interns, giving the legal protection to the indigent that, by all rights under our Constitution, they should have. In this way, too, the interns would gain the courtroom experience that they need, for, as I have said, it is only in the courtroom that reasonably skilled young trial lawyers can be developed.

I was lucky when I got out of law school because I went with a large firm in Washington. They had an extensive volume of trial practice and for five years I was in the courtroom almost every day trying cases. There is just no substitute for this experience.

In a trial, a lawyer makes mistakes and he finds out where he made them. He can never learn this from a book. No one can learn to cross-examine by reading, not even by reading all the greatest books ever written on cross-examination. A lawyer learns to cross-examine only by facing an agile, skillful witness, by moving in and finding out the do's and the don't's. There is only one way to learn this—in actual courtroom combat.

Besides learning from this experience, there is so much else that a lawyer learns in the courtroom, so much that he is forced to learn. In the great variety of cases in which a trial lawyer must necessarily take part, many of them involving facts of an expert nature—medical, economic, scientific—he discovers that he must educate himself so that, for the life of that particular trial, he will know as much about these facts, in the narrow area in which he is directly concerned, as the most expert man in the whole world.

Here is what I mean. Several years ago I tried a case in Washington involving a bank merger. My clients were stockholders in a smaller bank which was merging with one of the big banks in Washington, and they were resisting the merger.

I knew nothing about bank mergers, absolutely nothing. So I found the man who is widely heralded as the outstanding authority in the United States on bank mergers, and I went to him in New York. My clients were able to pay for this and I took a course from him. For one week we worked sixteen, maybe eighteen hours a day, an intensively concentrated one-week course in the narrow area of bank mergers with which we would be concerned in this case—not the whole field, for I was not concerned with this and did not attempt it, but a concentrated study of the direct area that would confront me.

When I emerged from this course, I knew as much about this narrow area as some people who had been in the field all their lives. They knew hundreds of times more about the over-all subject than I did; but I had been concentrating on this one facet and I knew as much about it, and maybe more, than they did.

The result was that when adverse witnesses got on the stand and began to paint with a broad brush, I could button them down. They quickly realized, from my questions, that I knew what I was talking about. This put a bridle on them and prevented them from using generalities. In fact, it flustered some of the witnesses quite badly. People who consider themselves experts, wiser in some particular field than anybody else, do not like to be questioned by someone who is as knowledgeable in that narrow area as they are. They think that this particular little region belongs only to them and it confuses them when they find that it does not, and they often show their confusion and sometimes their anger. This produces an adverse effect on the jury, and a favorable effect for the lawyer who is doing the questioning.

So for this immediate month, in trial practice, there may be a bank merger with which you are concerned. Next month it may be a ruptured intervertebral disc, then a manipulation of the stock market by a specialist in some kind of stock. So it goes, month after month, always shifting as you move from trial to trial.

And you wonder, perhaps, how you can possibly learn enough and be prepared to try all these technical cases. This is the way it works. Perhaps in college you had the experience of getting behind in a course, then staying up for two nights and just pounding the subject into yourself, getting ready for a big exam. You pass the exam, maybe you do well on it, but a week later you do not know any more about the subject than before you crammed. This is the way it is with a lawyer. I do not know anything about bank mergers any more. I do not know any more than I did before I started, but I knew an immense amount for the life of the trial.

This takes a certain kind of mind that is able to endure intensive concentration and is capable of absorbing innumerable details, having them ready instantly at any moment in the trial. It also requires an unusual memory, not only for immediate details but also for the background and the history of the subject at issue. Such memory is tremendously important to a lawyer, both in the preparation of a case and in the actual trial itself. He must remember everything.

In preparing a case for trial, a lawyer must understand that he has one purpose: the complete development of all the facts. Nothing less than this will suffice. Every detail must be examined. *Every* person who has *any* knowledge of *any* fact in issue must be interviewed. I mean exactly what I say. All facts. Every person. This is the preparation so often overlooked by trial lawyers, and this is why they fail in the courtroom.

It is not enough in preparing a case to interview only the obvious persons who are known to have information about it. A lawyer who is rightfully and conscientiously preparing his case must interview every person who *may* have information about it. The odds may be ten to one against some person knowing anything that might be wanted, but that person still must be interviewed. Statements must be taken, compared, tested, and searched for any possible detail that could be useful. These statements, along with all other listed facts, must be compiled in a fact file, indexed by subject matter, indexed by witnesses, and cross-indexed. Sometimes these files can become huge, and, obviously, all the work of gathering the information and making the files cannot be done by the lawyer alone. Here is where it is entirely proper for him to have assistance in the development of a case; but always, no matter how big and complicated the case may grow, he himself must be directly watching and supervising the development of the facts.

At the same time, he must also be developing the law, finding out every possible legal subject, every legal question, that might be involved in the case. This sometimes requires the preparation of perhaps fifty questions of law, though only two of them may arise later in the trial.

It is like preparing a football team. The coach prepares defenses against fifty or sixty combinations of plays that his opponent may use against him, and maybe only one of them is used. When he stops it cold, everybody says, "What a brilliant defense against that play. What an inspired genius is that coach to have foreseen that they were going to use that offensive weapon against him."

It is not inspired genius at all. It is brains, sweat, and toil. It is going over every single possible play that could be used against him, and working out his defense against each of them. Then, when one of them comes, he is ready for it. He could not take the chance of picking out the plays that his opponent would use. If he did, and omitted even one play, then, sure as fate, that would be the one his opponent would use.

So it is in preparing for a trial. A lawyer must be prepared for every question of law that might arise against him. He dare not omit one.

In careful preparation, I believe that a lawyer should always have the devil's advocate. In my office, the devil's advocate searches each of our cases as we prepare it, persistently finding the holes and forcing us to prepare specifically against each of

them. Whenever I go into court, I have completely prepared both sides of the case.

Some trial lawyers do not want to do this. They say, "My opponent is skillful. He will find all the law on his side. I am going
to prepare only my side." But I don't like it that way, and I don't
think it can be done that way. I believe that a lawyer must prepare both sides, so that he will not be surprised by whatever may
be hurled at him. After he is prepared in this way, even if his opponent does come up with some detail that may have escaped
him, it cannot be so far from the facts already known that it will
completely surprise him, or put him at a total disadvantage.

There is a curious side light to the preparation of both sides of
a case; it can afford a lawyer some interesting experiences in a
courtroom. Sometimes he looks in wonder at the way his opponent
has *not* prepared his case. He thinks of all that could be done with
the other side, all that the other lawyer could do if he had only
worked on his case hard enough and prepared it thoroughly. It
can be worrisome to sit in a courtroom and see justice affected by
the lack of industry on the part of a lawyer.

Of course, no matter how much a lawyer prepares, how ready
he may think he is, he is sometimes confronted with the unexpected. No lawyer can do a really perfect job; if he could, then
the unexpected could never happen. He just does the best he
can, and yet sometimes he will get a jolt that will affect his plans.
When he does, then comes the test of the really great trial lawyer.
What does he do about it? Can he meet any variance or turn
in the trial with the resilience and flexibility to shift gears, perhaps
very suddenly, in the middle of it? If he does not have that
ability, he loses when he is surprised. But if he has the resilience
and flexibility, he changes quickly, without displaying the slightest
disturbance or fluster, and goes on in another direction.

The effective trial lawyer of today is quite different from the
old hambones of the past, the men who depended on high-flown
oratory and lung power to play on the emotions of the jury. Some
of them are still around, but they are getting fewer in number
and less in influence. Trial law has now become a much more

refined and sensitive type of thing, and simply shouting, and cry-
ing, and waving the flag is looked on as insulting to the intelligence of the jury. And one must never underestimate the
jury's intelligence. One must always treat them as if they were
very intelligent people, even when they are not.

This mention of courtroom behavior raises another question.
Does a lawyer consciously change his manner and his behavior
according to the impression he wants to make on a jury? I have
said that a lawyer wants a jury to like him, and they won't like
him if he is affected and unnatural, and yet I doubt if any lawyer
is always the same before every jury. Was Clarence Darrow the
same in his courtroom manner in the mountains of Tennessee as in
Chicago?

While I do not think that this is really a big factor in the thinking of a young man or woman concerned with the law as a career,
I believe that it should be explained to them, particularly to
those who are interested in trial law. One fact, however, should
be understood immediately and should be emphasized: it is far
more important for them to remember that the impression the
lawyer himself makes, whatever his manner, is quite incidental
when compared with the impression he wants his case to make.
A successful lawyer is always thinking of his case first, but, consciously or unconsciously, there may be some shifting of his
manner as he appears before different juries.

I try cases around the country and I live in Washington.
When I go to New York, I do not think of myself as an outsider
and the juries there do not regard me as an outsider. I can feel
no difference in trying a case in New York and trying one in my
home city.

But if I go out to the Midwest—for example, to Duluth, Min-
nesota—I do not take it for granted that the people there are
exactly delighted to have me. They have, in Duluth, some very
able lawyers whom they like, and they feel that they do not really
need somebody from the East coming in and trying to tell them
how to decide a case.

So I always put it right out in the open and say, "I am from the
East and I have come here to try this case. I appreciate the

courtesies that you have shown me by receiving me in your community for the purpose of this trial." I think that a lawyer should articulate his awareness of his position, and from then on, in Duluth or almost any other city where he is an outsider, he will probably be a little more deferential to the court, more deferential to the jury, than if he were back in his home town.

Now, since we have started discussing courtroom behavior, I think I would like to say that some lawyers can develop some very bad habits in the courtroom. For instance, there is the trial lawyer who is always objecting.

In my opinion, the objector who objects merely to show off how right he is on the law—and he may be very right—is a fool. The only time to object is when something is coming into evidence which, if the lawyer does not object and stop it, is going to hurt his client. Many times when evidence is objectionable legally, and a trial lawyer can make an objection and be sustained, he is very poorly advised to do it. Juries naturally resent the man who blocks them from hearing things which they think they might like to hear. Objections, for the sake of demonstrating how much a lawyer knows about the law, are ridiculous. They hurt him. Watch two good trial lawyers try a case and there will be a minimum of objecting. Only when something is about to happen that is truly prejudicial will the objection be made.

There is something else in this general area of courtroom behavior that I should mention. Bullying is always bad. There is never a reason for bullying a witness, regardless of who he is. There is never a reason to demonstrate bad manners in a courtroom. The really great trial lawyer is carefully a gentleman in the courtroom. This is the impression that he wishes to make on the jury, and it is a good impression.

It is the impression, also, that he wants to make on the court and a good relationship with the court is very important. I consider that a lawyer has an obligation to be as courteous and as respectful of the court as possible, always taking care, of course, that he never indulges in any suggestion of fawning or of flattery.

In return, I think that the trial lawyer is entitled to the same courtesy and respect from the court. Unfortunately, there are occasions when he does not get it. The court may have predilections and may demonstrate these predilections by bullying counsel. When this happens, a lawyer is very unwise to respond in kind. Instead, if he handles the situation properly, and dramatizes to the jury the fact that he is being treated a little unfairly, he can convert this disadvantage to an advantage.

In regard to the relationship between a lawyer and his client during the trial, I think that the best relationship is no relationship. The client is there present, he sits with the lawyer, and further than that there is nothing.

By the time a lawyer gets into court, all talking with his client should be history; the case should have been completely talked out between them. There may be occasions when it is necessary to speak to the client, but they should be minimal.

So far as any relationship with the other lawyer is concerned, that should be governed by the same rules that apply to the relationship with the court. The defending lawyer is a gentleman and he treats the prosecutor as one. He shows the prosecutor courtesy and respect, and I think it is even more important to do so when the prosecutor is failing to demonstrate courtesy or is showing a lack of respect. This will always be noticed by the jury, and in the defending lawyer's favor.

Commenting on the other lawyer, criticizing him, taking notice of him personally, is, in almost every instance that I can conceive of, a mistake. It is hard to make an abstract general judgment about the relationship with the other lawyer; but courtesy, I am sure, is always advisable.

Also—and most important—if the prosecutor is criticizing the defending lawyer, is attacking him in any way, it is essential to guard against anger. Anger is a base emotion at any time and a lawyer always loses when he gets angry. If he lets the prosecutor upset him in court, even slightly, then the prosecutor has accomplished something that is helpful to him and harmful to the defense. Moreover, any time a lawyer lets his opponent get him angry, he will not be thinking clearly. In the courtroom, anger is a petty luxury that no trial lawyer, no matter how skillful he may be otherwise, can afford.

Now about the crowd. What about the people in the court-room and the lawyer's relationship with them?

The answer is quick. The crowd has no place so far as the trial lawyer is concerned. If he is able, and is really doing his job effectively, he does not waste any time, any effort, any energy, any thought of any kind on the people in the back. And the reason is clear and certain: they do not have a vote. All his energy, all his thinking, all his imaginative powers, all his resourcefulness are being poured, not into the people who do not vote, but into the jurors who do.

The mention of the crowd brings us to another factor in the courtroom that must be considered—the press. What of the news-papermen? What, also, of the men from radio and television who want to get into the courtroom, bringing their broadcasting equipment and their cameras with them?

One of the problems that we have in the administration of justice, especially criminal justice, is what is called "trial by newspaper." So often newspapers will generate a lot of publicity around a trial and create preconceptions in the minds of prospective jurors. They will print stories and confessions, print past records, and this, almost always, is adverse to the defense.

I do not think that the newspapers should be blamed for this. I do not believe that anything should be done to curb them from printing anything to which they can get access. If they were curbed, we then would be in conflict with our concept of the First Amendment. I do not advocate adopting the English system which holds a newspaper in contempt for printing pre-trial in-formation that might influence a possible juror.

It is my belief that we would eliminate a large part of this prejudicial publicity if we would only enforce the canons of ethics that now exist, and clean up our own house, in this regard, within the legal profession. This is what I mean: I do not think that any lawyer, whether he be a defense lawyer or a prosecutor, should ever make a comment to the press evaluating his case or any evidence.

Second, I do not think that he should state to the press what he is *going* to prove. He should never say what he intends to show at any future time in court, whether that time is one hour later or three days later.

I believe, too, that the responsibility of a lawyer actually engaged in a case carries over to his subordinates, so that nobody on the defense side should ever give this kind of information or this evaluation to the press.

On the prosecutor's side, I think that his responsibility should carry over to the police, so that we do not have statements coming from the police which are damaging and prejudicial to the defense.

If we carefully enforced these rules, we would eliminate a great percentage of prejudicial publicity and eliminate most of the things that now are objectionable with respect to newspapers and trials, especially criminal trials.

Finally, in our consideration of the lawyer and his relationship with the different elements in the courtroom, there is his relationship with the jury. This I have saved for last, trying to indicate its significance. The importance of his relationship with the jury simply cannot be overemphasized. All that he thinks is centered on the jury. All that he does is aimed at them.

Sometimes I am asked if I conceive of the jury as a unit or as twelve individuals. They are, I assure you, twelve individuals. A lawyer can never think of them in the abstract as merely a unit. If the jury ever becomes simply an abstraction to him, then all his skills as a trial man are lost.

He may not be looking directly at the jury at all times; but always he is conscious of those twelve people, and of each of them as an individual. Always he is watching for reactions, and sometimes he gets them.

However, he must learn to be extremely careful about this because sometimes the reactions can totally deceive him. He interprets a reaction one way, and it may be completely the opposite. A juror may grimace at some evidence and the lawyer thinks he has done it because he finds the evidence so damaging; whereas, in fact, he grimaces because he finds the evidence so incredible that he just does not believe this witness.

These are things that one looks for and sometimes sees, but one must always remember that they can be misleading. A lawyer can never be sure of anything about any jury, except that it is there.

In a trial there is so much for a lawyer to take into account; but suppose we begin our discussion of an actual trial by considering the picking of a jury.

I often wonder how much any of us really knows about picking a jury. We all think that we know at least some things—but then so many other things also apply. So many different factors can become important, depending on the case that one is trying. For example, a lawyer will, of course, strive for one kind of jury for one kind of case; he will go after quite a different jury for another kind. If he is trying an antitrust case, he will look for different jurors than those he wants in a narcotics case. In a case involving a labor leader, a lawyer would certainly seek to avoid a jury of employers; instead, he would want people who had some sympathy with the labor movement. In the antitrust case I mentioned, he would be happy to have some members of the Union League sitting on the jury, men involved in big industry perhaps, because from them he might expect to elicit more sympathy for the defendant and his problem.

Always the lawyer is trying and hoping to get jurors who might, as he skillfully pleads his case, project themselves into the position of the defendant, thus making it possible for him to win sympathy from them.

At the beginning of every trial, there arises the question of the opening statement. Always, in a civil case, one makes an opening statement; but one may, or may not, make an opening in a criminal case. I generally do, because I think that first impressions are important.

If the prosecutor has an hour to give the jury a first impression, and they hear nothing to countervail it, then that first impression may be detrimental to the defense. This is a detriment that the defending lawyer wants to avoid, if possible, and when it comes his turn to make an opening statement, he is wise to do it if he can. By making his statement, and telling the jury what he intends to prove in the course of the trial, he can dissipate the effect of the prosecutor's opening.

In his opening, he can particularly impress on the jury the necessity of keeping a free mind throughout the trial, letting them know that they are going to hear one side of the case first, namely, the prosecutor's side, but that immediately thereafter they will hear the defense evidence. What he is really doing, in his opening, is to keep the impression at the beginning of the trial in a state of balance.

Let me say, in passing, that in the opening statement, as well as in all other statements in any trial, the lawyer will do his best to keep it as clear, as concise, and as simple as possible. That is *his* law—always, in all the years of his practice of trial law.

During a trial, the defending lawyer will have the opportunity to question his own witnesses and also those of the prosecution. The questioning of his witnesses is in direct examination, and is comparatively simple; for the good reason that he knows exactly how his questions will be answered. He has already prepared the witness to testify before he goes on the stand, and there is no opportunity for a defending lawyer to be surprised in direct examination.

He does not go into court to question his own witnesses for the purpose of learning any facts. He already knows every fact about the case from A to Z, from Alpha to Omega, before he goes in. He is not there to get educated. He is there to make a demonstration. Therefore, whenever he asks a question, he is only going over old familiar ground.

As a matter of fact, a careful defense lawyer never plays *anything* by ear in the courtroom. If I put a witness on the stand, I know him, know his background, know his character, know how to handle him. If he is smart or dull, reticent or voluble, I have already taken all this into account.

I will also have gone over his testimony with him, every shred of it, and gone over it with him again, and still again. He knows each question I will propose, and I know each answer. If, by any chance, I get an answer that is different from the one I expected, it will mean that he has changed his mind after he took the stand.

The direct examination of one's own witnesses is obviously simple; but let us go now to cross-examination, where one deals with the witnesses of the prosecution.

Cross-examination is the most complex art in the whole trial field, and the most difficult part of the trial to master. Let me repeat that no one can learn it by reading about it. One learns to cross-examine only by cross-examining.

The cross-examination of a shrewd and agile witness, adverse to the defense, is the most important part of a trial. Here is where a lawyer can be most effective, for if he can elicit from this witness a fact advantageous to the defense, it is like bursting a bomb. The lawyer might have brought out exactly this same fact in his own case, in direct examination of one of his own witnesses; but the fact at that time would have been no more than a little smoke puff, or, at most, a small firecracker going off.

Once a lawyer can skillfully manage an adverse witness, he has learned the greatest art in trial law, but again let me raise a warning. Even when he thinks he is being most skillful, he may be on the verge of hurting himself. He can hurt himself at any moment in cross-examination unless he knows exactly what he is doing and where he is going.

To begin with, he never asks a question when he does not know the answer. This may seem difficult in cross-examination, and it is. But only a very foolish lawyer asks a question, whether in direct or cross-examination, when he does not know the exact answer, or at the very least the exact area into which the answer is going to lead him.

There are some basic rules in cross-examination, and the first is this one I have just mentioned—you never ask a question when you do not know the answer.

Second, you never ask an adverse witness *why* he did something. Why! You never ask him why. Ask a man why he did something and he can talk for twenty minutes. He can give all his motivations. He can make a speech, every bit of it unfavorable to you.

I once watched a case being tried where the man on the witness stand was testifying for the Government that the defendant had sold him a narcotic. He was testifying with obvious feeling against the defendant. The defense lawyer got up after the direct examination was concluded. He had not prepared his case and did not know what to do. So he just shook the Christmas tree to see what would fall off for him.

He asked some meaningless questions, just fumbling around, and then finally he blurted out: "*Why* are you testifying against this defendant with such obvious relish, such obvious pleasure?" This was not really a question, he was just trying to make a statement in front of the jury, and he put it this way in the form of a question.

And this is what he got, this was the witness' reply: "Mr. X, I will tell you why I am testifying against your client with such obvious relish, as you put it. I am fifty-six years old. Ten years ago I had a family. I had a wife and four lovely children. I lived up in Rye, New York. I had a good business. I was living a happy life and then, somehow, I got addicted to barbiturates as a result of taking a lot of medicine at one point. Pretty soon, I was caught. I was hooked, as they say in the jargon of the addicts." He went on: "Within two years I was groveling in the gutters of the Bowery. I lost my wife. I lost my business. I lost my family. I was alone.

"I was within perhaps a month of death as a result of the use of that rotten stuff that your client peddles. But through the grace of God I made a comeback. I got off the stuff. And I promised that same God who redeemed me that I would devote the rest of my life to putting skunks like your client in the penitentiary."

Finished! That was the end of that case. The lawyer asked why, and he found out.

Let me give you another illustration of this. I once tried a case involving a man who had been killed by a street car in Washington. There was some suggestion that he might have been drinking before he was hit, but there was no proof of this. He did have a tendency to drink too much, but there was no evidence that he had had a drink when he was hit by the street car.

I put the man's son on the stand. Although he had not witnessed the accident, he had come upon the scene shortly thereafter, and he testified.

When the defense lawyer took him over on cross-examination, he said to him, "You went out in the street, didn't you? Your father was lying there, wasn't he?"

The boy answered, "Yes."

The lawyer said, "You went out and leaned over him, didn't you?"

"Yes."

"As a matter of fact, you put your face right down close to him, didn't you?"

"Yes."

The lawyer said, "You were sniffing for alcohol, weren't you? Looking for a bottle, weren't you?"

"No, sir."

"Weren't you bending over looking in his pockets, trying to get a bottle out of his pocket?"

"No, sir."

"Did you smell alcohol on him?"

"No, sir."

"Well, witnesses have testified that you leaned over him, lying there in the road. *Why* did you lean over him?"

The boy said, "Because he was my father and he was dying, and I leaned over and kissed him."

That jury—well, that jury was ready to come out of the box to grab that lawyer. They wanted to get him and flog him.

There was no recovery from that. There could be no recovery. Why? The lawyer had found out why, all right. He knew now why that boy had leaned over his father.

Every time you ask why, it is as though you were in the ring with the champion, just standing there with your hands hanging loose at your sides. He is surely going to hit you, and he may knock you cold.

When one lawyer asked why about the narcotic, and the other

lawyer asked why about the boy's father, neither of them knew what he was going to get, but you see what happened. If you do not know what is ahead, and do not know where you are going, then don't start. It is better to have no cross-examination at all than to have a bad one.

An adverse witness, like an unbroken horse, is going to try to break away and take you where you don't want to go. But you know *exactly* where you intend to go, and the idea is to keep the witness bridled and to bring him, however reluctant, down that course to where you want him.

Never give him a chance to break away, to go where *he* wants to go, by asking him a question when you don't know what the answer must be. Hold him on the course that you have been over again and again while preparing the case, knowing every dip, every bend, every inch of it. You may ask him a question and get an answer different from the one you expected; but this can mean only that his answer is different from the truth, from what he should have answered. When he does this, you are standing right there with the stuff to hit him over the head with it and bring him back.

If he gets into conflicting testimony, and gives conflicting statements, you just tighten your grip on him and bring him right down the course that you are taking him, holding him steady no matter how hard he tries to swerve and break loose. He may be trying to trick you or give you a shock, but you don't let him. You just hold him and keep asking him what *you* know, and you move him from *your* A to *your* B, and on to *your* C—wherever it is you intend to take him.

And once you get him there, turn him loose *quick*. In cross-examination you must always have a starting place and a termination place. When you get the witness there—quit!

To ask "why" is foolish. To ask a question when you do not know the answer is foolish. To hang on and ask an extra question is just plain silly. There can be no reason for it and no possible good in it.

The classic story about the extra question has to do with the man who was charged with mayhem. The allegation was that he

was in a fight and the fight got rough and he bit the complainant's
ear off. Just bit it right off.

So the case went to trial. A witness was on the stand and
the defense lawyer took him over on cross-examination. "Now,
you saw this fight, did you?"

"Well," he said, "I didn't see all of it."

"As a matter of fact, you didn't see very much of it, did you?"

"I didn't see very much of it, no."

The lawyer said, "As a matter of fact, you never saw the defendant bite the complainant's ear, did you?"

And the witness said, "No, I didn't."

Stopping place! Exactly here. This answer gives the defense
the advantage. Sit down.

But this lawyer could not stop. He had to go on and he said,
"But you testified that he bit it off, didn't you?"

"Yes."

"Well, how did you know that the defendant bit the complainant's ear off?"

"Because I saw him spit it out."

Finished! One question too many!

After this, there could be only one verdict, and the stupid
lawyer had brought it on himself.

I am not suggesting for a moment that a case should be won
by the wrong side because some crucial question is left unasked.
If at any time cross-examination leaves the jury with a misleading impression, then the best person to correct that impression is
the lawyer who called the witness in the first place. The whole
system of adversary litigation breaks down if we try to impose this
additional duty on the cross-examiner himself.

Besides learning to avoid these fundamental errors that I have
mentioned, one learns, while continuing in trial practice, that
the facts gleaned in cross-examination can be used in a number of
different ways. A lawyer finds out that some of these ways are a
great deal more effective and favorable to him than are others.

He can score a ten-strike, perhaps, in cross-examination by getting a witness to admit something. But at that time the strike
may seem unrelated, even insignificant at the moment, and he,

in his eagerness, may be afraid that it will be lost on the jury. The tendency of many trial lawyers, and almost all inexperienced lawyers, I think, is to hurry in and pick up that fact at that very moment. They want to show the jury immediately just how significant it is. They have not learned to wait.

This hurrying in may be a very bungling and a very foolish thing to do. Maybe the lawyer should just take that fact and put it away in the icebox and let it lie there for a week, or two weeks, or however long it may be until the time comes for him to sum up. The summing up at the end of the trial is the last thing that the jury hears, and this is the time to take that important fact out of the icebox, exhibit it, and evaluate it. It is a lot better for him, in his summing up, to point out the significance of this crucial fact, and for him to explain it, than to have given the adverse witness a chance back there in cross-examination to explain it—and also a chance to belittle it and maybe throw some mud on it.

I will give you an illustration of this. I tried a case, some years back, involving the Reconstruction Finance Corporation in the Truman administration. A lawyer in Washington was charged with having committed perjury in front of the grand jury investigating the RFC, by denying that he had ever given anything of value to anyone employed at the RFC. It was subsequently developed that he had given a television set to one of the employees a few years before at Christmas.

His defense was that he had forgotten about it at the time the question was asked, and that he had later returned to the grand jury to give this fact, when his mind was refreshed, but that the grand jury by that time had gone out of session.

At the trial, one of the lawyers who had worked on the case as an investigator was on the stand. In cross-examination I asked him an almost irrelevant question. It was so irrelevant that my opposing lawyer, who was a very able man, did not object because he did not figure it could possibly hurt him. I asked the man on the stand: "Now who were the other lawyers from the Department of Justice who worked with you on this investigation for the grand jury?"

He said, "Mr. Smith. Mr. Brown. Mr. Black. Mr. Blue. And Mr. Johnson."

"Now you worked on this investigation for a whole year and those are the only lawyers who worked with you?"

"That's all. Those are the ones. There were six of us."

So later in the defense, I called Mr. Smith and under the guise of simply testing the accuracy of the transcription of some testimony, I asked a couple of questions that appeared meaningless and boring. Then I asked him one that appeared even more meaningless and boring: "Who were the other lawyers who worked with you on this?"

And Smith said, "Well, there was Mr. Brown. Mr. Black. Mr. Blue. Mr. Jones"—then he named the man who had testified earlier—"and Mr. Murphy."

So then I called the next one and I asked him the same question, burying it in a lot of dull and meaningless other questions. Pretty soon it turned out that Mr. Blue left out Mr. Brown. And Mr. Brown left out Mr. Black. And Mr. Black left out Mr. Murphy. Every one of the prosecutors had omitted a name or added a name of those who worked with him.

And nobody—of course this was a long trial and these questions were buried in a melange of hundreds of pages of testimony—but *nobody* in that courtroom had any concept of the significance of what had happened. And I did not tell them! I just put it away in the icebox.

But at the end of the trial, in the summing up, I took it out and I said, "Now here we have the Department of Justice asking that you return a verdict of guilty beyond a reasonable doubt against this man whose reputation to this point has been unsullied. They are unwilling to accord him the benefit of a mistake in recollection, and yet the very lawyers who got the indictment all have mistaken recollections about the very same grand jury that indicted him. All six of them have mistaken recollections.

"I am not asking that they be indicted, because I would be laughed down the courthouse steps if I made such a ludicrous request as to ask that these six men be indicated because each of their recollections failed them about a transaction of *one* year ago. Yet they are asking you to convict this man whose recollection failed about a matter *three* years ago."

Well, you know, this was a belly shot. It created a tremendous impact on the jury.

Now just think back to that day in cross-examination and suppose, when the first man was testifying, I had said, "But you forgot Mr. Jones, didn't you?"

"Oh, yes, I forgot Mr. Jones."

Then, right away, all of them would have gotten together in a huddle, and they all would have quickly prepared themselves. From then on, they would all be right, and there would be nothing in it, either then or later, for me or my client. I would have lost the impression that was rightfully ours, and lost its favorable impact on the jury.

Every young man interested in the law, and contemplating trial law as his specialty, wants to know the future of the trial lawyer. This is understandable and he should know.

I have been around the country for the past several years talking at law schools, urging men in law schools to go into the trial field because there is a very great dearth of really able trial lawyers in America. There are a number of reasons for this and I would like to elaborate on them, making this whole question of entering trial practice as clear as I can, for I believe it is terribly important that there be a resurgence of good trial lawyers to answer the urgent need for them. After all, the conduct of the whole judicial system can be only as good as the ability of the men who are contesting.

Some men say that if they had the flair, talent, eloquence, resilience, imagination, resourcefulness, and the sharp and penetrating judgment to be fine trial lawyers, they would go into the field. But many of these men also say, "I know, however, that I can rate myself only a little better than average, perhaps no more than mediocre. Wouldn't it be safer for me to stay and work in an office, rather than to risk going into the courtroom?"

The answer to these men of doubtful trial ability is, of course, yes. A man who may have the capacity to become a good office lawyer is foolish to become a poor trial lawyer. But what I decry is the fact that there are men with the flair, and the talent, and all the various abilities to be fine trial lawyers, but they just are not going into the trial field.

One reason is that it is *very* hard work. Furthermore, the work, you must understand, is always on the trial lawyer himself, no matter how high he may rise in his profession.

If I am a really great tax lawyer, and you have unbounded confidence in me, then you will bring your personal or your firm's tax problem to me. I take on your problem, and you go away from my office with the feeling that you have been to the best tax lawyer there is. You know that I am going to solve your problem for you.

Well, the first thing I do is to call in some junior and delegate a large portion of the job to him, telling him to do all the spade work, and maybe 90 per cent of the actual work, coming back later and presenting it to me for a final evaluation and check-over, and maybe touching up here and there. Then I call you in and I say, "Now here is our opinion." So you go away again, this time highly pleased and in the belief that you have received the opinion of the best in the business.

On the other hand, if you have a problem concerning yourself or your firm, in which actual litigation is involved, you go to see the best trial lawyer in your city. You ask him to take on your case and he does.

But no matter how big he is, he cannot call in a junior and say, "You go argue the motions on this case next week." The day he does that, you are going to be very upset about it because you did not hire the junior. You hired the best trial lawyer in your city and you expect him to be there working for you.

The difference between the two situations is that a person knows when there is delegation in the trial field, and he does not know when there is delegation in the tax field, or in other fields. But the fact of his knowing is not the only reason for my not wanting to delegate responsibility in the trial field. I have strong beliefs about this, for my experience has been that it is very, very hard to split responsibilities in the conduct of a trial. A lawyer just can't try a case by committee. He must try it himself.

Since the opportunity for delegation is so much less in trial work, the volume a person can handle is much less and, therefore, the financial rewards are less. For an equivalent amount of talent and effort, I am convinced that a lawyer can get much greater financial rewards in other forms of practice.

Finally, the physical attrition in trial law is so much greater because of the strain of being in contest every day of your working life. So the young law student asks, "Why should I do this? With all these disadvantages, with all these things against it, why should I go into trial law?"

One reason is that the trial lawyers who walk into court and fight the great cases are regarded as the great lawyers. Those lawyers who do not go into trial law can never know the satisfaction that comes in this profession when a man goes into a hard, tough fight for someone who is in trouble and gives him help. This is more than financial gain and the man who has the ability to accomplish this and aborts it by not using it, can never be really satisfied as a lawyer.

The greatest admiration and esteem in the law profession is historically reserved for the trial lawyers. One seldom reads in history about office lawyers. The lawyers who have made great names for themselves, and are regarded as having made real contributions to the administration of justice, have been trial lawyers.

This is not because of the drama in trial practice which causes these lawyers to be noticed by the public. It is because law is civilization's way of settling fights between individuals, and the men who make the greatest contribution to the settlement of these fights and disputes are the men who do the contesting in the courtroom, the trial lawyers.

Now I suppose that here is where I should have a word to say about another kind of trial lawyer, the "shyster."

In every profession, regardless of what it is, there are some people of whom the respectable members are not very proud. I don't care what the business or profession, there is always somebody who is trying to cut corners and do something dishonorable. There are a number of such men in trial work, and, because they are more exposed in what they do, they are more easily noticed. But finally, for each of them, a lack of character always emerges, and character determines the staying power of any lawyer, whatever his practice may be. If he does not have character, he will not be around very long.

The first penalty he pays is the loss of the respect of the other members of his profession. This is a horrible price for any lawyer to pay because, without the esteem of the bar and the bench, he is not only a kind of personal outcast, but it is impossible for him to be really effective in his profession. He may never be disgraced publicly for something he has done, and he may drift on and make a living, but he will always be thought of as a "shyster" and looked on as a second-class member of the profession.

At this time, while I am tying up loose ends, I might as well speak of Perry Mason.

I am asked a lot of questions about Perry Mason and I should tell you that I have never watched one of his complete shows. I rarely watch television shows that purport to deal with courtroom practice, because most of them are simply too awful to watch. Most of them distort and misrepresent actual trial practice to such an extent that I cannot bear to watch them. The simple fact is that their melodrama supersedes the realities of the situation to the point of absurdity.

Perry Mason, I understand, never loses a case. You show me a trial lawyer who has never lost a case, and I will show you a trial lawyer who has never tried more than two.

There is a tremendous delusion about the effectiveness of trial counsel. In actual fact, the area of efficacy for a trial lawyer is very narrow. Suppose we take a hundred cases involving hypothetical situations, any hundred cases. The best trial lawyer in America might win sixty and lose forty. The most incompetent will win forty and lose sixty.

The greatest football coach in America, working with the material that some schools might offer him, could win only four and lose four. Maybe, in a squeeze, he might win five and lose three. But win them all—like Perry Mason!—that's absurd.

Yet such shows create the impression among the laity that they can go into the office of a great trial lawyer, and he can win the case for them, no matter what the facts are, no matter what the merits of the case. This just cannot be. It is impossible to take an impossible case, and win it.

Anyone can see how misleading this is when it causes people, even in a true courtroom, to sit around waiting for the defense to use spectacular tactics, and win. This is the effect of certain television shows, and similar spectacular and misleading effects would taint actual trials if the networks were allowed to put the trial on television.

I am dedicated to keeping television cameras out of the courtroom. There are many reasons for this. One is that the networks would never show the full trial. They would leave out the boring parts, showing only the sensational and overlooking the fact that sometimes the least exciting part of a case is really the most significant. They would manage, also, to give a story treatment to the trial, thereby creating a completely wrong impression of the administration of justice.

The search for truth in a courtroom is difficult enough without putting it on stage. Let a witness realize that he is in front of a camera, and he may become more concerned with his histrionics than with his oath. This applies not only to witnesses, but to judges and jurymen and lawyers, all primping and nudging to get on camera and stay there as long as they can.

I have been asked if my objection to televesion cameras carries over as strongly to still cameras and news photographers in the courtroom, and I cannot say that it does; but I oppose their being there, nevertheless. Over the Department of Justice in Washington, facing Pennsylvania Avenue, is an inscription: "The place of Justice is a hallowed place." I think it should also be a quiet place where one searches for the truth with care and dignity. Every touch of the carnival, of the circus, should be eliminated.

Some people always bring up the old, and seemingly proper

argument, that trials are public. They say that as means of communication increase, so the publicness of trials should increase.

They overlook the fact that trials are held in public to guard the rights of the individual, and not to satisfy the curiosity of onlookers. The founding fathers knew the terrible abuses that can take place in secret trials, and they determined to have open trials as legal protection for the man accused. This protection can suffer, and be partly lost, when a witness is elaborately testifying into television cameras and jurors are posing for photographers.

Our rights to public trial involve all our rights: both our rights to life and liberty, and our rights of property.

In a consideration of these rights, I am particularly concerned with the liberties of men because there is so much unconcern about them; yet at one time I spent five years trying nothing but civil cases, defending corporations that were sued. Insurance companies. Public utilities companies. Day in and day out, I was in court in these cases. I would never de-emphasize for one moment the importance of property rights. In our form of society, the right of private property is not only important to our nation but it is the bedrock of our whole system.

There are basic and tremendous differences, however, between the legal rights that safeguard the freedom, reputation, and liberty of men, and the rules that safeguard property. This is because our laws have become archaic, I think, and we overemphasize property rights to the exclusion of human rights. We do this because our laws, even today, stem back to feudal times when a piece of property was more valuable than a man. We still continue to safeguard property rights with procedural rules that are far more advantageous and efficacious than the rules that safeguard human life and liberty.

The facts are that if your firm were sued today for $500, you could, under the existing rules of procedure, get the names of all the witnesses your opponent was going to use against you. You could take their testimony before trial in the form of sworn depositions, and get all documentary evidence that was to be offered. When time came for you to go into court in defense of your $500, you would know every scintilla of evidence to be used against you and you could be prepared for it.

In contrast, if you were indicted and faced five years in the penitentiary provided you lost the case, you could not get the names of witnesses who were to testify against you. You could not take their depositions. You could get only a few documents.

The unfairness of this procedure is most obvious when it affects innocent men. The man guilty of a crime goes to trial knowing what the witnesses have told the grand jury, fully aware of all facts that the prosecution has gathered and all information it has. Of course he knows, since he is the man who broke into the house, who picked the pocket, who stole the clothes. He knows everything about it and goes into court with the advantage of this knowledge.

But the innocent man, the man falsely accused—and our records are filled with the names of such men—goes into court in ignorance of the prosecution's case, not knowing what was said against him before the grand jury, and, even more, not knowing who said it. This procedural injustice can affect any of us, at any time.

The liberty of a people depends in notable part upon the procedural safeguards of these people. A fundamental difference between a democratic and a totalitarian society is in their criminal procedures, the way that crimes are prosecuted. This becomes clearer when we consider the difference between a country with open courtroom trial for any man openly accused, and a country where a trial can be unannounced and held in secret, or where trial, evidence, and conviction all are in the mob shout of "To the wall!"

One reason for the continued archaic inequity that distinguishes the criminal and civil procedures in our country is that the law schools continue to place so much emphasis on property rights and so little on human rights. The graduate comes out of law school thinking that the *ne plus ultra* for him is to go to some Wall Street firm and handle segments, no matter how small they may be, of antitrust cases. It is declassé for him to stand beside some poor downtrodden figure that society is trying to put in a cage.

You have only to scan the curricula of the law schools, the best ones in the country, and you will find that they are steeped in courses on personal property, real property, trusts, taxation, corporations, partnerships, damages, wills, all dealing with property.

Look again. What courses are there that deal with the freedom of men? The right of a man to express his thoughts? The right to worship? The right to confront his accuser face to face? The right to cross-examine him? These are the rights that affect freedom, but one does not find much about them in the curricula of the law schools. In a curriculum of twenty courses in a law school, there may be no more than one course, or possibly two, devoted to the rights and freedom of men.

We must certainly continue our concern for the safeguarding of property rights, but there also needs to be a far greater emphasis on human rights and individual liberties, particularly where the poor and the friendless, the weak and the degraded, the unpopular and the unorthodox, are seeking to be heard in the courts.

With a vast disregard, we ignore the fact that the lowly and the helpless always are the first to be touched by the strong hand of authority when it reaches out in its probing intrusion into human rights. We disregard the fact that in protecting the rights of the lowly, we protect the rights of all men. Justice Frankfurter said, "It is a fair summary of history to say that the safeguards of liberty have frequently been forged in cases involving not very nice people." We fail to remember this until it is our own segment of society that is touched, as the hand of authority reaches ever higher, and probes ever deeper, in its invasion of liberty.

It is the obligation of lawyers to oppose every infringement of human rights, and to defend these rights in the courts. The freedom of man lies in the law, and the history of our liberties has largely been written in the criminal courtroom.

This is why I suggest to young lawyers that they disregard criticism, misunderstandings, and pressure, and dedicate themselves to advocacy in causes involving human freedom. Here is where men of intellect, character, and determination are needed. Here is where liberty is in delicate balance now, and will be tomorrow and thereafter.

_6_ *You in*

CORPORATION LAW

BY PAUL CARRINGTON
Dallas, Texas

PAUL CARRINGTON

Born: 1894, Mexico, Missouri

University of Missouri: A.B., 1914
Harvard Law School: LL.B., 1917

2nd Lieutenant, US Army Signal Corps: 1918–19
Instructor, Primary Flying

Admitted to Texas Bar: 1919
Practiced Civil Law in Dallas: 1919—
Senior Partner: Carrington, Johnson & Stephens

General counsel and Director:
Mercantile National Bank at Dallas
Burrus Mills, Inc., and other corporations

Dallas Bar Association, President: 1940

Texas State Bar, President: 1960
First Chairman, Section of Labor Law
First Chairman, Section of Corporation, Banking and Business Law
Chairman, Committee on Revision of Corporation Laws: 1950–56

American Bar Association, Assembly Delegate: 1958—
Chairman, Committee on Post War Planning: 1943–45
Chairman, Committee on Commerce: 1952–54
Chairman, Committee on Lawyer Referral Service: 1959—
Chairman, Section of Corporation, Banking and Business Law: 1955
Member, Committee on Corporate Laws: 1949—

American Bar Foundation, Fellow: 1956—; Member, Committee for An-
notating The Model Business Corporation Act: 1958—
Southwestern Legal Foundation, Trustee: 1948—
American Judicature Society, Director: 1958—
American Law Institute
American Arbitration Association, Director: 1935—
American Society of International Law, Executive Council: 1961—
Harvard Law School Association, President: 1959–61

The creative corporation lawyer . . . does not merely
steer his client around pitfalls to avoid needless legal risks.
He actively directs and moulds the institutions and instru-
ments of the pertinent law. Says Cardozo: "He is much
more than a traffic officer, warning of obstructions and
keeping travelers to the traveled path. He is a creative
agent. . . . In our complex economic life new problems
call from day to day for new methods and devices." [1]

I F YOU consider yourself a prospect for becoming a corporation
lawyer rather than some other kind of lawyer, it would be
well for you to talk with at least one each of four or five different
kinds of corporation lawyers who are successful in their diverse
fields of activity. It is my purpose to describe very briefly the
different kinds of corporation lawyers there are today, to tell how
the fields of activity of most of them have grown up during my
years of practice, and to predict that during your years of practice, should you become a lawyer and decide to work wholly or
chiefly in corporation law, you will encounter greater and yet
more challenging changes.

I suggest that you learn as much as you can as to how and
why each of the four or five lawyers who have practiced in differ-

[1] *Corporation Lawyer, Saint or Sinner?* 1961, by Beryl H. Levy, page 43,
quoting Mr. Justice Cardozo of the Supreme Court of the United States in
a memorial to a lawyer friend, John G. Milburn.

ent fields of corporation law entered his field, and briefly what his experiences in his field have been. It will be easy to find the successful lawyers on whom you decide to call, and I feel sure they will be willing to discuss these matters with you. In the light of my prediction that each of them will discard his reticence about his own personal experiences, I will try in this chapter, in like manner, to discard my own reticence about mentioning any of my own experiences which tend to explain how and why I am now where I am in corporation law. These personal references may be of interest to you and I think will be more so after you have talked with four or five corporation lawyers. I feel sure you will find that each of these with whom you talk will have had experiences materially different from mine and from each other's. The contrast between their various professional careers and mine should be enlightening, especially since I have not been a rifleman in any one field of corporation law, but have been more like a corporal shouting signals when to fire to specialized riflemen working with me.

First of all, as you consider whether to become a corporation lawyer at all, let me suggest that you think of yourself at a later time, as one actually in practice and participating in the direct action and joys of accomplishment of an expert rifleman. As you do, it will be fun to read this chapter, I hope, thinking of yourself as first in one field of corporation law and then in another. Having an imaginary choice at this stage of your life between several different sorts of rifles, with one of which you may become expert, may be intriguing to you. Please do not expect to decide with finality as you read this chapter, or even after you have the visits with lawyers in various fields of corporation law, as I am suggesting, just what rifle you may choose; for in my judgment you clearly should make that choice later after you complete your legal education.

Now, some of my personal experiences. In college I worked harder at debate and oratory than anything else. In law school, I enjoyed moot court briefs and arguments most of all. In my law school days, Louis D. Brandeis (later Mr. Justice Brandeis of the

Supreme Court of the United States), then in his prime as a Boston lawyer, was more my hero than anyone else I knew then active in the practice of the law. I joined the Harvard Democratic Club and during some two weeks each fall went from town to town in a motor caravan every night in order to be with him, in order to visit with him and to hear him speak for Democratic nominees. If a lapse occurred where one speaker had finished in one town before the next speaker arrived, I would fill the gap. Above all, I then dreamed of a career as a trial lawyer, and, as I hoped for a career like his, probably trials involving important business matters. Though the First World War intervened just as my class was about to graduate, I retained throughout my few months as a soldier my dream of becoming an outstanding trial lawyer in New York City.

Upon being discharged, however, in January, 1919, I was advised that I could get more and better trial experience in such a city as Dallas, especially during the first few years of my practice, than I could get in a New York firm. Furthermore, if I did noteworthy trial work in Dallas, I might hope to be invited into a New York firm at a higher level and achieve my ambition sooner, perhaps, than if I had started with that same New York firm. I succeeded in attaching myself as a protégé—more of a shadow at first—to the man I understood was then the best trial lawyer in Dallas. Before I had practiced as long as ten years in Dallas, I no longer wanted to practice in New York or to devote my professional career to being exclusively a trial lawyer. So I will never know how good the advice was on which I acted in first coming to Dallas.

In Dallas, in the early 'twenties, there were so few lawyers that we all knew each other. Some practiced criminal law only. Some practiced commercial law—collections, foreclosures, bankruptcies. A few others were business lawyers devoting their time to banks or corporations. The balance, with the exception of those who merely hung on with whatever employment turned up, were civil trial lawyers. The lines of demarcation between the groups were not sharply drawn, and opinion might vary as to how to classify some of the lawyers. But if we exclude those who merely hung on, the civil trial lawyers greatly outnumbered those in all the other classes put together.

There are no statistics to prove or disprove my rough guess, but I would estimate that two-thirds, and probably more, of the successful Dallas lawyers at that time were trial lawyers who devoted their professional work to civil matters that would either be settled by agreement or would be tried. If they were tried, they would be strongly contested and quite likely would be determined only after the last possible appellate recourse had been exhausted. Throughout this period of my first ten years of practice, I did practically nothing but work on trial matters and on appeals from trial court decisions.

Teaming with our senior partner in many of his important cases, I read the books, carried them to court, prepared some trial briefs, and later participated in minor parts of major trials. Then I began undertaking small trials on my own, and later more difficult trials, until, before my first ten years were over, I had a trial docket of my own that kept me busy. As I look back now, I realize that it was not by my design but by accident that my major cases at the end of the 'twenties, and the first year or two of the 'thirties, involved state-court recceiverships and the reorganization of corporations coming out of state-court receiverships. Naturally, therefore, and without my planning it, I began representing some corporations and then a bank. Before I realized what was happening, I found myself busy with corporate problems which were relatively novel to me.

Since those years, I have been surprised to note how frequently other lawyers in entering corporation law have had experiences similar to mine. I have watched numerous corporate executives choose lawyers to serve corporate enterprises and I feel confident that they often have chosen them for the same reason that I was chosen for my first corporate employments, because I had impressed someone favorably in connection with the trial of lawsuits. Success in trying lawsuits does not normally prepare one to practice corporate law. Thirty years ago, even more than now, I think, business executives did not appreciate the fact that there are very capable lawyers who are extensively experienced in some legal matters but wholly inexperienced in others—hence, less able to serve a client in a field of law new to them than lawyers experienced in that field.

Although I had completed a broad law-school course with excellent teachers of the traditional subjects, a war and ten years of trial practice had intervened and I sincerely felt that I then knew far too little about corporation law. Instead of declining these new challenging employments, however, I took a correspondence course in accounting, read up on taxes, read general texts on banking, on corporation law and on business finances, and, of course, read the pertinent corporation statutes of my state and the court interpretations of them. Only after several months of such self-schooling did I feel that, giving myself the benefit of doubts, I could justify my decision to accept the new corporate employments.

This whole experience in study and training for my earlier corporate employments has had an additional significance for me. It taught me to appreciate, far more than otherwise I would, the opportunities that law schools and the organized bar have given to lawyers to continue their legal education and keep up to date by attending institutes and courses devoted to that purpose. I am a strong advocate of this as a great benefit to all lawyers.

It was some five years later that I concluded to abandon completely my long-standing dream of being primarily a trial lawyer. Only then did I cease keeping up as fully as possible with the current literature relating to trials and trial procedure with which every ambitious lawyer desiring to become a better trial lawyer should be familiar. During the early 'thirties, holding on to my law-school dream, I had been trying to stay abreast of trial law as well as the current literature on corporation, banking, and business law.

I wish to emphasize that the extent of my trial experience has been of great value to me in my later years of corporate practice. It has permitted me to evaluate problems with greater confidence and to make recommendations relating to business decisions about issues which might develop into controversy or which threatened actual litigation. If, knowing that you intend to practice corporation law later, you were to have the chance of gaining the experience of at least five years of general civil trial work, I would strongly urge that you accept the opportunity. Corporation lawyers are concerned with avoiding or minimizing the pitfalls of litigation; experience in the pit sharpens the ability to appraise potential problems of litigation.

I have long felt that the timing of my entrance into corporation law, just prior to the beginning of the New Deal, was most fortuitous. During the New Deal years of the 'thirties, broad new areas of regulation of corporation business developed, and, as a result, new fields of corporate law sprouted. This involved a reversal in trend of much that had been written, prior to 1930, in the literature of corporation, banking, and business law. The transition was not so difficult for me as for lawyers who had spent many years in the practice of those fields of law, years in which I had been working in trial law or even before I began to practice.

The political and economic issues which were before us all in the presidential campaign of 1932, and which were dramatized so effectively during the first one hundred days of the new administration in 1933, resulted in a splurge of federal legislation that may permanently have revolutionized corporate enterprise and the practice of corporation law. It is interesting, in thinking back over those years, to recall the increasing emphasis on legislation involving corporations at that time. President Hoover, during his administration, urged economic legislation to combat the Great Depression, having chiefly to do with corporations and corporation finances, such as legislation creating the Reconstruction Finance Corporation and the Home Owner's Loan Corporation.

Then, as soon as President Roosevelt took office, his aim was first in the corporate direction. He declared a bank holiday, and later reopened the banks with insured deposits. He sponsored federal legislation which, for the first time, regulated the issuance of corporate securities. With the National Industrial Recovery

Administration, he expected to reorganize business, industry by industry.

Many of the acts of Congress, enacting this first New Deal, ran into trouble in the interpretations of the Constitution by the "Nine Old Men" of the Supreme Court. The result of their decisions was, however, not to defeat the New Deal, but to change its emphasis from industrial reorganization and reform to economic recovery by the expenditure of federal money. The Supreme Court decided that Congress, and not the judiciary, should make decisions as to the amounts of money to be received by the federal government from taxes or from loans, and as to the expenditure of such funds directly by the federal government or through grants by the federal government to state or local governments. A *new* New Deal continued to spawn federal legislation regulating business and corporations in many ways, but its major emphasis was on spending us all out of the depression. Hence businessmen in all parts of the country became tax-conscious as never before.

Because of this new consciousness, and this new trend, I began, near the end of 1935, to look about for a man to join our firm— the first to do so as a specialist—one who would devote himself to federal tax law. About the same time each of several other Dallas firms was making room for a man to devote his time to federal tax matters. A field so long assumed to be one involving mathematical computations and details was being discovered by the legal profession to have reached a stage of development bristling with legal difficulties of major importance. Within a decade, no law firm could serve corporate clients adequately without at least one reliable tax lawyer, and without consulting him in advance as to the tax impact of every large transaction planned or guided by the firm for the client.

Hence, first among those who have developed a specialty of their own in corporation law, let me mention the *tax lawyer*. He need not be, and indeed usually is not, dealing exclusively with corporations and corporation law; but almost all tax lawyers, whether in private practice, in government service, education, or private industry, deal with corporation law for a substantial part of their time. While the federal income tax law dates back to 1913, its real impact on the practice of corporation law began about the mid-'thirties, and has steadily increased since then. For that reason, I mention the specialization of the tax lawyer first because a corporal in a firm practicing corporation law must have, more surely than any other specialist, one or more tax lawyers in his squad of riflemen.

Next—at least this is my experience—such a corporal needs, as a full-time specialist, at least one *corporate finance and securities lawyer.* With the enactment of the Securities Act of 1933, the Securities Exchange Act of 1934, the Public Utility Holding Company Act of 1935, the Trust Indenture Act of 1939, the Investment Act of 1940, and the Investment Advisors Act of 1940, Congress has created wide powers of regulation of many corporations with the result that nearly all corporations need to know the extent of their obligations under these federal statutes, and the rules and regulations issued under them by the Securities Exchange Commission. In my own practice I have often wanted and needed in my squad one or more rifleman who knew, much better in detail than I, the ins and outs of this important area of corporation law.

With the enactment of the National Labor Relations Act of 1935 (as later amended in 1947, 1954, and 1959) and with the enactment of the Federal Wage and Hour Act of 1938, the federal regulation of a large proportion of corporations in this new area began. Where not pre-empted by federal regulation, the control over these matters by state legislation meanwhile became more detailed. Before the Second World War commenced, I found that I needed help here, too. Most law firms with a substantial corporate practice have found it necessary to have one or more specialists devoting full time as *labor lawyers.*

A field that has been intensely interesting to me, dating back to my law-school days, is that of antitrust law. The Sherman Act of 1890, the Clayton Act of 1914, and the Federal Trade Commission Act of 1914, and court decisions under them, were studied in law school. At that time I thought that anyone working in this field was preparing to try, or was actually trying, a lawsuit; but, as is true in almost everything else, the antitrust field has become much more complicated than it used to be. Today one must know, in order to advise clients in this field, the basic statutes above mentioned and in addition: the Robinson-Patman law; numerous other supplemental acts of Congress; the decisions, rules, and regulations of the Federal Trade Commission, and the impact of a much greater bulk of court decisions on all this. The antitrust and fair-trade laws of one's own state and neighboring states, and the rules and practices of the agency dealing with each of these laws, must also be kept in mind. The importance of these subjects to corporate clients has made it urgent that our firm retain more than one experienced specialist as *antitrust and trade-regulation lawyers*.

My experience in the late 'twenties has made me keenly interested also in the work of *corporate organization and reorganization lawyers*. Under an amendatory act of Congress, state court receiverships as a vehicle of re-enlivening corporations in financial stress were largely superseded by proceedings for reorganization under the new Section 77B of the Bankruptcy Act. I spent a considerable part of my time in the 'thirties engaged in such efforts, partly litigious in character, but chiefly office work, planning, documenting, and supervising the steps taken in carrying out the rehabilitation of corporate enterprises.

However, with the defense build-up in 1940 and 1941, and with federal expenditures in the next few years again greatly increased in connection with the conduct of the war, the need for corporate rehabilitation practically evaporated in our part of the country. Since then, there has been little use by us of the Chandler Act amendments to the bankruptcy provision. For the same economic reasons, there has been more than an offsetting need for the talents of lawyers experienced in advising on the organizations of corporations, their mergers, consolidations, and expansion. Every law firm engaged in the corporate field would prefer, of course, to be devoted to these constructive services, and in services concerned with the problems about taxes, securities, labor, antitrust, and trade, that grow out of the development of corporations, than to be at work in bankruptcy or rehabilitation litigation that arise out of business failures or difficulties threatening liquidation of the corporate enterprise. (May I mention, in passing, that the economic theory generally accepted in my college days was that businessmen, and hence corporate lawyers specializing in organization or reorganization problems, should expect a rotating emphasis affecting them and their services—a depression to be followed by a recovery, by overenthusiasms, boom, and depression again, all in recurrent cycles?)

The specialists in the five fields I have mentioned—tax, labor, corporate finance and securities, antitrust and trade regulation, corporate organization and reorganization—are those I believe are most likely to be found in law firms. But there are other areas of specialization included in many firms, such as the *patent lawyer* and the *admiralty lawyer*. The type and volume of corporation practice of any firm weighs as a controlling guide in determining how many corporate practitioners in specialized fields the firm shall have, and in what divergent fields they shall work.

In the opening of this chapter I referred to changes in the practice of law, as well as changes in business and public affairs, that I believe lie ahead. In taking these into account, one should recognize that specializations of today may well prove to be the specializations no longer needed a decade from now, or even in less time. Hence a broad legal education will, in my opinion, serve as a better start for future activities as a corporate lawyer than any limitation a young man might impose on himself in law school—or, even more unwise, before law school—by dedicating himself prematurely to some particular specialty.

The lack of wisdom in a premature choice is indicated by the changes that have occurred during my years of practice, and in the kinds of specialization most needed in the general practice of corporation law; yet these changes will be followed, I sincerely believe, by changes equally important and far-reaching in the next twenty years or so. As one example of what is occurring, as one important change, I wish to mention a specialty which, until recently, has received comparatively little emphasis in some parts of the country. I hope, and believe, that our economy is to be increasingly dependent on international trade. I believe, too, that the corporate clients of law firms of interior cities, such as Dallas, will in the years ahead be keenly interested in legal problems involving international trade, international finance, and international trade practices. Law firms in our largest cities, and especially New York City, now have a rich experience and a recognized expertise in this field. Increasingly, I believe, a need will become apparent in other cities, even those well inland, for lawyers to specialize in this field of corporation law. A lawyer in the international field will need an extensive basic knowledge of laws of one or more other nations, as well as our own generally; he will need great information about international affairs; and he must know the statutes creating a labyrinth of federal agencies and the pertinent decisions, rules, regulations, and practices of these agencies.

In the offices of many law firms engaged in the general practice of corporate law there are, besides the specialists I have mentioned, other lawyers who devote themselves to no special field of corporate law but serve the needs of an individual corporation, or a number of corporate clients within the same industry. In our part of the country, there are partners in law firms who devote themselves to the general corporate practice by especially serving one or more clients in these lines of business: banking and financial institutions; oil and gas companies; insurance companies; transportation corporations. These lawyers, serving an individual client, or some particular line of business or industry, will, of course, have available for assistance and joint effort the firm's various specialists in separate fields of corporate law.

In our office, for instance, in recent years we have had, for a bank, three men devoting themselves almost wholly to bank matters, and they, in turn, have had the assistance of specialists, the riflemen referred to above. Also in recent years, we have had two men who devoted most of their time and attention to oil and gas matters, serving no single client but meeting the needs of several clients engaged in that industry. For the needs of other corporate clients, we have attempted to divide the responsibility among the various partners according to their interests and specialties.

A lawyer in a firm who devotes his entire time to a single client has an opportunity to learn the routine business practice of that client, the policy decisions and how they compare with others in the same industry, and thereby is in a much better position to be of service than if he were without such a background.

Some corporations have such volume of legal work that they develop legal departments of their own. Undoubtedly, there is an advantage in having a general counsel and his staff immediately available in the office of a corporation. But lacking such counsel and staff, a corporation will find that a lawyer from a firm engaged in general practice can well fill its needs. Beside the corporate lawyer primarily consulted, and the specialists within his firm that he can work with, there will also be available to him for consultation still other lawyers in the firm who are proficient in fields of law other than corporate law and whose experience may prove to be of substantial assistance when requested.

Many other corporations retain a lawyer, either a full-time official or employee of the corporation at its office, who is the only lawyer in its official family. Of course he should be, and usually is, authorized to employ a law firm in general practice on all corporate legal matters that he thinks he should. But the tendency, especially if the corporate enterprise has not yet attained maturity and substantial size, appears to be that such an office counsel will be less likely to call on a law firm for assistance than would the same man acting as general counsel who might readily call in partners of his own firm to assist him. Reliance on a single lawyer in the office of a corporation, without enough assistance from specialists, is much more common in smaller corporations while still in the formative stage; though it would seem that for them specialized assistance to the general counsel would normally be of more than usual value.

A recent report, issued by the American Bar Foundation,[2] shows that the number of lawyers in *private industry*—that is, lawyers employed and salaried by private industry—has doubled in the past decade. It is safe to assume, I believe, that substantially all of these lawyers so employed are engaged in one area or another of corporation law.

Though I do not have statistical proof of this, it is my belief that the number of lawyers engaged in the practice of corporate law, not in industry but in *private practice,* has also doubled in the past decade.[3]

Nor is this growth in corporate practice limited only to private industry and private practice; growth [4] in two other areas of corporation law must be considered: the practice of corporation law in government service and in educational institutions.

It is reasonable to assume, I believe, that more than half of the lawyers employed by the federal government are employed in those agencies that deal with corporations, and that these lawyers have to do with the formulation, interpretation, and enforcement of decisions, rules, regulations, and policies of these agencies. Besides the lawyers in these particular agencies, there are many others employed by the Federal Government who are active in corporation law. The opportunities for corporation lawyers in government service have been notably increasing, and this trend will probably continue.

Many other lawyers now active in corporation law over the country have had the advantage of experience in government service. Surely one avenue of investigation that anyone will want to make, as he considers corporation law as a career, should be in regard to what suitable government position might be open to him, either as permanent employment or as a steppingstone to later private practice in corporation law.

Government service is not the only area of corporation law that

[2] Statistical Report, "The 1961 Lawyer," American Bar Foundation, December, 1961, page 63.

[3] Id., Compare pages 63 with pages 62 and 121.

[4] Id., pages 63 and 76–77.

has increased with the many increasing statutes relating to the regulations and supervision of corporate enterprise, both federal and state. Opportunities for teaching in the field of corporation law have also increased and presumably will continue to do so. Such opportunities will continue to be few when compared to opportunities in federal service, yet I recommend that you should consider both possibilities.

I have already advised you to visit four or five lawyers in private practice, preferably lawyers with experience in different fields of corporation law. I also advise you to visit one or two corporate lawyers in private industry. In addition, I suggest that you visit a teacher of corporation law and that you call on one, or more than one, corporation lawyers in government service. In each of these visits you will, of course, seek from these lawyers the benefit of their experience and advice.

The trend of American life during the past fifty years has been steadily toward an urban and suburban society and an industrial economy; that trend, it seems to me, is likely to be yet stronger during the next fifty years.

The trend of American business has distinctly been toward the growth and development of corporate enterprises, not the growth and increased influence of big corporations, but chiefly the organization and development of corporations for the conduct of small business and the growth of many of these in size and influence as they succeed. This trend in business, it seems to me, is likely to become notably stronger in your day than in mine.

What the part of the counsel of America's developing corporations shall be in all of this has been most effectively stated by two of them:

. . . the vast accumulation of wealth lodged in a (one large) modern business corporation belongs not to those who administer that wealth, but to many thousands of equitable owners—the stockholders. This places every member of corporate management, including general counsel, in what is tantamount to a position of public trust. Through his training and experience as a lawyer, general counsel is the one who should be most acutely sensitive to the exacting nature of this fiduciary obligation. Accordingly, one of his principal functions should be to act as guardian of the corporate conscience.[5]

To begin with, the present-day corporation stands not on the periphery of the democratic process, as it did in the last half of the nineteenth century, but in its dead center. The democratic process is a continuing and sensitive series of rising pressures and inevitable responses. As a major element in our capitalist society, the corporation occupies a unique place. It has a personality that can be credited or blamed; but unlike the individual, it has very little margin for error because it is without any inherent value. It is valuable only insofar as it serves people. It cannot, therefore, behave cavalierly, as some individuals can. If it makes a mistake, and certainly if it repeats a mistake, something will happen sooner or later to ensure that it will never make the same one again. Pressures will rise to police it tighter, to impose new regulations, to restrict it in new ways, sometimes to punish it. And the response will come through the courts, through the legislatures, through labor unions, through consumers; indeed, through all the means available for the people in a democracy to express themselves. . . .

An alert corporation counsel should be seeking constantly to learn the direction in which society is moving. Today's aspirations are reflected in tomorrow's laws; and no counsel wants his corporation limping along, surly in protest, bringing up the rear in those constantly changing frontiers in human relationships that give the law its flexibility. Let me emphasize that counsel has a determining voice here, and a highly creative part to play, because there is an opportunity for him to give guidance and point to future laws.[6]

---

[5] Lloyd F. Thanhouser, general counsel of Continental Oil Company, "The Corporate Counsel's Viewpoint," *The Business Lawyer* (quarterly professional magazine published by the Section of Corporation, Banking and Business Law of the American Bar Association), issue of November 1961, page 83.

[6] William T. Gossett, general counsel of Ford Motor Company, 1947–1962; President of the American Bar Foundation 1960–1962; quotations are from his lectures to the Washington and Lee University School of Law, 1956, as published in the *John Randolph Tucker Lectures*, 1953–1956, pages 194, 203, and 208.

I urge you, therefore, as a prospective lawyer, to consider carefully the possibility of taking part in the molding of these developments in the years ahead, not only because of the satisfactions that you yourself can enjoy but also because of the part that you can have for the good of all.

7 *You in*

INTERNATIONAL LAW

BY PHILIP C. JESSUP

JUDGE

INTERNATIONAL COURT OF JUSTICE

The Hague

PHILIP C. JESSUP

Born: 1897, New York, New York

Hamilton College: A.B., 1919
Yale University: LL.B., 1924
Columbia University: A.M., 1924
    Ph.D., 1927
LL.D.: Hamilton College, Brown University, Western Reserve University,
    Middlebury College, Seoul National University, Rutgers University
L.C.D.: Colgate University, Union College
Litt. D.: University of Hanoi
J.D.: Oslo University, University of Paris

US Army (A. E. F.): World War I

Admitted District of Columbia Bar: 1925
Admitted New York Bar: 1927
Member: Parker & Duryee (New York): 1927–43
Columbia University:
    Lecturer, International Law: 1925–27
    Assistant Professor: 1927–29
    Associate Professor: 1929–35
    Professor: 1935–46
    Hamilton Fish Professor of International Law and Diplomacy: 1946–61
Judge, International Court of Justice: 1961—

Legal adviser to federal government offices in numerous instances, 1924–53,
    at international conferences, embassies, and to United States delegations
    at United Nations
United States representative to United Nations General Assembly: 1948–
    52; Deputy Representative UN Security Council: 1948–49
Appointed Ambassador at large: 1949. Resigned: 1953
Member of several associations in the field of International Law and Diplo-
    macy

Author: *The Law of Territorial Waters and Maritime Jurisdiction*
    A Modern Law of Nations
    Transnational Law
    The Use of International Law
    Elihu Root
    Controls for Outer Space & The Antarctic Analogy (with H. J. Taunben-
    feld)
Formerly: Supervising editor, Columbia University Studies in History,
    Economics and Public Law. Board of editors: *Columbia Law Review;
    Yale Law Journal; World Politics; American Journal of International
    Law; International Organization*

It WOULD have been September, 1946; first-year students were registering at the Columbia Law School. There was a knock on my office door in Kent Hall: a tall young man and his pretty bride came in.

"Are you the Professor of International Law, sir?"

"Yes. What can I do for you?"

He was direct and to the point. "I piloted fighter plane escorts for bombing raids over Germany. When we were on our way back to England, we had time to think. I used to wonder what I would do if I got back home. I made up my mind the only thing worth while was to help prevent another war. Mary and I got married as soon as I was discharged. We've talked it over and she agrees. It seems to me you have to have some law against war. I suppose that's international law. How can I learn enough so I can help?"

I wish I could have pointed out to him a quick and certain path. Actually, I had to say, "'Before you can be an international lawyer, you must be a lawyer."

My mind went back to 1919 and to an earlier war. I had returned from some months as a light machine gunner, Pfc., at the front in Belgium and northern France. I came back to Hamilton College, in Clinton, New York, to finish my senior year. On the edge of the college campus lived one of the great men of the American bar and of statecraft—Elihu Root. I went to see him and I told him substantially what the young pilot, years later, said to me.

"First," Mr. Root said, "before there is any question of international law, you must be a lawyer."

My father was a lawyer in New York City, author of the standard book on Surrogate Practice. He knew Professor John Bassett
Moore, first incumbent of the Hamilton Fish Chair of International Law and Diplomacy at Columbia University, a man with
wide experience in the State Department, author of the great
international-law digests which bear his name, successful counselor to governments and private clients, later a judge of the
World Court. At my father's request, Professor Moore gave me an
appointment; I told him that I wanted to specialize in international law and needed his advice.

"To specialize in international law . . . ?" He thought about it
for a moment. "Well, after you have finished law school . . ."

I am sure that the advice which I got then, and which later I
gave, was wise advice. It would have been taken for granted in
Europe where international law is a standard part of the law curriculum. But in the United States, international law was then a
curiosity, an odd specialty like Roman law or legal history. Few
law schools taught it and, as a matter of fact, no state bar examination requires a knowledge of international law even today.

Even so eminent a lawyer as John Bassett Moore, while given
a "courtesy seat" on the Columbia Law Faculty, held a chair established in the Faculty of Political Science. Most young Americans interested in international law approached it in those days as
a part of political science and studied for a Ph.D., instead of an
LL.B. I was faced with this choice and eventually took both degrees which actually—and I shall explain this later—I think is useful training.*

The late Frederic R. Coudert, a leading member of the New
York Bar, once said that if a fellow practitioner introduced him
as an "international" lawyer, he suspected him of trying to steal
away his best domestic clients—the Coudert firm had among its
clients not only foreign embassies but also corporations and indi-

---

* There have been and are eminent Professors of International Law in the
United States who never took a law degree; they have had to teach themselves to be lawyers in knowledge and in intellectual approach, although
they did not become members of the bar. This is the hard way and I know
no reason to recommend it.

viduals. When I was first admitted to the bar, in 1925, if I told a "common-law lawyer" that I was an *international* lawyer, he would smile tolerantly and then perhaps guffaw, asking, "Is there any such thing as international law?"

If one were in a position to chat with such a questioner, then one had an opportunity to counter with a few queries (forgive the anachronisms!): "Why do you suppose the Constitution of the United States includes among the powers of Congress the power 'to define and punish. . . . offenses against the Law of Nations'?

"Why has the Supreme Court of the United States said: 'International Law is a part of our law, and must be ascertained and administered by the courts of justice of appropriate jurisdiction, as often as questions of right depending upon it are duly presented for their determination'?" (One could cite constitutions and case law of many other countries, but my common-law lawyer would be more impressed with American precedents.)

"The Constitution also says that treaties are part of the supreme law of the land—but our Constitution does not bind other countries, does it? So if a treaty is binding on the other party as well as on the United States, it must be because of some rule of *international* law.

"Perhaps you don't know that to make sure the United States would observe its international obligations, Congress in 1789 passed a law (*still on the books*) providing that the federal district courts should have original jurisdiction . . . of any civil action by an alien for a tort only, committed in violation of the law of nations or a treaty of the United States.

"Do you remember that after the American Civil War we were paid $15,000,000 by England, which was the amount of damages assessed by an international tribunal in the Alabama claims for England's violations of international law?

"Did you know that the United States has pressed and defended claims for breaches of international law before some thirty different international tribunals? One of these tribunals, established with Mexico under a treaty of 1923, had 3,617 different claims presented to it—and most of the claimants undoubtedly retained lawyers to prepare their cases. Also, there were some 13,000 claims before the American-German Claims Commission set up in 1922.

"Have you ever examined even one of the decisions of the World Court; that is, of the Permanent Court of International Justice which functioned under the League of Nations system from 1920 to 1945, and its successor, the present International Court of Justice, which is 'the principal judicial organ of the United Nations'?"

In answer to these queries, our hard-boiled practitioner is apt to say, "That's all very well, but how do you enforce a decision of the international court? And what's more, do you really think the World Court can decide all the disputes between the United States and the Soviet Union?"

"Of course it cannot," I would answer, "any more than the Supreme Court of the United States was able to settle all the disputes which led to our War Between the States. Internationally, no state can be forced into court without its consent; but the experience of a century and a half shows that once governments agree to submit a case to an international court, there has been a refusal to comply with the judgment in only a fraction of 1 per cent of the cases decided."

Now let's abandon our interlocutor for the moment and return to you and to law school. If you want to be an international lawyer, do you specialize in law school? To a certain extent, yes; but always bearing in mind that *first of all you are going to be a lawyer*, a member of the bar. (You have already been wisely warned in this book against pre-law specialization.)

You will have a much wider choice of courses in international law today than was available to a law student twenty-five years ago. The change is quite recent and is due, I think, to two influences. At the risk of some inaccuracy, we can say that one influence is spiritual and the other material. What I would call the spiritual influence is the impact upon the American spirit—or the American mind, if you will—of the *Second* World War and the position of the United States in the world after that war.

If one goes back to the 1920's and considers the postwar impact of the *First* World War, he will see that student interest even then was stimulated in international studies; but he will be reminded that this was also the era of American isolation. Not only did we reject the League of Nations, but, despite the urging of every President from Woodrow Wilson to Franklin D. Roosevelt, the requisite two-thirds of the Senate was never willing to approve American membership in the World Court.

Then came World War II, and after this war great changes came about in this country. The United States led the way in establishing the United Nations with the provision in its charter that made the International Court of Justice an integral part of the UN organization. In the years that have followed, the cold war has intensified and perpetuated American consciousness of the inescapable international role of the United States.

The American Bar has come to take its rightful place of leadership in legal matters of international concern. It was leadership from within the ranks of the bar which checked the isolationist effort—by the so-called Bricker amendment—to hamstring the President in the exercise of his constitutional role in control of foreign relations. It is under the aegis of the American Bar Association that there is now being carried on, by a former president of the Association, a well-financed world-wide campaign for "World Peace Through the Rule of Law."

These are among the symptoms, the signs of the existing awareness of American concern with international legal problems, and the central problem which concerned my air force pilot—the problem of the prevention of war. This awakening is especially notable and of interest here, inasmuch as it concerns lawyers (though, in fairness, one could point to innumerable examples of the same lively interest in other professional and civic groups). It does no harm to have lawyers suddenly "discover" international law or its desirability as when the Attorney General of the United States several years ago encouraged the Assembly of the American Bar Association, gathered in Westminister Hall, London, by telling them that "Creating a system of law for the nations of the world should not be beyond" the competence of a civilization which "has brought forth the methods of the common law and developed the Bill of Rights." In reality, the "system of law for the nations" has existed for three centuries and more; what is lacking is the willingness to use the system.

I have suggested that, besides any spiritual influence, there has also been material influence behind the growing interest in international law and the reflection of that interest in law-school curricula. This material influence again is twofold.

In part I have in mind that, as the international interests of the United States government and of American business increase, so do the demands on the American lawyer for counsel on international legal problems. At the present time, for example, American interests in legal problems affecting foreign investments, and also in the effects of the European Common Market on American business, are demanding the intensive exertions of some of our best legal talent. (I will venture to say that if someone like you should read these pages, say five years from now, he might need to change these two illustrative examples, but there will be equivalents in their places.)

More directly applicable to law-school curricula, but at the same time not wholly unrelated to the point just made, is the program of the Ford Foundation for promoting international legal studies in American law schools. Large grants have been made to a number of law schools to enable them to develop new courses and research activities in this area. The consequence is that in a number of the leading law schools today you would have opportunity—generally in your second and third years—to acquire some familiarity with international legal problems. You are also likely to find courses or seminars labeled and designed to acquaint you with "international business transactions." One might say, in passing, that if these are not "bread and butter" courses, they are at least *"croissants avec confiture."*

Probably, too, you will find some courses in comparative or foreign law which will alert you to the fact that other legal systems, perhaps of greater antiquity than the common law which is at the root of most of your courses, have evolved very different legal concepts or principles and that adequate currently operating codes of law and procedure are based on them. If you can absorb something of the Roman law roots of the modern civil law, so much the better. So much the better, in particular, for our international lawyer because much of international law was developed, particularly in the seventeenth century, by "civilians"; that is, by lawyers trained in Roman and civil law.

The courses I have mentioned are either modern practical courses in international legal studies, or related background courses; they are not courses in *"public* international law" as the term is understood outside of the United States and as the content used to be in American law schools.

Do you wonder why I suddenly speak of "public" international law, as if some international law could be "private"—which may well sound like a paradox? I shall come back shortly to indicate what kinds of problems are covered by *public* international law; but, somewhat parenthetically, let me first explain that there is, indeed, a subject which generally, outside of the United States (and to some extent other common-law countries), is called *"private* international law." In American terminology it is called "conflicts of law," and that is a better descriptive label. Conflicts of law, just to give one example, deals with such questions as this: "Which national law applies to a contract made by two Germans, in Argentina, to be performed in the United States—is it German law, or Argentine law, or United States law?"

The "conflicts" course is one which you, as a potential international lawyer, certainly want to take even though you may find the course largely directed to problems of conflicts among the laws of the several states of the United States and therefore blending into some aspects of American constitutional law. But the subject matter of "conflicts," or private international law, has more than once figured in judgments of the World Court. Indeed, the United States is one of the few countries which has not made treaties with other countries to regulate these conflicts of laws.

Treaties are a most essential part of the international legal framework, and one of the principal topics in *public* international law. To an extent, treaties are contractural agreements between countries, and, to that extent, rules of international law exist to deal with the form of contracting, the validity of the contract, its interpretation, its termination, and like aspects which you will have studied first year in a common law course on contracts. If you ever have to plead a case before an international court, the chances are that you will, *inter alia,* have to argue some point of treaty law.

Public international law is also concerned with problems which arise if a citizen or corporation of one country makes a contract with the government of another country, *e.g.*, to build a railroad, or a dam, to dredge a port, to develop mineral resources, or to loan money. If the government defaults, repudiates, or fails to perform its obligations, what recourse has the private contractor? Here one meets the interrelation of law and politics, the role of the State Department, its embassies and consulates, in extending diplomatic protection to citizens abroad. Such diplomatic interposition may lead to arbitration, often in the form of a mixed claims commission which will decide on the basis of international law. Perhaps, as in several cases in the past, the governments will refer the case to the International Court of Justice at The Hague.

But when you, as an international lawyer, are concerned with a citizen's claim against a foreign government, you are not left wholly to international remedies. You may sue the government in a national court. When? Where? How? All these questions your client will ask. Can you libel in an American port a ship owned by a foreign government, or does the government have "sovereign immunity"? Can you attach the funds which the foreign government has on deposit in a New York bank? Can you serve a summons on the government's ambassador? On his consul? These are among the multiplicity of jurisdictional questions with which public international law is concerned. Also, in these days one finds examples of governmental expropriation, or nationalization, of aliens' property. If the expropriating government seeks to sell the seized property abroad, and assuming no compensation was paid to the original owner, will a foreign national court question or deny that government's title on the ground that it was acquired in violation of international law?

You may also have opportunity to argue an international law

case in a special type of national court. As far back as 1831, France paid the United States some five and a half million dollars as a lump-sum settlement of claims of American citizens against France. The United States Congress then set up an American commission of three persons to decide the merits of the individual American claims according to the applicable treaty "and the principles of justice, equity, and the law of nations." There have been a number of similar lump-sum settlements creating a fund out of which American claimants were paid after decisions by some special American tribunal. Since World War II, Congress has established the Foreign Claims Settlement Commission which, among others, decided on claims against a seventeen-million-dollar fund paid to the United States by Yugoslavia to cover cases where the property of American citizens in Yugoslavia had been taken by that government between 1939 and 1948.

But, you will say, this may be all very well to show that international law, like national law, can be involved in the practical affairs of business and everyday life, but is that what the air-force pilot wanted to learn about? Is that the star which leads one on the road to the abolition of war? Yes and no. But before grappling with that issue, let's pursue a bit further the career of the international lawyer as practitioner.

You have taken, we will suppose, as many as possible of the internationally oriented courses that the law school offers. Perhaps you have taken extra international law courses during the summer, as at The Hague Academy of International Law. You are looking for a job in a law office and you have an appointment in the office of Smith, Smith, Jones, Johnson and Scott.

Mr. Scott (looking at his file): "Now, let's see—you are at X Law School, aren't you? Not on the *Law Review* but in the top third of your class. That's good because the standards at X are high. Have you a pretty clear idea of what you want to do as a lawyer?"

You: "Yes, Mr. Scott. I'm specializing in international law and I know your firm handles international cases——"

Mr. Scott: "Very interesting indeed is international law and

I'm sure you'll find it so. My own specialty happens to be wills and estates. But the firm is not taking on any specialists now. We just need three good young lawyers to do pretty humdrum clerking jobs at first. It has been a pleasure to meet you. Good day."

If you had said you were a specialist in real property, or corporate reorganization, or admiralty, or patents, you might have gotten the same reply. Certainly it would be most unusual to be able to *begin* the practice of law as an international lawyer. As I have said before, but can hardly emphasize too much—you must first be a lawyer. If you are fortunate enough to be taken into an office which handles international cases, it is quite possible that after six months or so you might be able to let it be known that a point involved in the XYZ case in the office is one on which you wrote a seminar paper in law school and perhaps you could be useful.

But it is only fair to recall the position of M., a very able lawyer who had been a Minister of Finance in his own country before he took refuge in the United States and started his legal career all over again. He was naturalized here, admitted to the bar, and found a place in one of the big New York law firms which handles numerous international cases. At the outset, the partner handling a public utility rate case in New Jersey needed help and M. was assigned to him. Eight months later another partner, who knew M's background, asked for help on an international case. "Absolutely impossible!" said the public utility partner. "I can't possibly spare him until we finish the hearings before the Commission." Flattering of course, but M. soon resigned and successfully started a firm of his own for the practice of international law. You must please observe, however, that M. was quite a bit older than the average law student and had contacts of his own. Ordinarily a person just out of law school would not be wise to hang out his own shingle as an international lawyer, unless he was endowed not only with optimism and patience but also with a reasonable amount of private income.

So let's assume that you are in the office of a law firm—and I must admit that I am thinking largely in terms of a firm in one of the big cities since I am discussing international law and one is not apt to look for that kind of practice in a small community. You will probably find your work in the office fearfully exacting, with many long evenings and weekend tasks, and probably none of them having anything to do with international law. But you need not forget your interest in international law. When you join the American Bar Association you can elect membership in the Section on International and Comparative Law. There may be an international law committee in your local bar association. You can become a member of the American Branch of the International Law Association and of the American Society of International Law. Able young members of the bar, with expertise in international law, are usually in demand in the associations and there are frequent opportunities to take part in a discussion at one of the periodic meetings. Also, both for contact and for content, and to find opportunities for service, membership in some local association or council on foreign relations is something you should welcome when you are eligible.

Perhaps you think that all this is enough to keep you busy and you are right. Nevertheless, you may find time to write an article or a note for publication in some law journal. It may be that some problem on which you have been working in the office will lend itself to that treatment, or some seminar paper you wrote in law school can be developed and polished. I have known quite a few such papers which have later appeared in print. Use your writing energy for writing on an international legal topic; such publication will stand you in good stead.

A year passes and you have had a taste of the practice of the law—you are a lawyer. But even now if you get the opportunity to continue in practice with all, or even much of your time, devoted to international law cases, you will be one of a lucky small minority. It would be pleasant, but surprising, if you have been able, so soon as this, to establish a reputation as an international lawyer. If at this time, therefore, you find your surroundings and work congenial, your prospects good, and your personal circumstances conducive to staying where you are, then you might well stay there and continue in your work. You would not be the first lawyer to become well known as an international lawyer after having climbed pretty far up the ladder of common law practice.

But suppose you prefer to press more directly and immediately along the lines where your deepest interest lies in international law, what are your alternatives? I will suggest two, emphasizing the while that your choice will depend on personal preferences and very likely on family and economic factors.

The first alternative I will mention is government service. If you know that you like wrestling with legal problems, you might see if there is an opening in the Office of the Legal Adviser of the Department of State in Washington. There may be sixty or more lawyers in that office and there are apt to be two or three vacancies a year. They usually don't like to take on lawyers who want merely a very brief experience in Washington, and in the ways of government; but, on the other hand, it has not heretofore been usual to exact a commitment for a long period. That office handles many kinds of international law problems and is also involved in a considerable amount of statutory drafting and interpretation. (You can read about this in an article in *The American Journal of International Law:* July, 1962, Volume 56.) It is a useful experience for an international lawyer, though it must be said that not everyone will find it congenial as a lifetime career.

There is international legal work to be done in other government departments in Washington. A few years ago the Committee on International Law of the Association of American Law Schools made a survey of the frequency with which a long list of international law questions arise in many different departments— Defense, Justice, Treasury, *et al.,*·and also in agencies like the Federal Communications Commission, the Atomic Energy Commission, and the Civil Aeronautics Board. It was astonishing to find in how many offices these questions arise.

This is partly explained by the fact that the United States is a member of all the specialized agencies of the United Nations whose very names suggest the range of subject matter: International *Labor* Organization; *Food and Agriculture* Organization; World *Health* Organization, International *Maritime* Consultative

Organization, the International *Bank* and the International *Monetary Fund*. All organizations, it is safe to say, have legal problems and in many instances, when the United States is involved, they are dealt with in the government department concerned with the subject in question. As an example of this, the status of our American forces in NATO and other countries raises very many problems of international law that are handled in the Pentagon. Moreover, if you examine the journals and other publications of the armed services and the curricula of the several War Colleges, you will see what an active interest is taken in international law. Naturally the Navy has a special interest in the law of the sea, and the Defense Department as a whole is intensely concerned with the law of the air and the newly developing law of outer space.

But, you remind me, I was speaking about the legal problems which arise in international organizations. Why, you ask, shouldn't you get a legal job in one of those specialized agencies or in the Secretariat of the United Nations itself? If you get the chance, take it. American lawyers are rendering valuable service today in the UN and in some of the agencies; but all these organizations face the problem of "geographical distribution"—the appropriate allotment of jobs among the some hundred members. The "quota" of the United States is generally oversubscribed and you are not likely to find many openings. If you do find one, the work will be excellent experience for your career as an international lawyer. You may, as others have before you, find that despite all the frustrations, this itself is a career which satisfies not only the *lawyer* in you, but also your desire for international service in the cause of peace.

So, it seems, we have perhaps come back again to our air force pilot and his goal. And yet, we still may not be ready to talk with him and try to answer his questions. In the spirit of his visit, however, of his desires and his purpose, let me lead you back to Washington once more to consider still another possibility.

You are now a well-trained lawyer, but for reasons of your own the general practice of the law, the constant attention to what may appear to you to be highly meticulous detail, may fail to stir your continuing interest. This is no defect. "Everyone to his own taste" is a saying which is quite applicable to the professions. Some like trial law, some do not. Some like mortgages, or patents, or wills and estates, and some, as we know, like international law. Still others, many of them among our ablest practitioners, have been wooed away from their law offices to executive positions in banks and industrial corporations. Perhaps, therefore, instead of limiting yourself entirely to international law, you will decide to use your now well-trained mind, and your practical experience, in more general kinds of international service.

I have in mind, at the moment, what a good many lawyers have done; they have entered the Foreign Service of the United States. Furthermore, they have gone up to high places in that career service, on both the diplomatic and the consular side, and I venture to say that they have found their legal training was useful. (I am tempted to digress on a favorite argument raised by the contention of such eminent diplomatists as Sir Harold Nicholson, and, to some extent, by George Kennan, that lawyers make bad diplomatists. I have contended that this conclusion was due to a lack of understanding of lawyers and what they are and what they do, particularly a lack of realization that a very large part of the negotiating in American business life and in labor-management relations is done by lawyers. Let it suffice here to name only two great American lawyers who also, as Secretaries of State, were great diplomatists—Elihu Root and Dean Acheson.)

You need a real sense of dedication to enter the Foreign Service. Here, definitely, you do not start unless you intend to make it a career. Although Congress has reluctantly improved somewhat the compensation for our Foreign Service Officers, you will never get rich in the Service. You may well face real hardships and danger. You are likely to hear yourself called a "striped-pants cookie pusher," even though you don't own striped pants and cookies are not served in the tropical backwater where you are stationed for the time being. You will suffer the slings and arrows of outrageous Congressmen. Even worse, you may have to bear the boredom of a training period of shuffling ships papers or visa applications in some great but dull European industrial city. And yet the chances are good for interesting assignments, for a gratifying sense of participation in forwarding your country's foreign policy, for satisfaction in a worth-while job well done.

I have suggested that one does not nibble at the Foreign Service just for a year or two of experience. On the other hand, it may happen that for reasons of your own health, or the health of your wife or children, or some other impelling personal reason, you may find it necessary to resign. If so, you will be glad that you have another string to your bow, that you are a member of the bar and are able to resume practice.

We have been talking about government service as one of the alternatives open to you, if for one reason or another you decide not to continue in ordinary law practice. There is a second alternative open to you—teaching. And here, no doubt, you will call me a prejudiced witness because teaching is the basic career which I chose for myself. While I was in law school I was fortunate enough to be hired by one of my professors of international law to do some research on an international claim then pending before an international tribunal. I was also fortunate to have a year just after law school in the State Department as an Assistant Solicitor (The Legal Adviser was then called Solicitor) on the staff of an eminent international lawyer, Charles Cheney Hyde, with whom at the end of a year I went to Columbia to teach. (Perhaps I should mention that while I was at the State Department in my humble capacity, I came into the presence of the Secretary of State only once; but I was quite conscious of the fact that the Secretary, besides holding his high government position, was also a great lawyer—Charles Evans Hughes, later a judge of the World Court and Chief Justice of the United States.)

In those days, the legal office of the State Department was not so large as it is now and I had a varied experience not wholly dissimilar to that in a practitioner's office except that all the cases were international in character. For instance, while there I worked on part of a brief in a domestic court and on another in a tribunal of the Permanent Court of Arbitration. I helped to draft regulations to be applied by consular officers in a new immigration law. There was also abundant work in interpreting statutes relating to nationality of American citizens.

Subsequently in New York, after leaving the State Department,

I was a partner in a law firm for sixteen years; but aside from some matters of accommodation, or family need, I did not participate in general practice. During these years I was also teaching, and the cases for a foreign government, with international claims and a few other international matters, were not sufficiently numerous to interfere with my work at the university which was now my principal interest. Again one is tempted to digress into a eulogy of the academic career, but this is once more a question of taste, and here we are concerned with it only as it relates to the potential career of an international lawyer.

Perhaps, at this moment, it may be something of a shock to ask your thoughts to climb back down the ladder, particularly after you have envisaged the possibility of being Ambassador, Secretary of State, Legal Adviser to the United Nations, or senior partner in a big New York law firm. But we must remember that you, as you contemplate your career in international law, are actually still at the foot of the ladder—so let's draw back in order to make a longer jump, as the French expression goes.

In doing so, I would like to point out that as a result of the development of international legal studies in the law schools, which I have already described, there are many more opportunities than formerly to get a position on a law faculty with at least part time devoted to teaching international legal courses. In a recent bulletin of one of our leading law schools, I find fourteen persons listed as offering courses or seminars in a program of international legal studies. It is true that a beginner will often be asked to teach also a section of one of the basic first-year courses, and one should keep in mind that international law is still widely taught in faculties of political science in the United States; indeed, in some universities one may be called on to teach in both that faculty and in the law school. The facts are, however, that there are now careers in the teaching of international law, and the scope of these careers is widening.

At this time I need to recall what I said about the advantage of taking both the LL.B. degree and a Ph.D. I am not particularly concerned with the fact—though unhappily it *is* a fact—that if you plan to teach in a faculty of political science, a Ph.D. is almost (but not absolutely) essential. It is the hallmark which proves to the dean, or head of a department, that you yourself have experienced the training which it is expected that you will now give to graduate students. Yet I hope I am correct in believing that it is becoming more and more widely recognized that there are other experiences which may be the equivalent of the Ph.D., including, for example, a graduate degree in law in a law school.

The professional usage of the Ph.D., however, is not our prime concern at the moment and our interest in that degree has to do with its possible value, within its training, for the international lawyer. It is true that expertise in international law is promoted by familiarity with bodies of knowledge which are not included in a *law school* curriculum. It is also true that in the work for the Ph.D. you would almost certainly study "international relations," which is a convenient catch-all label to suggest the analysis of the historical, political, economic, psychological or idealogical, geographic, or other factors which influence governmental foreign policies. In some universities, moreover, it is still likely that more intensive work in public international law and international organization can be pursued by the Ph.D. candidate than by students in the law school; this is because, for the Ph.D. degree, the candidate is required to have the benefit of at least a reading knowledge of one or two foreign languages. Then, too, the candidate must write a dissertation, often of book length, which sometimes—but by no means always—is publishable. If it is published, and is favorably reviewed in legal journals, it undoubtedly aids his career, academic or other.

In this discussion of degrees and teaching, it should be recognized that universities nowadays have taken into account the international legal specialist and have made adjustments in their curricula to further his training. By way of illustration, I will mention a plan with which I was familiar; there are no doubt others of equal value and even the one I know best has undergone some changes. At Columbia University, there was, in addition to the Law School and the Graduate Faculty of Political Science, a School of International Affairs with which were affiliated a series of regional institutes—on Russia, East Asia, the Middle East, East and West Europe, and later Latin America. The School of International Affairs had a two-year graduate course leading to the degree of Master of International Affairs. (Of course one really could not "master" them in two years, but then you can get a "bachelor's" degree after you are married, and you don't need to be a philosopher to get a Ph.D.) Each student in the School of International Affairs had to choose a regional specialty in one of the Institutes and also a substantive specialty —law, economics, business, or government affairs.

To the law student there was offered a "combined program" in this way: regular first two years in Law School, then a transfer for one year to the School of International Affairs, then back to the Law School for the third year of law, at the end of which he received both the LL.B. and the M.I.A. degrees. In his second year of law, the student would be able to select some public-law courses, international law, perhaps constitutional law, and so on. In the School of International Affairs he was urged to avoid legal courses, to concentrate on the language, culture, government, history, politics and economy of the region of his choice. In his last year in Law School he would go into seminars on international business transactions, legal-economic problems of American foreign policy, and international law itself, with a broad base for understanding the backgrounds of the legal problems.

There was a particular reason for dovetailing the two courses, instead of having the student do a year of graduate work just after taking his LL.B. We found that if the law student postponed his bar exams, he had more trouble preparing for them. Also, if he did not go job hunting at the same time as his law classmates, he was at a disadvantage. While I think it is less and less true, the law offices at that time were a bit dubious about the value of "graduate" work outside of a law school; they wondered if the man might not be a bit rusty on his law and also whether he might expect to be treated as a "specialist." On the other hand, I know of one case in which a man who had taken the combined course was offered more than the usual starting salary because of his additional training. In any event, I believe there is real value in entering the third year of law with a year of related non-legal studies under your hat.

In planning your career in international law, provided you have already determined that your eventual goal is to be a teacher, a professor in that field, I would urge you to go straight through law school for your LL.B. You then pass your bar examinations, and, after this, go on for the necessary one or two years required for the Ph.D. While carrying out this plan you might, in between years of study, get in a year's experience in a law office or in government. With two strings to your academic bow, the LL.B. and the Ph.D., you can shoot at either a law faculty or a political science target—in either one still concerning yourself with your specialty of international law.

What then? Where are you? These are natural questions to ask in the United States, for an American professor is not without honor save in his own country—if the prophets will pardon my paraphrasing the familiar saying. In Europe the tradition is rather different. Most of the European international lawyers who are called upon by governments and the big companies to give consultative opinions on international-law questions, to argue cases before various international tribunals, including the International Court of Justice, are professors. Inevitably they have been trained in the law at a university, and, while still acting as professors, they may well have a private practice or some position in government. The situation in Latin America is much the same.

Perhaps a comparable tradition is in course of development in the United States. Certainly a large number of the great names in international law in this country have combined academic careers with international-law practice and some government experience. In this century, John Bassett Moore, Edwin M. Borchard, Charles Cheney Hyde, Manley O. Hudson are illustrations. On the other hand, there have been other great international lawyers who followed the career of the practitioner—Root, Choate, Coudert (father and son), for example.

Whether it be law or economics or sociology or engineering or physics or some other subject, American universities are now ac-

customed to the outside demands upon the skills of their leading
professors. In particular regard to the law, it is usually realized
in the university that the most vital teacher is the one who keeps
in personal touch with the actualities of the law. While the professor is still fair game for the cartoonist and the columnist, he
is in constant demand in government and in business. The ivory
tower these days does not claim all professors as tenants. Inevitably there are cases of teachers who become so interested in the
actualities (and perhaps in the extra income which they provide) that they neglect their courses and their students, but a
balanced combination is possible and fruitful. Leaves of absence
for public service have become usual.

Now let me pull you right back up to the top, or near the top,
of the ladder again. Let's assume that you are established either
as a professor of international law, or as a practitioner, or perhaps
some combination of the two. What kinds of cases are apt to
come your way?

You may be asked to give an expert opinion on a question of international law in a litigated case in court. This, however, is not
usual, since the prevailing doctrine is to the effect that international law is part of the law of the land; it is, therefore, *argued*
like any point of domestic law, rather than being *proved* by experts as is customarily done to establish the law of a foreign country.

More frequently you will be asked to give an opinion to some
business interest or to some foreign government. Perhaps the
X Oil Company wants an opinion on the validity of a concession
in Ruritania. In considerable contrast to this are the so-called
off-shore oil cases which recently were litigated in the United
States federal courts; in them, international lawyers were retained to give opinions to state governments, such as those of
California and Texas, concerning the international law on the
continental shelf and the extent of territorial waters. Sometimes
such opinions are printed as appendices to the briefs.

If countries A and B are disputing a boundary, or the interpretation of a treaty, or some other question, you and other international lawyers may be asked to give an opinion, either for

the private guidance of the government which retains you or for the avowed purpose of publishing it in order to help persuade the other government or eventually some tribunal to which the dispute may be submitted.

You may also be called in by a law firm which represents a government, or has some other client involved in a case before a claims commission or other tribunal. Depending on the forum, you may be asked to prepare a memorandum or to participate in writing the brief. Finally, you may be asked to argue the case before the tribunal.

Perhaps you wonder how you can become admitted to the bar of the "World Court"—The International Court of Justice. Unlike the Supreme Court of the United States, the International Court does not have a "bar" in this sense. Any person designated as agent, counsel, or advocate, by a government party to a case before the Court, may plead before the Court. It is quite usual for each party to be represented by several lawyers, each one arguing some particular part of the case. Consider, for instance, a recent case decided by the International Court of Justice. It was a boundary dispute between two Asian States, Cambodia and Thailand. Each country used one of its own lawyers, but Cambodia's case was chiefly argued by one American lawyer, a practitioner and a former Secretary of State, and two professors from the University of Paris; for Thailand, there was one American (also a practitioner, but one who has served in government and has done some teaching), an English barrister who had been Attorney General, and a Belgian lawyer-professor-senator.

All proceedings before the Court are in both English and French; usually a lawyer will talk for ten or fifteen minutes and then pause for the translation. There is no limit on the total length of time which may be devoted to the arguments. The case mentioned above took exactly a month from the beginning to the end of the oral proceedings, but they included, rather unusually for cases in the International Court, extensive examination and cross-examination of experts and witnesses.

This is not the place for an extended description of this world tribunal, but I may be excused if I add just a few salient facts.

There are fifteen judges from as many countries on the bench of the International Court of Justice which sits in the Peace Palace at The Hague in Holland. The judges are elected by the General Assembly and the Security Council of the United Nations for nine-year terms, five judges being replaced every three years. In addition to cases which two governments may agree to submit to the Court, the Court, as the principal judicial organ of the United Nations, is authorized to give advisory opinions on the request of the General Assembly, or of one of the Councils, or of other authorized organs or agencies of the UN. The discharge of this advisory function, which is strictly judicial in character, dealing with legal questions, has been an important part of the work of the World Court, both in its earlier form under the League of Nations and now as a part of the United Nations.

Do I see my air force pilot looking over my shoulder and sadly shaking his head? Is he discouraged? I hope not, though I think that by now he will agree with me that there is no quick, short road to the abolition of war. John Bassett Moore used to remind us that with all the perfection of domestic laws and government institutions, civil wars still break out in various countries of the world. How then shall we expect that the still somewhat primitive form of international organization, and the admittedly incomplete acceptance of international law, can prevent international wars?

That some governments have submitted what to them were very large and important territorial claims to adjudication by the World Court is encouraging. That the International Law Commission of the United Nations is making useful progress with the codification and progressive development of international law, is also welcome. Such trends are likely to continue and to multiply; they can also be stimulated and urged on. It is a truism that we must have peaceful alternatives for the settlement of international disputes, even though they are not always utilized. Here is the challenge to the international lawyer, not only today but through almost infinite tomorrows.

_8_ *You in*

LABOR LAW

BY ARTHUR J. GOLDBERG
ASSOCIATE JUSTICE
Supreme Court of the United States

ARTHUR J. GOLDBERG

Born: 1908, Chicago, Illinois

Northwestern University: B.S.L., 1929
    J.D., 1930

Office of Strategic Services: 1942–43
Major, US Army: 1943–44

Admitted to Illinois Bar: 1929
Practice in Chicago:
    Kamfner, Horwitz, Halligan & Daniels: 1929–31
    Pritzker & Pritzker: 1931–33
    Private practice, Arthur J. Goldberg: 1933–45
    Partner, Goldberg & Devoe: 1945–47
    Senior member, Goldberg, Devoe, Shadur & Mikva: 1947–61
Practice in Washington:
    Goldberg, Feller & Bredhoff: 1948–61
Professor of Law, John Marshall Law School: 1945–48
Lecturer, University of Chicago School of Industrial Relations: 1945–48

General counsel, CIO: 1948–55
General counsel, United Steel Workers: 1948–61
Special counsel, AFL-CIO: 1955–61
General counsel, AFL-CIO Industrial-Union Department: 1955–61
Counsel, AFL-CIO Ethical Practices Committee: 1955–61
Secretary of Labor: January, 1961– August, 1962
Nominated Associate Justice of Supreme Court of the United States by
    President Kennedy; August, 1962. Confirmed by the Senate and took
    office: September, 1962

Author: AFL-CIO: *Labor United*
Editor-in-chief: *Illinois Law Review*—1929

BECAUSE I happened to specialize in labor law, I have been asked to write on some of the characteristics of a practice in that field.* Any discussion of labor law, however, must begin with consideration of law in general. And any discussion of law must begin with consideration of education in general.

To be a labor lawyer, one must first be a lawyer. To be a lawyer, one must first be a cultivated man. Mr. Justice Frankfurter has said this well in his introduction to this book and in his earlier words, written in a letter in 1945, which his introduction reproduces.

Perhaps the best illustration of the truth and force of Mr. Justice Frankfurter's observation is the importance, in the practice of law, of an ability to write. A lawyer writes wills and contracts and trust indentures, as you might expect. Beyond that, he writes such things as speeches and magazine articles. Any writing that a client may require, a lawyer may be called upon to produce. Writing in many fields of course requires education in many fields. And whatever the field, writing requires a facility with language. This facility comes most readily from extended and frequent contact with language, contact which, in turn, comes most readily from widespread reading. Quite apart from the intellectual broadening which cultivation offers, and which is an asset not just in a professional career but also in life, generalized edu-

* Note: This chapter was written by Mr. Goldberg while he was Secretary of Labor; before he took his place as an Associate Justice on the Supreme Court.

cation has a very practical purpose for the lawyer: it helps him write.

Law school itself might well be considered part of a generalized education rather than the beginning of a specialty. A good illustration of the utility of a legal education as preparation for a career other than law is the great number of lawyers serving in important nonlegal positions in government. Lawyers have traditionally occupied a prominent place in government at every level. President Kennedy's Administration is no exception. Six Cabinet officers are members of the bar, and only one, the Attorney General, has an office primarily legal in character. There are in addition, some thirty important sub-Cabinet posts held by lawyers, such as the Under Secretary of State, the Under Secretary of the Treasury, the Deputy Secretary of Defense, and the Under Secretary of Agriculture. In the Congress, over sixty Senators and more than two hundred Representatives are lawyers. And, as might be expected, through the broad range of government, there are many, many more lawyers in public service.

These public servants, performing a wide variety of tasks, are daily aided by their legal education. It is true that a number of them may be considered as temporarily in government, likely to return to private life and, perhaps, the practice of law. But many are not; and government service is only illustrative. Many more men trained in the law are pursuing active careers in the various walks of business life. They, too, are aided in their work by having gone to law school.

Because generalized education is the best preparation for the practice of law, and because a legal education is helpful to any career, decision as to which field of law to specialize in should not be made at the time one is first considering the prospect of law school. Indeed, the decision to specialize in any given field perhaps should not be made at any time. All areas of the law hold forth the promise of great interest to anyone who enjoys any area. If one area is to be preferred over another, it can only be after considerable exposure to both. As one gains more and more experience not merely in law school but in the general practice of law, he may develop a bent for one particular field or against one particular field. He may not. But there simply is no way of knowing in advance of the event.

Many young people today enter law school with a defined ambition to specialize in a given area. This ambition may be formed from the best possible motives. Often, it is not. There seems to be a current rage for tax law, which I fear may be based on the idea that this field offers more favorable financial reward than others do. The college student so motivated makes sure he takes accounting courses in undergraduate school and enters law school determined to take as many tax courses as possible. All other courses become burdens that must be borne in order to become a lawyer and enter a tax practice. The difficulty with this type of approach is the obvious one: the student never gives subjects other than tax a chance. He predetermines disinterest in other subjects. This not only detracts from his legal education; it also precludes him from developing an interest in a field to which he may be better suited and, indeed, in which he may well be more interested. It may even keep him from entering a field in which he would make more money, if that is his motivation. Lack of knowledge or interest in other areas, moreover, may prevent him from becoming a good tax lawyer.

Actually, decisions as to which field of law to specialize in are rarely made—the specialization just takes place. I personally had arrived at no firm determination to be a labor lawyer in my law school days or in my early days of practice. Had I resolutely pursued some special field in the early days, it might well not have been labor law. The events which have since taken place prove that such a course would have been a mistake. I would think the same is true of many if not most lawyers. Specialization in a given field somehow comes about; conscious decision to specialize holds forth a great threat of error.

Specifically in labor law, the practice today is so varied that any specialization in law school might well penalize one's later career. The labor lawyer runs the gamut of subjects studied in law school and encountered in any field of practice. Trust law, contracts, tax law, real and personal property, criminal law, administrative law, trial and appellate practice—these are merely illustrative of the many and different fields the practice of labor law entails.

The kinds of labor lawyers are as varied as the areas their practice embraces. Labor lawyers represent unions, employers and the government. Labor lawyers act as arbitrators and mediators in labor disputes. And, of course, labor lawyers like any lawyers serve as professors. All of these labor lawyers in all of these roles perform important functions.

Each of the roles demands certain qualities—qualities which are also demanded of all lawyers, but which are of particular importance in the emotionally charged and volatile field of labor law.

The first of these qualities is independence, a quality particularly necessary in the practitioner. It is in the ancient and best tradition of the law that the lawyer have an independence of his client. This independence lies at the core of the lawyer's obligation to the cause of social justice; it furnishes the basis of the lawyer's capacity to serve society at the same time that he serves his client.

In its clearest context, this independence moves the lawyer to urge that a course of action dictated by the client's narrow self-interest not be followed, or that a different course more consonant with the public interest be adopted. A sense of public conscience is demanded of the lawyer when his advice about proposed action is sought. Independence serves to bolster that conscience and promote its assertion in the formulation of proposed courses of conduct.

But action may be taken despite the contrary urgings of a lawyer or without prior solicitation of his advice. The lawyer may be presented with an accomplished fact and asked to defend the person who caused its happening. The quality of independence —allowing the lawyer to stand apart from his client—then requires that the lawyer represent a client with whom, or with whose cause, he may not wish to be identified. Personal disagreement with the cause, or adverse public opinion, does not excuse the lawyer from society's demand that a man be given legal representation. The Right Honorable Sir Hartley Shawcross, speaking

in 1953 as Chairman of the General Council of the Bar, summed
it up thus:

I have recently heard it said that certain members of the Bar in one
of Her Majesty's Colonies refused to accept a brief to defend an Afri-
can, accused of offences of a quasi-political nature against public
order. The suggestion is that those barristers made excuses and declined to act, their true reason being that they thought that their popularity or reputation might be detrimentally affected by appearing for
the defence in such a case. For the prosecution they might appear,
but not for the defence.

If this report were true it would disclose a wholly deplorable de-
parture from the great traditions of our law and one which, if sub-
stantiated, both the Attorney-General and the Bar Council, would
have to deal with in the severest possible way.

Among laymen on both sides of politics there are some foolish and
shortsighted enough to think that a barrister may and should pick and
choose the cases in which he is prepared to appear.

It would be well if those people remembered how the present rule
—that a barrister must accept a brief on behalf of any client who
wishes to retain him to appear before any court in which he holds
himself out to practise—was finally established. It arose in 1792 over
the prosecution of Tom Paine for publishing the second part of his
Rights of Man. The great advocate, Erskine, who accepted the retainer to defend Paine, and was deprived of his Office as Attorney-
General to the Prince of Wales for doing so, said—and said truly—in a
famous speech; 'From the moment that any advocate can be permitted to say that he will or will not stand between the Crown and
the subject arraigned in the Court where he daily sits to practise,
from that moment the liberties of England are at an end.' "

These important words, uttered in Great Britain about criminal
law, are of course as meaningful in the United States in the context of labor law.

Corollary to independence is objectivity. The labor lawyer
must remove himself from the interested vantage point of his
client and view the issues in a dispassionate light.

Dispassion must also characterize the lawyer's arguments—
oral and written—in favor of his client's cause. Representation

must, of course, be advocacy. And advocacy must be vigorous. But vigor is distinct from passion. The lawyer's involvement in the client's cause is representational, not personal. Passion blinds judgment. A lawyer—an advocate—must not be a zealot.

With dispassion comes professional courtesy to one's colleagues at the bar and to those with whom one deals. Courtesy and a scrupulous regard for ethics not only are the measure of a professional man—or, indeed, a civilized man—they are also indispensable to a successful practice. For labor law involves continuing relationships with the same people, and these people, like all people, do not appreciate discourtesy or shady ethics.

The fact that labor law does involve continuing relationships with people is one of its strong points. For my part, a practice that was confined to the library would not be enjoyable. Nor would I be content in a passive practice in which one spent his days thinking but not acting. Research and reflection are crucial components of any law practice. Research and reflection are crucial to the personal intellectual need that every lawyer feels. But in my view they cannot alone do the job. Personal contact and action are essential.

Labor law furnishes abundant opportunity for personal contact and action. An obvious illustration is negotiation over a collective bargaining agreement.

Collective bargaining is mistakenly considered by many as involving an unthinking rigidity on both sides of the bargaining table. This erroneous impression is well brought out in a story that is supposed to describe the beginning of a typical collective bargaining session. Management opens the session by greeting the labor representatives and stating, "We don't know what you want this year, but whatever it is the answer is 'no.'" Labor allegedly then returns the greeting and adds, "We don't know what we want this year either, but whatever it is we won't take 'no' for an answer."

Let me assure you that collective bargaining does not proceed on any such basis. To be sure, each side has its own interests, which it values very highly. Each side has its own goals, which it wants very much to achieve. But each side well knows in advance that the bargaining will result in a compromise, that there will be a give and take, and that neither side will achieve the precise position it urges.

And this is what collective bargaining should be. Quite apart from the fact that compromise is the keystone of negotiation, neither side is alone able to determine what is best for the interests of both. Compromise serves not only to accommodate the demands of both sides, but also to produce a workable solution that otherwise might never have been considered.

In practice, compromise seems to be more available at late hours. As negotiations draw closer and closer to the deadline for agreement without strike, the sessions last longer and longer into the night. Whether for good reason or bad, each side seems to feel that the other will become more reasonable as the hour grows later. You might say that each side attempts physically to wear the other down. I doubt that this is actually so, but it is true that most agreements in collective bargaining situations are reached in the wee hours.

This phenomenon makes collective bargaining the more enjoyable. Of course there are frustrations. And fatigue. But a session that lasts from morning to night provides a tremendous amount of excitement. There is also the additional challenge of remaining attentive for extended periods, of assuring yourself that the other side is in fact bargaining and not just trying to wear you down. The requirement of constant alertness has its physical cost, but this is give-and-take lawyering at its finest.

The pressure of hard bargaining over many hours has some interesting by-products. I remember one negotiation when both sides had agreed that there should be absolutely no "leaks" to the press during the progress of the bargaining. One day after we had negotiated for some time, I realized that there were two men sitting at the bargaining table whom I had not seen before. Assuming that they were new members of the management team, I asked the management representative, who had been present throughout the proceedings, to introduce me to his colleagues.

Both of us were taken aback when he replied that he had assumed they were with me. It turned out, of course, that they were both reporters.

The amount of time consumed in extended negotiations explains another most enjoyable perquisite of the practice of labor law—the development of close personal associations with interesting people. Collective bargaining sessions, involving as constant and lengthy interactions between people as they do, are ordinarily conducted on a first-name basis. Despite the old saw about familiarity breeding contempt, the resulting relationships often become quite close. This is true regardless of the side of the bargaining table on which any given person may be sitting. Friendships develop between representatives of both sides. I have made many lasting friendships with management representatives whom I met in negotiations, and these developing friendships are good not only for the people involved but also for collective bargaining as an institution. With friendship comes respect and understanding. And respect and understanding are at the forefront of the attitudes that promote fruitful bargaining.

The greatest pleasure in the practice of labor law lies in the sense of satisfaction that comes from serving the cause of social justice—the abiding justification for the existence and efforts of all lawyers.

Through his work on a host of matters, the lawyer plays a role in the development of the law that governs society. The labor lawyer has, in addition, the opportunity to participate in the fashioning of private systems of law—systems that, for a branch of society, involve a genuine body of governing law.

This opportunity for service and satisfaction is well shown in the process that brought about the merger of the American Federation of Labor and the Congress of Industrial Organizations.

The split of these two vast federations of international unions was caused in large part by a difference of philosophy on the proper organization of labor unions. The AFL believed in organization along trade or craft lines—plumbers, carpenters, and the like. The CIO, in contrast, considered that unions should be organized on an industrial basis—automobile workers, steel workers, and so on. There were other differences between the AFL and the CIO, of course, but the major problems in the final analysis derived from these contrary views on the fundamental question of organization.

The achievement of unity—the merger of the two into the AFL-CIO—involved the creation of a new system of private law. It is not possible for me to tell the whole story within the confines of this chapter. For those of you who are interested in a more complete history, I have written a book on the subject, *AFL-CIO: Labor United.* I would like, however, to go into a few of the high lights of the process so that you may appreciate what I mean by a system of private law.

The process of merger began with an effort to solve the problems that had occurred when unions in one federation tried to acquire as members workers who already were members of unions in the other. The solution accomplished was the voluntary agreement of unions in both federations that they would not engage in this practice against each other. This agreement became known, understandably, as the "no-raiding agreement."

The next step was negotiation of the merger agreement. As might be expected, the number of questions, and differences of opinion, that had to be resolved in order to arrive at an agreement for merger was anything but small. Nor were these questions and differences insignificant on the merits. Yet, somehow, after a day's discussion, the subcommittee representatives of the AFL and the CIO were ready to instruct their respective general counsel to prepare a draft. J. Albert Woll for the AFL and I for the CIO developed a draft, and the next day it was adopted by the full committee on unity. The executive bodies of the two federations subsequently ratified the agreement, and the way was cleared for the drafting of a constitution.

The constitution of the AFL-CIO contains a statement of twelve objectives and principles. These objectives and principles express a philosophy which emphasizes the labor movement as traditionally American and instinctively democratic in character.

The first objective is the most fundamental of union programs and aims, "to aid workers in securing improved wages, hours, and working conditions with due regard for the autonomy, integrity, and jurisdiction of affiliated unions." All democratic unions share these goals today; they shall remain the foundation of the labor movement of the future.

The second objective calls for helping the unorganized worker to improve his situation by making effective unionism available to him; for encouraging stronger unions to help weaker ones; for guaranteeing the craft union and the industrial union—the two traditional forms of American labor organization—equal status in the new federation. This objective reflects the fundamental belief of the labor movement in worker-to-worker mutual aid.

Third, the constitution provides for the creation of new unions and organizing committees.

Fourth is the objective to "encourage all workers without regard to race, creed, color, national origin, or ancestry to share equally in the full benefits of union organization."

The fifth objective—giving content to the preamble's pledge to serve the entire community—calls for efforts to secure legislation not only to promote principles of free collective bargaining but also to protect "the rights of workers, farmers, and consumers, and the security and welfare of all the people."

The sixth objective is similar: to protect and strengthen American democracy, the people's rights and liberties, and our heritage of freedom.

Seventh is co-operation with other free and democratic trade unions to promote world peace and freedom.

Eighth is the objective to eliminate raiding between unions of the AFL-CIO and to encourage the elimination of disputes about jurisdiction.

Ninth is to encourage use of the union lable, and to promote the labor press and other means of advancing the education of the labor movement.

Tenth, to adopt stern and effective measures to protect the labor movement from communism and corruption. Both the AFL and the CIO had at various times faced some problem of infiltration into a minority of their affiliated unions by Communists and by racketeers. While both federations suffered both problems, the AFL was the principal victim of racketeer infiltration and the CIO the principal victim of Communist infiltration—perhaps by reason of the basic Communist dependence on industrial workers for support of its revolutionary goal. In any event, the solutions to these undesired and undesirable infiltrations—ultimately involving the expulsion of some unions—were effected with scrupulous regard for due process. Care was taken to insure that any action was based on fact, not suspicion, and that the positions and arguments on all sides were heard and understood. This experience of the AFL and the CIO separately underlies this objective of the merged organization.

The eleventh objective is to safeguard "the democratic character of the labor movement" and the autonomy of its unions.

Twelfth and finally is an objective on political action and civic responsibility: "While preserving the independence of the labor movement from political control, to encourage workers to register and vote, to exercise their full rights and responsibilities of citizenship, and to perform their rightful part in the political life of the local, state, and national communities."

These objectives and principles constitute a comprehensive charter for the American labor movement. They provide the outlines of a legal system for that movement. They furnish the foundation of a system of private law.

Further developing this system of private law, the merged AFL-CIO adopted ethical practices codes, which define the rights of a union member and his union. Six rights are involved: first, the right to a democratic union; second, the right to due process of law in union disciplinary proceedings; third, the right to a clean, honest union; fourth, the right to an effective union; fifth, the right to a union free from discrimination because of race, creed or color; sixth, the right to a responsible union—responsible not only to its members, and to its employers, but to the community and the nation as a whole.

The principles and objectives of the AFL-CIO constitution and the ethical practices codes together comprise a considerable body of law. My colleagues and I had great satisfaction in being the legal architects of these policies. Other labor lawyers have enjoyed the satisfaction of participating in the development of the recently established procedure for resolving internal disputes.

I do not mean to exaggerate, or to understate, the role or importance of lawyers in this process. Obviously, the principals had to be willing to agree. Yet the important and satisfying task of giving inspiration and vitality to that agreement remained—and remains—for the lawyers.

Similar opportunity for service can be found in the joint efforts of labor and management.

The paramount illustration lies in the pension and insurance agreements collectively bargained by labor and management. Working together over the bargaining table, labor and management have in many industries developed pension plans and insurance arrangements which provide workers with the opportunity for a decent life upon retirement and protection against the risks of life and death. Collective bargaining to these ends has served not merely to accommodate the private interests of labor and management; it also provides for persons too old or too infirm to work without causing them a loss of dignity, or creating an economic burden on society by making them dependent on the community for support and survival.

Let me give you another illustration. In the automobile, steel, and other industries, labor and management jointly developed, through collective bargaining, comparable programs known as Supplemental Unemployment Benefit plans (SUB). These plans call for employer contributions to funds which are used to pay benefits supplementing unemployment compensation. That is, through the operation of these plans, workers who become unemployed receive weekly amounts in addition to those made available under the unemployment laws.

In these days of high unemployment, workers find themselves jobless entirely apart from their own desires or their own doing. They are the victims of economic conditions beyond their power to control.

When the demand for a given product, say steel, diminishes, the demand for workers to make that product also dwindles. Persons who have devoted a substantial portion of their lives to working in steel mills suddenly find themselves without work. Skills which these people have developed throughout their working careers suddenly are no longer needed by the industry in which they were learned. These skills, moreover, may not be readily adaptable to other industries. No matter how desperately the people seek new employment, no jobs may be available. Despite their efforts, these people remain jobless. They have become statistics in a labor market in which there are no buyers.

These workers without work find themselves on the list of the unemployed, making weekly trips to the local unemployment office to collect unemployment benefits that on the national average in 1962 totaled less than $35.00. To the worker with a family, $35.00 is a weekly sum that hardly rises to a subsistence level. Yet try as he will, the worker may be completely unable to find any means of increasing that amount. He is caught up by the economic conditions that surround him.

SUB then takes over. It furnishes the unemployed worker with a supplementary benefit, increasing his weekly income. In a real sense, SUB puts food into the mouths of the unemployed worker's family.

SUB does more than that. The dollars SUB provides are quickly spent. They travel from hand to hand in payment for goods and services that are necessary to everyday living. Because these dollars are of such high velocity, they go beyond the function of helping the unemployed worker and his family to that of providing stimulation for the economy. SUB itself, of course, cannot bring about an economic recovery. But the dollars it provides do constitute a force in the upturn of business conditions, and it does thereby help not only to provide for the worker and his family during a period of unemployment but also to create a promise—held forth by a business upswing—of ending that unemployment.

Here, then, is an area of great service and great professional satisfaction for the labor lawyer. From his efforts in negotiating SUB plans, the lawyer is rewarded with the knowledge that he has served to help people in need. He is rewarded to know that unemployed workers and their families will be cared for, that business activity will in some degree be stimulated, and that the period of unemployment will be to that degree reduced. Comporting with the private interests of both labor and management, SUB thus serves the public interest in full measure.

Lawyers on both sides can experience a sense of purpose in the practice of labor law. This sense of purpose finds expression in the lawyers' efforts to help bring justice into the labor-management relationship. The labor lawyer should always strive to promote true understanding and harmony in this relationship.

Labor law, like any field of the law, is a developing institution. Justice is blind to prejudices and personalities, but not to social and economic developments. As institutions of society and government evolve, the law grows with them. Lawyers must have the foresight and flexibility that is inherent in the law they practice. They are not merely technicians who perform services for a client. They are officers of the court and servants of social justice. They are the sculptors of the law that governs and protects the society in which they live.

The time has long passed when the parties to collective bargaining sent the lawyers out of the room so that a settlement could be achieved. Today, the lawyers are invited into the room to consummate the settlement. Labor lawyers must well discharge this responsibility.

_9_ *You as a*

DISTRICT ATTORNEY

BY EDWARD S. SILVER

DISTRICT ATTORNEY

Kings County, New York

EDWARD S. SILVER

Born: 1898, New York, New York

Erasmus Hall High School: Brooklyn
The City College of New York: B.S.S., 1920
Harvard Law School: LL.B., 1924

U. S. Navy, Apprentice Seaman: 1918

Admitted New York Bar: 1925
Assistant United States Attorney: 1925–29
    Chief of Bureau of Indictments: 1927–29
Special Assistant U. S. Attorney: 1929–31
Commissioner, Alien Enemy Hearing Board
    Eastern District of New York: 1942–45
Chief Assistant District Attorney, Kings County, Brooklyn: 1946–53
District Attorney, Kings County: 1954–57
    Re-elected: 1957–1961
    Re-elected: 1961–

President: New York State District Attorneys Association: 1957
    National District Attorneys Association: 1959–60
    Civic Center Clinic (for psychiatric treatment of offenders): 1955–
    Brooklyn Council, American Jewish Congress: 1942–44
    National Council of Young Israel: 1928–29; 1944–48

Chairman: Committee on Prosecution Problems American Bar Association:
    1960–
    Committee on Penal Law and Criminal Procedure, New York State Bar
        Association: 1954
    Technical Advisory Committee Detached Workers Project (Juvenile
        Delinquency): 1950–

Member-at-large: National Council Boy Scouts of America: 1951
Honorary Member, Detective Endowment Association, Police Department,
    New York, New York
Public Service Award, Police Reserve Association, City of New York: 1957
Award of Merit, New York State District Attorneys' Association: 1958
Furtherance of Justice Award, National District Attorneys' Association:
    1962

WHAT IS a district attorney and what does he do? How does a lawyer become a district attorney? Why should a young man, interested in law and a career in the law, think about being a district attorney?

These questions, and others, will be answered as we go along in this chapter; but before any decisions about being a district attorney can be made, there are others that must be made. First, a person must decide that he wants to be a lawyer, because, of course, he must be a lawyer before he can be a district attorney. Such a basic decision as this one concerning the law, which may determine a person's whole career, sometimes is made early. The shaping and directing of one's life, influenced at times by happenings that may seem almost incidental, can occur when one is still a young man. For that reason, I would like to begin this chapter with something of my own early life. I shall ask you to understand that I am writing this, personal as it is, with only one idea—that my experiences, which are not unlike the experiences of so many other men, may be of some value to those young men of today who are now in their time of wondering and deciding.

In June, 1916, I graduated from Erasmus Hall High School in Brooklyn. That summer I worked in Coney Island selling popcorn. My employer was a man named Potter and we boys started at 11 A.M. and worked until midnight, except on weekends when we worked until one or two o'clock in the morning. We held rolls of popcorn in our outstretched hands and shouted, "Five a roll—five a roll—six for a quarter—Potter's popcorn—best on the Island

—get 'em fresh." Potter sat nearby on a shoeshine chair and now and then he would call out, "Come on, boys. Let's hear it." We did all right, so long as we kept hollering. Old man Potter did all right, too, for people said that he was very rich.

One thing about the job was that every morning when I got up, I had no voice. One morning a letter came telling me that the University of the State of New York—the State Education Department—had awarded me a scholarship, provided I attended a college in New York State. I was doing my best to tell my mother, but I just stood there shaking the letter, for I had no voice.

"All right," she said. "I'll give you a glass of warm milk." That was the daily procedure: a swallow, a few grunts, a swallow, a few grunts, and gradually my voice came back, a bit hoarse at first, but building up until I was ready for another day's work with Potter.

When I told my mother about the letter, she said in her matter-of-fact way, speaking, as she usually did to me, in Yiddish. "That settles it. We didn't know whether you could go to college, but now we'll have to work it out." That was the way she always made decisions for the family, calmly and positively.

Each summer during my high school days I worked at some job at the Bush Terminal, a long line of industrial buildings that are still on the Brooklyn water front. It was not hard to get a job there if you knew how. You put on a pair of long pants, went in and said you wanted to go to work. Somebody always asked, "What class were you in when you quit grammar school?" You answered, "Six A." If you said you had gone higher, they did not want you—they thought you might be too intellectual and wouldn't do hard or dirty work. During my school summers I worked as a sweeper, an oiler, a truck loader. I worked in a knitting mill and was sort of all-around boy in a match factory.

I could tell a lot about those jobs, but I'll just tell about the Sirio Match Company. My main job was to remove the book matches as they came from the machines, then take them to the tables where the girls packed them into boxes. The boss of the plant was an Italian engineer, Mr. Caesar, who had invented the machine. A large roll of paper was fed into one end, passed through a series of clever gadgets, and the book matches dropped out at the other end. To get advertising on the paper, it had to be sent out to a printer.

Mr. Caesar had me doing other jobs than removing book matches and one was to tidy up his office every day, which involved cleaning out his spittoon. I was at this one morning when a man was trying to sell Mr. Caesar a printing press so that he could print the advertising himself. Mr. Caesar finally admitted that it would save him money. "But," he said, "if I used it, I'd have to deal with the printers' union, and I want no part of unions." Pointing at me, he added, "See that boy, that's what I want— dummies."

In the fall of 1916, I matriculated at The City College of New York and started out for a B.A., but I did not have the language requirements and I switched to a Bachelor of Science in Social Science.

The scholarship I had received from the State Education Department helped, but it could not fully meet my needs, and I got a job as a shipping clerk for a firm that manufactured ladies' dresses. I did my work at the college in the morning and got to the plant at two o'clock. CCNY is at 137 Street and my job was at 33 Street and Seventh Avenue, so I had to hustle. I worked there until eight o'clock, went home to Brooklyn, did my studying, and it was midnight when I got to bed. Next morning I rode the subway for an hour and a half to meet my nine o'clock class. It sounds pretty rough, and it was, but a lot of boys at the college had tougher schedules than I had.

In those days the soft-goods industry was almost all in the hands of Jews. The firm I worked for was Freidman Bros. & O'Brien, and whenever I mentioned the firm, the name brought a grin. One day, years later, after I had become an Assistant U. S. Attorney and was picking a jury, the judge asked if any of the jury knew counsel or the Assistant Attorney. A man I did not recognize arose and said that he knew Mr. Silver. "He used to work for me as a shipping clerk." That was Mr. O'Brien. After some questions, he remained on the jury.

My first contact with the law was in the summer of 1918. With

World War I under way, there was a shortage of farm help, and it was announced that any student who volunteered to work on a farm would receive a passing grade in the subjects he was taking. I was taking Physics IV and some heavy courses in Math, so I decided I would volunteer for farm work.

With three classmates and two Japanese visiting students, I went to work on a tobacco plantation in Tariffville, Connecticut. In describing our employer, Mr. M., the other workers told us: "He's a good man—better dead." But it was stay and work for him or go back to Physics IV and Math, so I stayed. We set out plants, and worked rain or shine.

One afternoon, after we had worked in a downpour, a cool wind came up and I was asked by the other boys to go to the tobacco-drying shed, where we lived, for some sweaters and jackets. Mr. M. spotted me and asked why I was away from work. I told him. "You and your friends are through. Tell them to get packed and get out. When picking time comes, and the leaves are sopping wet, you'll quit on me just when I need you. You city bums are no good for me." He went to where the other boys were and he fired the lot of us. "I'll pay you what I owe you. Now get packed and get out."

We went back to the shed and asked if we could stay the night. "Get out," Mr. M. said. We told him we weren't going until the rain stopped.

Half an hour later, the sheriff and two deputies arrived. They were armed with shotguns because Mr. M. had told them we had threatened to kill him. We were arrested, except the Japanese, and taken a mile away to await the Justice of the Peace, who was a barber in an adjoining town. I asked the sheriff if I could get a lawyer and he pointed at the telephone. I called several lawyers in Hartford, but none of them was interested in us. Each of them gave the same advice: "You'll probably be fined anyhow, so you had better plead guilty. It will be easier that way." Not one of them seemed concerned in the slightest about whether or not we were actually guilty or innocent.

When the Justice of the Peace arrived, we were charged with trespass and assault. Mr. M. told his story, including his statement that we had threatened to kill him. We told our story, interrupted constantly by Mr. M.: "Watch those New York bandits. They're lying. They ought to go to jail."

The Justice of the Peace knew Mr. M. and was as fair to us as he dared to be, acquitting us of assault but finding us guilty of trespass. The fines and costs came to $36.04—$9.01 apiece—or three days in jail. We said we would go to jail, but the Justice of the Peace explained that transportation costs to jail would be $25, so we paid the fine. That same day, after we had walked several miles, another farmer hired us and I worked long enough to get credit for my courses at college.

I believe that this incident with Mr. M., and the injustice of it, greatly influenced me in my decision to study law. I had no idea what I wanted in law, or in justice, but I wanted something and that feeling stayed with me. When I went back to college that fall, I kept thinking about the law.

It is that way sometimes with a young fellow—something happens and he gets an idea. It may be hazy at first, but it stays with him. Maybe it is something that he has never thought of before, nor anything his father has done or anybody in his family. My father was a tailor, and a good one; but, so far as I know, nobody in my family had ever been a lawyer. However, what happened in Tariffville—the Justice of the Peace, the lawyers in Hartford, the whole curious process of the law that day—set me to thinking. Usually the big decisions don't come all at once—they grow, and I am reasonably sure that what happened in Tariffville started me toward the law.

In July of 1918 I joined the Navy and for four months was attached to the USS *Granite State*—moored with heavy chains at 72 Street and the Hudson River. We wore our sock caps at salty angles, but we couldn't help feeling that a sailor ought to be at sea. The war ended November 11, and the next day we were mustered out—rank, Apprentice Seamen.

By the time I graduated from CCNY in February, 1920, I was firm about being a lawyer. Also, somewhere along the way, I had determined to go to Harvard Law School. I did not have the money—tuition in 1920 was $200 a year, and I would need $700 more; $900 for the year. The only way I could get it was to earn it. I knew that I would have to miss one year to earn enough, and this meant that I would work from February, 1920, until September, 1921.

Besides saving $900, I felt that I should pay my way at home. Then, too, as an orthodox observant Jew, I had to find a job where there would be no work on the Sabbath. The job I finally found was as traffic manager in a concern that imported wood pulp from abroad and from Canada. I knew nothing about railroad rates or routing freight cars, but the head bookkeeper was a friendly man and he helped me.

I had hardly started to work when I was told to divert a car of pulp coming from Canada to a destination other than the one on the bill of lading. Somebody just dropped a bill of lading on my desk and told me to take care of it. A freight car out there somewhere was traveling fast to one point, and I had to stop it and send it to another. I had no idea what to do, so I telephoned the railroad people and asked them. It turned out to be simple. I gave them information about the car, its place and time of starting, its route and new destination, and they took care of the rest of it.

My dad had taught me about this. A man has a place to go, but doesn't know how to get there. He has a task to do and doesn't know how to do it. Why should he wander around from one wrong place to another? Why should he fret and fume about a strange task? Ask! There is nothing wrong in not knowing.

In my job I soon learned that one does not necessarily accept the exact way that things have always been done—there may be a better way. Our system of records was out of date and wasteful of time, so I figured out a card index that showed what pulp had been bought, what had been sold, and what we had on hand. It was an obvious thing to do, but nobody else had done it, and so I ruled a number of cards and charts, wrote an accompanying explanation, and took everything to the manager of the company.

I was startled by my reception. He told me that he had not been waiting for me to come along and tell him how to run the company; he had been doing all right before I showed up, and for me just to stick to my job. I couldn't figure out why he was acting that way, and I went to my friend the bookkeeper. He told me that I would meet a man, now and then, like the manager who was jealous and did not want any change because it might threaten his job. He said that sometime later, when he saw the boss privately, he would talk with him about my plan for the records.

Not long afterward, the owner of the company, who had not spoken a word to me in the months I had been there, asked me how much it would cost to have the forms printed. It did not cost much, and so the system I had suggested was started. I thought it sort of strange that the boss never gave me a word of praise or encouragement for the idea.

The truth is that I was finding out something about the world outside of college, and about the kind of men you meet. I was finding out, too, about a passing mark when you are out working on a job. In high school or college, 60 per cent or 70 per cent can pass you and 90 per cent gets you an A. But you learn pretty soon, when you are out working, that there are no A's and B's and C's. There is just one mark—100 per cent! The whole thing, whatever it is, has got to be right, or you flunk. I kept finding this out, sometimes in little ways, sometimes in ways more important, and then one day I had it impressed on me even more strongly.

Mr. G., the owner, sent word for me to give him the amount of a particular kind of pulp on hand. I figured it out and sent it to him, along with the card on which the figures were based. But I made an error in adding one of the columns. Then came the only time that Mr. G. ever spoke to me during the year and a half I worked for him, except when he had asked me how much the forms would cost. He came to my desk, tossed the card on it, and said, as he walked away, "Where did you learn to add, in college?" I had done everything right except one little thing, but 90 per cent was a flunking mark.

I never imagined that my job at the wood pulp company would help me at law school, but it did. A freight car sometimes can get misdirected and lost, and occasionally I had to go to the Weehawken freight yards in New Jersey and look for a car that was missing. The yards stretched over many acres and while I tramped them, I had a chance to talk to the railroad men and learn some of the practical problems of railroading. When time came for me to take the Interstate Commerce Course at Harvard, I took it under Professor Felix Frankfurter, and I became the practical railroad man of the class. I didn't really know so much about railroading, but Professor Frankfurther thought I did, and I liked that.

At the end of my work with the pulp company I was making $40 a week, and had saved about $900. I had paid my way at home and had guarded every penny. Throughout that year and a half of work, I had budgeted myself and my budget called for 35¢ a week for entertainment. If I spent 45¢ any week, then next week's entertainment allowance was 25¢. But I was going to the Harvard Law School, and all the work and the saving were easy.

One of my classmates at City College had entered Harvard in the fall of 1920, and, when he came home on vacation, he terrified me. He told me that one-third of the class flunked out at the end of the first year, that everybody studied ten or twelves hours a day, that there was one examination at the end of the year and the professors made it as tough as possible. He had me really worried because I didn't consider it an honor to be flunked out, even from Harvard; but I had intended to go there and I wasn't backing down. It turned out that a part of what my friend had said was true, but a part was just the tradition of second-year men worrying first-year men.

I got to Cambridge a few days before school started and found a room on a street a few minutes' walk from Langdell Hall. I guess it was a good thing that I went to Cambridge scared, and started out scared, because I set a schedule of study that I followed for three years.

Five days a week, we had classes two hours a day. Besides these classes, I spent two hours each morning in the library; then I had lunch for an hour, a walk and some talk with friends. I was back in the library at two o'clock and remained there until five. To the gym for calisthenics or a game of squash; then dinner and a walk to my room for mail or a package. Each evening back to the library at seven o'clock and I stayed there until ten when it closed.

On Saturdays I quit at five o'clock, and did little or no work on Sundays, except perhaps to read a few cases for Monday's classes. This was my regular schedule and it took something really unusual to break it. In fact, I am pretty sure that I did not break it more than three or four times during the three years I was at Harvard.

They were the most wonderful years of my life. The books and study were fine, but the men under whom I worked would have inspired anybody—Pound, Williston, Beale, Frankfurter, Chaffee, Joe Warren, Ed Warren, Scott, Sayre, Wambaugh. They were a part of the world I wanted, the world of the law, and their learning and their teaching would send us students hurrying back to the library to start studying again, wondering if we could ever learn as much as they knew.

After my first year at Harvard, when I went back to Brooklyn, in June of 1922, I had just about $5 left. That summer and the next I worked as a waiter in the Catskills, and I was graduated from the Law School in 1924, in debt for borrowed money, $640. In the second and third year, my marks had been good enough for a faculty scholarship, which had helped considerably.

During my last year at Law School, I had the privilege of doing some legal research because of the friendship and assistance of Professor Frankfurter.

One job I did was for Senator Beveridge of Indiana who had written to Professor Frankfurter for a student to do research on what he called ridiculous and onerous statutes that had been passed by various states. He wanted to show that some of these statutes made no sense, and we came up with some good examples. One statute regulated the size of bed sheets in a hotel. Another regulated the grading of apples—the grade was decided by the size of the blemish on the apple. When Senator Beveridge asked me for a bill for my work, I told Professor Frankfurter that I had not expected to be paid. He said, "Getting paid for his work is very important for any lawyer. Send the Senator a bill for $50." I did and soon received a check.

One day, in my second summer as a waiter in the Catskills, I was sweeping the floor, and there, in the doorway, stood a young lady wearing a gray tweed suit, and in her hand dangled a leghorn straw sailor hat from which hung a black velvet ribbon. I sort of caught my breath and looked at her a second time. I had seen that young lady before. But then she had been only a child of twelve, playing with a group of children of whom my younger brother was one. This was no child! This was a beautiful young lady and I hurried to the proprietor and told him that a girl I knew had come in. Would he please put her on the other side of the dining room from where I served? Once before I had gotten into difficulty with a girl I knew and served, and from whom I would not accept a gratuity. I did not want the same trouble again.

He did what I asked and I did not wait on her up there in the Catskills—but it is a pleasure to tell you that I have been happily waiting on her ever since, because she became my wife.

I called on Regina's father, Gedaliah Bublick, editor of the *Jewish Daily News,* during the Christmas vacation of 1923. The Bublicks lived not far from our neighborhood and he asked questions until he learned that the Silvers were not rich people; but they were God-fearing, decent people, and were liked by their neighbors. That was enough for him.

I had been graduated from Harvard in June and was to be married in November; but before I could practice law, or get a job in a law firm, or make an advance of any kind in the law, I had to pass the bar examination. And the examination was set for July! There was only one hope: to take a cram course in New York Practice taught by Harold Medina, who was a practicing lawyer at the time and a wonderful teacher. Later, of course, he became the famous Judge Medina of the 2nd Circuit Federal Court.

I took the examination, and, a short time later, while riding on the subway, I had a terrible experience. I was going for an interview about a job with a law firm, and, suddenly, as I read the New York *Times,* I saw the list of those who had passed the bar exams. Nervously, I turned to the "S's." My name was not there! I was stunned. My heart sank. What could I say? What could I do? I was to be married in four months and I could not get the job I was going for at that moment, or any other job. I kept looking at the list, as if in a trance, and then, not among the "S's," and completely out of place, I saw my name: SILVER, ED-WARD S.

By then, and in truth, I could not believe my eyes. I felt that I was only seeing things. I quietly folded the paper and held it still for a few minutes. Then I opened it and looked again. It was still there—SILVER, EDWARD S. But not among the "S's." My heartbreak turned to elation. I wanted to shout, to dance—and to tell some-body. Of course the person I wanted to tell was Regina and as soon as the train stopped I got out and called her. She was glad to hear it, but it was no surprise—she had expected it all along!

Those few minutes on the subway were a frightening experi-ence for a young man, and, to this day, I do not know how my name got misplaced—though, of course, as soon as I saw it, I didn't care where it was.

I got the job I was going for, with Hays, Hershfield & Wolf, and I spent most of my time in research, though I had the opportu-nity, now and then, to prepare cases for trial. Occasionally, too, I went into court when some of the great lawyers were in action. I would sit there and listen to them, and watch them, and wonder if I could ever do it.

There was a little problem about my getting the job with this firm because I was a Sabbath observer and there was hesitancy about hiring me. But, as the partners discussed the problem, someone spoke of Daniel P. Hays, who had been the senior member of the firm for many years, and who had passed away not long before I applied for the job. Mr. Hays, though a member of the Reform Group of Judaism, had never come to the office on the Sabbath, and someone said it would be an affront to his memory if I were rejected because I followed the same practice. I did not know about this at the time, but later, when I found out that I had a spiritual tie with Mr. Daniel P. Hays, I was proud of it and thankful to him.

Until now, in this chapter, I have been writing about one young man who wanted to be a lawyer. I have told my story slowly, with personal details, because I believed it might be useful to at least some of the thousands of young men who today have the same longings and difficulties that I had. They, too, want to be lawyers, and sometimes the wanting is so strong that it almost hurts, but they do not have the money to go on with their desires and ambitions. Nor do they have any "influence"—and some of them imagine that they need influence, that a young man, on his own, cannot make it. Let me tell that young man: this is just not the truth. He *can* make it!

I doubt if many of you are in a tougher spot than I was, and that is why I have told about my young manhood—not bragging, I hope, or saying, "Look at me," only trying to pass on some facts and encouragement to any young man, whoever he may be or wherever he may be in this country, who wonders about himself and doubts his chance to study law and become a lawyer.

Let me tell him again that he can do it, and, what is more, I can tell him his chances precisely. His becoming a lawyer *depends exactly on how much he wants to become a lawyer.* A lawyer grows from the desire of a man, and develops out of the determination of a man, and without these there is no lawyer.

I am the District Attorney of Kings County, the official name of an area probably better known to you as Brooklyn.

And what is a district attorney? What does he do? What part does he play in the fight against crime?

He has a number of names, varying in states and counties: District Attorney, State's Attorney, Commonwealth's Attorney, County Solicitor, Prosecuting Attorney, Circuit Attorney. But whatever his name, he is the public prosecutor.

The popular belief about the district attorney is a misconception created by novelists and spectacular television shows, leading one to believe that his chief desire is to get convictions. In reality, his desire and his purpose is to see that justice is done and that no innocent man is mistreated.

I have had the honor of being President of the National District Attorneys' Association. I have been President of the New York State District Attorneys' Association. I have worked with prosecutors in my own state and elsewhere, and, with possibly a few very rare exceptions, these men are more concerned with justice than with building any record of convictions.

About a year ago a young man was arrested in our county on a murder and robbery charge based on his own confession. The defendant's lawyer came to me and said, "Mr. Silver, my client has confessed to killing this elderly woman and robbing her. The confession was voluntary, but my client had been reading magazines and paperbacks, and he was scared and believed that the police were going to beat him up in a Third Degree. Nobody beat him or even threatened him, but he was so nervous and frightened that he confessed. I am turning over my complete file to you because my client did not commit that murder. He was at a beach, forty miles away, when the woman was killed. You check it out, and I believe you will come to the same conclusion."

If it were the desire of the district attorney only to get convictions, to build up a record for himself, I could have ignored the lawyer, taken his client into court, presented the confession and most likely have come out with a conviction. Instead, I put one of my best assistants on the case and he worked on it for four months, helped throughout this time by others in my office and by a number of city detectives. At the end of the investigation, we presented the case to the grand jury and the grand jury did not indict.

Kings County, an area roughly 8 miles by 10—80 square miles —has a population of near 3,000,000 people of many ethnic and racial origins. There are more people per square mile in Kings County than in any other county in the United States, and this density of population creates unusual problems for the police and the district attorney.

Because of the volume of work, I have a staff of 86 assistant district attorneys. They are assigned to various bureaus: Indictment, Supreme Court, Criminal Term (where felonies are tried), Appeals, Rackets, Criminal Court of the City of New York (misdemeanor cases), Investigations, and Complaints. We also have assistants in the various parts of the Criminal Court of the City of New York—preliminary hearings in felony cases, misdemeanor trials, parts for Gamblers, Vehicle deaths, and Adolescent violators.

In addition, I have a medical assistant and a complement of 147 other people, consisting of 25 detective-investigators, 15 racket investigators, 16 homicide stenographers, 6 grand jury stenographers, 5 accountants, 12 process servers, and 68 additional secretaries, stenographers, and clerks. To this should be added 79 detectives and patrolmen, including two female detectives, headed by a captain and lieutenant, who are assigned to my office by the Police Commissioner of New York City. This is a total of 313 persons.

An important part of the work of a district attorney is with the grand jury. In Brooklyn, we have at least two grand juries sitting each month of the year; more often there are three grand juries sitting, and sometimes four.

A grand jury consists of 23 persons, men and women from all walks of life chosen by lot from a panel made up by the Commissioner of Jurors. When they are empaneled by a justice of the Criminal Term of the Supreme Court, he designates one of their number as foreman, another as assistant foreman (technically called acting foreman), and one as secretary. They sit for a month and get $6 per day and lunch while they are in session. The court may extend the term of any grand jury and often does to enable it to finish work it has not completed.

The district attorney is responsible for the presentation of evidence to the grand jury. He charges that body on the law and explains what elements are necessary to make out a crime. The New York State Code of Criminal Procedure (Section 251) sets the rule when an indictment should be found: "The Grand Jury ought to find an indictment, when all the evidence before them, taken together, is such as in their judgment would, if unexplained or uncontradicted, warrant a conviction by the trial jury." It is proper to add that in New York State a defendant has a right to appear before a grand jury and give his version of the facts.

Besides investigating the general run of cases, a grand jury may, at the request of the district attorney, and with the consent of the court, inquire into special situations, and such investigations may require considerable time. For example, one grand jury, designated as the Rackets Grand Jury, was in session for years looking into the gambling racket and police corruption involved in this racket, into graft-taking by inspectors in various city departments, also the jukebox situation and racketeers connected with it, also phony labor unions run by unsavory characters, and other special situations that require long-term investigations.

Besides these ordinary duties of a grand jury, there are often special functions of that body. For example, there is the case of Abe Reles.

For ten years, there was considerable speculation in the press, magazines, radio, and TV about whether one Abe Reles, of "Murder Incorporated" fame, was or was not thrown out of the sixth-floor window of the Half Moon Hotel in Coney Island by the police in whose protective custody he was. In a hearing held by the Kefauver Committee, one United States senator—not Senator Kefauver—remarked, "There is no doubt that Reles was murdered."

Since there is no statute of limitation for murder, our office undertook to settle the controversy. A grand jury was extended for three months and with two assistants I undertook the inquiry. We interviewed over 200 witnesses, had 86 of them before the grand jury, and introduced 127 exhibits. This was the conclusion of the grand jury:

That Abe Reles met his death while trying to escape, by means of a knotted sheet which was attached to a wire, which wire was in turn attached to the radiator in his room. He fell to his death, while suspended from or supporting himself on this sheet, when the wire parted as a result of the strain of his weight on it.

We find that Reles did not meet with foul play and that he did not die of suicide.

It would be sheer speculation to attempt to discern his motive for wanting to escape.

This grand jury thus laid to rest the ghost of Reles, and the presentment is available to any who are interested in more details of this case.

It is interesting to note that when I invited the United States Senator to tell the grand jury why he thought Reles was murdered, he said it was just a remark he had made, and that he had no testimony to give.

It does not take a grand jury long, in its close work with a district attorney, to know whether he is seeking justice or only trying to get indictments. The treatment of witnesses, the treatment of a defendant, the keeping out of evidence, the clarity of the charge—all this soon shows the grand jury the spirit of the district attorney and his staff. I state with pardonable pride that I have often received letters from a grand jury praising the competence and the fairness of my assistants.

The cases that concern a district attorney are of infinite variety, and among the more serious are robberies, or what is colloquially called "stick-ups." When one occurs, the detective squad in that precinct gets busy at once, hurrying to the scene of the crime and immediately questioning the victim and other witnesses. As a result, they may arrest one or more persons. As soon as an arrest is made, my office is notified and an assistant district attorney and a stenographer are sent to the precinct where the crime was committed. They take question-and-answer statements from the witnesses. They also take statements from the arrested persons if they will make them, and they often do.

This procedure of "riding" on a case is not universally followed, but I find it helpful. We get statements when events are fresh in the minds of witnesses, and some witnesses might not be so co-operative if they have a day or two to consider. It is shocking how many citizens, on second thought, feel "It's not my headache. Why stick my neck out? I'll lose all that time in court." If, however, they have already given a statement to the district attorney, backing out and "loss of memory" become more difficult.

Also, if a defendant has more time to think, or be advised by his attorney, he is more likely to become mute. Caught soon after the crime, with witnesses who clearly identify him, he may feel the futility of denial and is more likely to make a confession.

It is a far cry from such factually simple cases as this, to cases that require the most demanding technical and scientific proof. In one murder case, for example, the victim, who was killed on Manhattan Beach and dumped into the sea, was found six days later off Fire Island, seventy miles away. It was a very serious task for our staff to learn the facts about tides, currents, and winds, so that they could question the expert witnesses properly and show the jury how that body had floated and been blown from Manhattan Beach to Fire Island in six days. In this same case it was necessary to show that the seaweed found in the cuff of the killer's trousers was the same kind of weed as that found in the waters off Manhattan Beach. (To satisfy the reader's possible curiosity, the killer was convicted and executed after his case had been reviewed in the Supreme Court of the United States.)

In another case, where a defendant was charged with murdering two women on separate occasions, the defense claimed that the defendant suffered from epilepsy which rendered him incapable of knowing what he was doing and was, therefore, in law, not responsible for his acts. We engaged an expert neurologist who testified that this was not so; but it took a very great deal of study and preparation for my assistant, who tried the case, to learn about this disease and its characteristics so that he was competent to examine his own witness and cross-examine the experts of the defendant. (The defendant was convicted, but the Court of Appeals sent it back for new trial. Ultimately the defendant pleaded guilty to Manslaughter in the First Degree in both cases and was sentenced to twenty to forty years.)

There are numerous crimes in which arrests are not made quickly, and the office of the district attorney must work on them for long periods of time with the hope of solving them. In such a situation, the police department and the district attorney's office work with especial closeness. Take the Arnold Schuster case as an example.

At about 9:10 P.M., on March 8, 1952, Arnold Schuster was shot and killed. He had recognized the famous bank robber, Willie Sutton, and the recognition had led to Sutton's capture. It was natural for everyone to feel that Sutton was involved in Schuster's murder. At three o'clock on the morning immediately after the murder, I interviewed Sutton in Queens County Jail and I was convinced that he had had nothing to do with it.

For eight years after this, we held a meeting once a month on this case. Always present for the police were an inspector, a lieutenant, and three detectives of the Homicide Squad. For the district attorney's office: the district attorney, his chief assistant, the heads of the Rackets, Appeals, and Investigation Bureaus. At this monthly conference over the eight years, every lead was checked out and suitable action decided on. Our investigations took us into almost every state in the Union and to some foreign countries, as far away as Australia. Over five thousand witnesses were interviewed.

We are still trying to locate one John "Chappie" Mazziota who had guns stolen from a pier in Brooklyn—of which one was the murder weapon. It is speculated by many, however, that if "Chappie" were still alive, he would have been located by now. Yet there is, for us, no acceptable evidence that he is dead and the police and our office still meet, though not as often as before, to review the Schuster case and to check out any leads.

Such a case as this is the exception, and, in contrast, is the case of the two boys, aged nine and eleven, who were found stabbed to death, each thirty times, in a deserted field overgrown with weeds. The representatives of the police and of my office met, reviewed the case, and considered what action to take. A co-ordinated plan was quickly worked out and within two days a young man, nineteen years old, was arrested. He made a full confession and re-enacted the crime.

I call these meetings, between the police and representatives of my office, "quarterback" sessions. Ideas and plans are suggested, tossed around, criticized, rejected, modified. One plan, though rejected, may plant the seed for another, possibly the right one. When knotty problems wholly within the district attorney's office come up, we hold "quarterback" sessions among ourselves and usually find a solution or at least a course to follow.

Sometimes, even in the midst of all the demands on the office of the district attorney, we undertake things that are not strictly within our jurisdiction. Not long ago, a letter came from Greece, asking whether I could locate a certain person. I could properly have disregarded the letter or written saying that this was not our function. Instead, I asked my police bureau to see what they could find. We were unsuccessful, but I wrote my Greek correspondent that we had tried. It is my feeling that people in trouble should not be ignored. Maybe we cannot always solve their problems, but often we can try, and sometimes we can help them.

While my office is divided into its various bureaus, there are no watertight compartments and no bureau acts independently of the others. For example, the Investigation Bureau, that "rides" when arrests for felonies are made, knows that its work is necessary in the trial of a case, for a poorly taken statement at the scene of a crime can be the cause of failure in a trial. Also, a case improperly presented to the grand jury can cause serious difficulties for the Supreme Court Bureau or Appeals Bureau. Each bureau is a part of an integrated whole, separated only for convenience in handling the total work.

There is one bureau in the district attorney's office that I want to speak about in particular—the Rackets Bureau. It is my considered opinion that no district attorney in any sizable community can do his job successfully without a Rackets Bureau. Crimes such as homicide, robbery, burglary, assault, most larcenies, and rape, usually happen rather suddenly and can be taken care of by the police and the district attorney in the customary way. But there are other crimes, serious and dangerous to the well-being of the community, that require long-term and patient investigation.

The TV "bait" advertising (described later in this chapter), the gambling syndicates, phony labor unions feeding on business as well as on labor, unscrupulous mechanics in many fields in this machine age, extortionists, grafters, and bribers in governmental services—all this can be rooted out only by the most careful investigations. Only a competent Rackets Bureau, with investigators and accountants, and guided by assistants trained in this special field, can cope with these threats to society.

We also have a Complaint Bureau that handles some three thousand to four thousand interviews each year with men and women who feel aggrieved and wish to report that, in their opinion, someone has violated the Penal Law in dealing with them. We are careful to give each person a full and courteous hearing, and frequently this bureau, listening to complaints, becomes aware of serious law violations.

For example, it was through such complaints that we learned of people renting apartments and taking a month's rent, a month's security, and a month's rent as commission, when they neither owned the buildings nor were authorized to rent the apartments. When this situation became known, the Complaint Bureau passed the information on to the Rackets Bureau and they developed the evidence against the racketeers. Nine persons were convicted and the racket was broken up.

Then there was the sewing-machine racket, which became another problem for the Rackets Bureau. We received a letter from a woman who claimed that she had bought a sewing machine which did not work and was of no use at all. She had bought it as a result of a TV advertisement which offered machines for $45, and which announced that the first fifteen persons who phoned, asking for a salesman to come to see them in their homes, would each get a pair of pinking shears worth $10, a fine table on which to put the machine, and also other gifts. One might be tempted to put such a letter aside and forget it. Any woman foolish enough to fall for such promises should have hard luck.

But we thought that we had better investigate, so we sent for the lady and heard her story. Then we began asking around and we found other ladies who had been visited by salesmen from this same sewing machine company. We got their stories and put them all together, and we decided that here was something that deserved our attention.

We hired seven or eight television sets and monitored all TV advertisements from this sewing machine company for a number of weeks. We recorded each advertisement, carefully marking the time and station from which it came. We did the same on their radio advertisements. While we were doing this, we also ascertained who their principals were and where they operated.

After some eight or nine weeks we were ready. We arrested the principals for false advertising, subpoenaed the books of the company, and began examining their records.

This was the story. They had taken in $350,000, but had never sold a single machine for the advertised price. The announced price was nothing more than bait to gain entrance to the homes of their victims. They would show the prospective buyer the $45 machine, which actually had cost the company itself more than $45, and then they would tell the lady that this machine was no good. They would say if the needle broke, it could not be replaced. They made the machine sound like a tractor by manipulating a bolt, and they said it would require whole cans of grease to keep it running.

Then they would bring out another machine, a different model, and say, "Now if you will just give us a few dollars deposit and sign a receipt for this fine machine, you can pay for it at only a little a week. You will save a lot of money and benefit from all the fine things you can make on this machine. We'll check your credit, which we are sure is good, and then you will have this wonderful machine at a great bargain."

But it was not a receipt they gave the woman to sign. It was an installment contract by which she agreed to pay some $20 a month. A few days later, a finance company would send her a booklet of installment payments that had to be made. The company legally and technically was a bona fide purchaser for value of the sales contract, and they were not subject to any action that the purchaser might wish to take against the seller.

In our investigations, we found that when husbands discovered what had happened, some mighty unpleasant situations sometimes developed between them and their wives.

The principals of this company were indicted and convicted,

and we put them and their racket out of business. But there was still more to be done about this kind of offense, and we invited representatives of twenty-one radio and television stations to a meeting in my office. I told them what we had learned about "bait" advertising and suggested that they themselves stamp out conditions which made possible such snaring of the gullible. "I have neither the power nor the desire to act as a censor," I said. "My job is to prosecute violators of the Penal Code, and that we will do; but I also believe that part of my job is to prevent crime and fraud. If I can help you in this matter of 'bait' advertising, I shall be glad to; but I think your industry ought to establish its own organization and police itself. After all, a person doesn't have to be a district attorney to know that nobody can sell, and keep on selling, $1 bills for 98¢."

Later that year, twenty-four stations in the metropolitan area voluntarily adopted standards to apply to all advertising offers, made on television or radio, which involved a salesman visiting the home of a listener.

Now about one more racket. We discovered that unscrupulous auto-selling companies were tricking some of our servicemen. A part of the racket was to sell cars to men while they were overseas on a sort of "lay-away" plan. A soldier would sign a contract for a car, make payments while he was in Europe, and then, when he disembarked in Brooklyn, salesmen would flimflam him on the kind of car and on the price. Another part of this racket was to "grab" soldiers as they disembarked, duping them into crooked and disastrous deals with promises of all kinds of bargains.

It would take a long story to recount the details of this affair; but my investigators, and also policemen assigned to me on a permanent basis, would dress as soldiers, yield to the fast talk of the crooks and deal with them, getting the evidence we needed. The result of the investigation was to put these cheating companies out of business, recover large sums for the servicemen, and put a virtual end to the contemptible racket. Furthermore, all servicemen overseas were alerted and did not fall easy victims to the racketeers.

Such investigations are a constant part of the work of the district attorney and his staff. Our responsibility is to expose and break up rackets of all kinds, and we have been successful in breaking up the TV-repair rackets, the auto-repair gyps, the TV-tube racket where old and used tubes are sold as new ones, the operation of bootleg taxis, false and short weights by butchers and oil dealers, bribery in various city departments, the fraud of phony labor unions existing only on paper, and corrupt relationships between crooked lawyers, bondsmen, and gamblers.

These are a few of the rackets we have had to deal with. There are others operating now. When we break these, there will be still others. The slick crooks are forever figuring out ways to steal. This is one of the many reasons why the office of the district attorney is such a complicated, busy, and interesting place.

The district attorney is vested with authority that is not known or understood by the public, or even by the legal fraternity outside of those engaged in the administration of criminal law. (The specific authority to which I refer is not always the same in every state, and the examples I use may not exactly apply everywhere, but the differences are slight.)

A man is arrested for homicide and the district attorney may, if the facts warrant, bring him into court charged with murder in the first degree. If he does, and the man is proved guilty, he will be sentenced to death.

It is also in the power of the district attorney to bring this same man into court, and, for this same offense, permit him to plead guilty to murder in the second degree, to manslaughter, and, in some really exceptional circumstances, to the comparatively negligible offense of assault. In these latter pleas, the death sentence is not permitted and the man can only be sent to prison. Furthermore, the plea that the district attorney accepts, whether second degree, manslaughter, or assault, will frequently determine the length of the prison sentence given by the judge.

Here is tremendous power, the power to spare a life, and the power to determine, within certain limits, the length of an imprisonment. The district attorney, in fact, exercises this authority with the consent of the court; but as a practical matter, the court generally goes along with the recommendation of the prosecutor. Thus, it iᴜ the district attorney's discretion and decision that prevail.

Such power or authority may seem strange to some, but a district attorney in his daily contact with people, many of them disturbed and twisted people, comes to know the reasons for this humanity of the law. My job is to prosecute for crime, and I do it; but it is also my responsibility to take into account more than the evidence, more than solely the facts in the case, more than "Guilty" or "Not Guilty." These are considerations where this exceptional power of the district attorney is needed.

Years before I became a district attorney, I participated in two cases that still influence me, teaching me something of the position of the prosecutor in dealing with men. I was an Assistant United States Attorney at the time, young and inexperienced, and in the course of my duties I procured the indictment of a boy. He was arrested for stealing from the mails while he was still in high school and was working as an extra in the post office during the Christmas rush. He had taken a mechanical pencil from a broken package that was open when he first saw it. I presented the evidence to the Grand Jury and an indictment followed. The boy had violated the law and that was that. The post office inspector who had arrested him was quite grave about the seriousness of the crime.

Shortly after the indictment, the boy's father came to see me. He had been a postal employee for many years and had a job where only the most trusted employees are used, handling registered insured mail. He had gotten his son the job so that they could work together and the boy could make some Christmas money. Between sobs he told me that his son had never been in trouble before, had a good school record and was a decent boy at home, obedient to his parents, friendly and attentive to his brothers and sisters. The father told me, and I believed him, that he could not feel worse if his son had died. I promised him that I would look into it.

I sent for the boy and had a long talk with him. All he could say was this: "I don't know why I did it. I didn't need the pencil.

It was just there, sticking out of the package and I put it in my pocket. Before I could even think what I had done, I was arrested." I believed him, and believed the father, and told him I would hold the case and see the boy from time to time.

I did see him, regularly, and I found that the father's report was true; he was a decent kid with a good record. Knowing that if I brought him into court he would be convicted, and that probably there would be a sentence for him to serve, I kept putting off the case each time it appeared on the calendar.

The postal inspector was in court whenever it was scheduled, and he kept asking when I was going to move the case for trial. I told him, to his great consternation, that I probably would never try it, and that sometime in the future I might *nolle prosse* it. He was shocked.

There is no finer body of men than the postal inspectors. They have great ability and integrity, complete pride in their corps and would do nothing to blemish the service. They work endlessly to find evidence and yet in no circumstance would they put words in a witness' mouth or twist a fact in the slightest to make it fit a case they are presenting. I have worked with them in many mail-fraud cases and I admire them no end, but this one particular inspector was a difficult man. A friend, who had been in the postal service for years, later told me that he was so hard to get along with that other men did not like to work with him, and he had been transferred repeatedly.

While the case against the boy was still pending, a second case came to me from this inspector. He had arrested a postal employee for mail embezzlement. The employee had broken off a lump of cake from a package that had split open in transit and the cake exposed. This employee had a Civil Service position, and, as soon as the charge was made against him and admitted, he was fired.

The inspector came to me and wanted the case presented to the grand jury. I told him that the man had been punished enough already, that losing his job was more punishment than he deserved. But the inspector was insistent and told me I had no right to take the law into my hands. He put it to me this way:

"How would you like for somebody to stick his hand into a cake that your mother had sent you?" I told him I would not like it, but I did not want a man hung for it either. This did not satisfy him and he kept insisting until I told him I would present the case.

When I took it to the grand jury, I told them the whole story and said I thought the fellow had been punished enough; but since the postal inspector was insistent, I was presenting it to them. I then called in the inspector and he told the grand jury the story, making it, I thought, as serious and as grim as he could. The man had received the broken package. He had seen the cake. He had broken off a lump and had eaten it.

The inspector and I walked out of the jury room together and into the anteroom. The door had hardly closed before the buzzer sounded. I walked back in and the foreman said: "No true bill." I reported the result to the inspector and he told me I was not fooling him; I had gone in there and influenced the grand jury, and I was responsible for the no true bill. I had no answer to make. In this particular case, I was willing to be responsible.

Now let's go back to my young defendant and his experience in the theft of the pencil:

I left the U. S. Attorney's office in 1929. The case against the boy had been adjourned many times and finally wound up in the files and just lay there. I had forgotten to dispose of it before I left. In the meantime, the boy had been graduated from high school, had attended Pace School of Accounting, and had graduated from there. One day he came to see me, and I was pleased to see him. He had grown into a clean-cut, decent young man.

We chatted a bit and he said that he wanted to take a Civil Service examination and did not know how to answer one of the questions: "Were you ever indicted for a crime?" As the record stood, I told him he would have to answer yes. While he was in my office, I telephoned the U. S. Attorney and later went to see him, explaining the whole situation and suggesting that the case be "nolled." The young man, however, still had to answer "yes" to the question, and he always will, though the "nolle" will help him some. I can only pray that the indictment did not prove too much of a stumbling block to him as he tried to find a job and make his way, and I wish that I had been older and more experienced when it had come up in the first place.

Concern about a boy and a pencil, and a man and a piece of cake, does not mean that a murderer, rapist, burglar, stick-up man, or dope pusher would get any easy treatment in my office. A district attorney who goes soft is a failure, decaying the whole system of prosecution; but I think it is entirely correct for the district attorney to have the authority I have mentioned, the leeway to use discretion. There are times, I believe, when he should act according to his experience and his understanding of crime and criminals, especially first offenders, rather than rigidly follow the unyielding formula of indictment, conviction, imprisonment. Suppose we take for consideration, in this matter of prosecution, the crime of Indecent Exposure.

In the vast majority of these cases the person involved is an otherwise respectable citizen, at fault only in this one serious aberration. Almost always, except for the crime of exposure, he has no criminal record. He is gainfully employed, usually is married and a father. Yet he finds himself in the hands of the law for an offense that strongly violates decency and offends all the moral senses of the community. It is an offense demanding the immediate attention of the district attorney and the authority of his office, but the problem that confronts us is more than this one immediate offense. Our real problem is whether this man is indicating a continuing condition and betraying evidence that he is on his way to more serious crime, possibly a grievous sexual attack and even murder, or is suffering from a periodic compulsion which, in some men, can be cured.

In most exposure cases it is easy for the district attorney to convict the defendant, send him to prison, and be temporarily rid of him and his problem. But the average imprisonment for this offense is three months, and the man soon is a threat to the community again and once more a liability to the district attorney. The real difficulty has not been considered, much less solved.

I would prefer, in most offenses for this crime, that the district attorney have the right to suspend the case, if he believes it wise, and allow time for examinations and tests—physical, possibly neurological, certainly psychiatric. This would be no "easy out" for the offender, for throughout the time of the examinations he would be under supervision and any untoward act on his part would bring him immediately into court and to trial.

By use of delay and examinations, we would detect those who might be successfully treated, and those others who are on their way to further crime. Refusing examinations and insisting on routine imprisonment can be a loss rather than a gain for a community, an action completely unproductive in the deeper adjustments of society, because a man, guilty of this offense, when released from prison, unexamined, untested, unknown, may soon be on the prowl again. The police may be able to catch him again, but this time the compulsion may have led him to more than exposure, and the police may be too late to prevent a tragedy.

No district attorney can seriously misuse this authority I have discussed, certainly he cannot continue malpractice for any length of time. If he does, the governor of the state can call a hearing and remove any district attorney who is slothful, incompetent, uses his office for political advancement, or for any other misconduct or offense. Besides protection through the governor, the people themselves have the ultimate protection at the polls. If they do not approve of a district attorney, they can always vote him out of office.

If one were to ask most persons what branch of the law they would prefer if they were lawyers, the chances are they would say, "I'd like to be a criminal lawyer." This is the part of law that they read about in books and magazines, that newspapers most often report, and that television portrays. The lay person, schooled in fiction and drama, likes to picture himself as the brilliant and infallible lawyer for the defense, cleverly trapping the witness and tying him up in his contradictory testimony.

Or if he is the prosecutor, what a thrill for him to fight the underworld! If we go by the record of the movies and TV, each night the D.A. is out on the water front shooting it out with the narcotic mob. Too often he displays more courage than brains, but his beautiful secretary always gets there in time, racing in to save his skin and his job and helping him capture the mobsters.

Actually, criminal law is one of the least popular of all branches of legal practice, and most lawyers know very little about it. Many a law firm that may occupy several acres of softly carpeted office space, with a dozen partners, a hundred lawyers and even more secretaries, stenographers, and clerks; with branch offices in foreign countries, and clients of national and international reputation, will go into a quick funk if one of their clients gets even slightly involved in any criminal matter. A civil complaint running to a hundred pages, and concerned with millions of dollars, would be just another piece of work for them—but a grand jury subpoena would throw the whole outfit into an uproar.

Great defense lawyers are sorely needed in the criminal courts, and one can understand why only a few are there. Criminal practice offers little income and less distinction, except for the very few men at the absolute top. Most defendants are indigent and other defendants, who could pay a proper fee, do not want a lawyer at all—they want a fixer or suborner. The inducement to criminal law is not an obvious one, but the need is plain and young men with a regard for public requirements will find their closest association with justice in the criminal courts.

They will find it either with the defense or on the other side of the table, the prosecutor's side. I have been on the prosecutor's side for a good many years, and I must mention it to all young men concerned with the law, admitting quickly as I do that the man who works for the public usually has poor pay and his prestige is nebulous. It is curious, though, that a man who gives his thought and his work to the public often finds how little he needs and how much he has.

In 1945, I was in private practice with an annual income of $50,000 to $60,000. Just before Christmas of that year I was offered the post of Chief Assistant in the office of the District Attorney. The job paid $10,500. I was paying more than that in tuition for the education of my three children and in charity contributions.

Why I took the job was not clear to me then, and is not much clearer now. I doubt if any man who gives up a successful private practice to take a public job which is more demanding, tougher, with less pay, could tell why he does it. He doesn't know the name of something that beckons, and I don't think he needs to know. I may have taken the job because of the excitement. Perhaps it was something in politics that drew me in. Anyhow, I thought I would try it for a year or two. Sixteen years have gone by and I am still in the job.

After I had been the Chief Assistant for eight years, I was elected district attorney in 1953; took office January 1, 1954, and have held the office ever since. I have never been sorry.

Yet I cannot honestly advise a young man beginning his law career to aim directly at the job of district attorney. There is so much about it that is sordid, so much daily association with selfishness and greed, pettiness, and the meanness and cruelty of men, that one must constantly bulwark his faith in God and a belief in the total mass of mankind, with its steady flow of goodness, or he himself can weaken into disbelief and a consuming cynicism. While not urging, or even suggesting, a career as a district attorney, I must say to every young man going into the practice of law that the time may come when that office may be open to him, and he be asked to accept it. What then for him? No man can think of himself alone. A lawyer, I believe, more than most men, has the training to play a part in a community. The life of the district attorney is hard, often unpleasant, always demanding, but it is an honorable, challenging, and exciting life.

The first and continuing claim on him, as a district attorney, is to serve his community in a constant battle against crime, against corruption, and against all the forces of the underworld in a complete effort to destroy them. This takes brains and it takes guts, and no man without both need match himself against the shrewdness and the ruthless determination of crooks and thugs, whether they are working alone or in mobs, whatever their racket may be,

or however they may infest society. And never underrate them!
They are smart, in a stupid sort of way, and they are more
cruel than hell. If you are dumb, they will run over you. If you
are a coward, they will stomp you.

To meet them, to assemble the evidence, to prosecute them
and send them to the electric chair or to prison, is the constant
job of the prosecution. Each district attorney is forever probing
to find some opening where he can break through the wall of
crime, knowing that another wall will form quickly, for they always form, and knowing that he must go on and break that one,
too. This is our job, our responsibility, our satisfaction, the endless
breaking down of the forces of lawlessness, sending to prison as
many of the professional criminals as we can detect in their
crimes, and keeping the others in law-abiding living for as long
as we can.

The job is full of anxieties. But if the district attorney makes
up his mind to tackle each situation honestly and to the best of
his ability, letting the chips fall wherever they may, then 99 per
cent of his anxieties will be gone. If this formula does not work,
he must be ready to go down with it. In doing his job, he may
have to hurt people he knows; but he can never let this make any
difference to him. He must be ready to withstand criticism that
often is caustic and sometimes is unfair—the public does not always know all the facts. He must be ready to temper justice with
mercy, even when it is the unpopular thing to do. He must be extremely careful in his use of power, for power is a heady thing
and can lead men astray.

The privilege of helping protect a community against corruption and violence is not the only reason that a man takes on the
tough, and, at times, almost brutal job of district attorney. Few
self-respecting, decent men like to think of spending years, perhaps the rest of their lives, in a world where daily they are raking
through the filth of crime as they search for evidence, and where
they are constantly coming up against liars, cheats, thieves, mur-
derers, pickpockets and prostitutes, rapists and forgers, sneaks
and pimps. This is no white-glove job, no ballroom and music,

no glamour. Yet no matter how tough the job, the open and blunt battle against crime is essential, and, like the battle against cancer, it must never let up.

But the satisfaction of winning against the forces of crime is, I believe, the lesser appeal of the office. There is another appeal beyond prosecution and conviction. There is the responsibility of dealing with a boy who stole a pencil, a man who stole a piece of cake. There is the chance, before the finality of the courtroom and the corrosion of prison, of sealing the crack in a character before the whole structure of the man is shattered.

10

The Practice of Law

IN A LARGE CITY

BY WHITNEY NORTH SEYMOUR

New York, New York

WHITNEY NORTH SEYMOUR

Born: 1901, Chicago, Illinois

University of Wisconsin: A.B., 1920; LL.D., 1962
Columbia University: LL.B., 1923; LL.D., 1960
Dartmouth College: LL.D., 1960
Duke University: LL.D., 1961
Akron University: LL.D., 1961
University of Manitoba: LL.D., 1961

Admitted to New York Bar: 1924
Simpson Thacher & Bartlett, New York, New York. Associate: 1923;
   Partner: 1929–31, 1933–
United States Assistant Solicitor General: 1931–33
Special Assistant Attorney General of the State of New York: 1954
Instructor New York University Law School: 1925–31 (part time)
Lecturer Yale Law School: 1935–45 (part time)

American Bar Association, President: 1960–61
American Bar Foundation, President: 1960–
The Association of the Bar of the City of New York, President: 1950–52
New York Legal Aid Society, President: 1945–50
American Arbitration Association, President: 1953–55
National Conference of Judicial Councils, Chairman
New York Joint Conference on Legal Education: President
American College of Trial Lawyers: President-elect
American Fund for Free Jurists: Vice-president
Attorney General's Committee on Anti-Trust Laws
New York Temporary Commission on the Courts
New York Advisory Committee on Commission of Civil Rights
Practicing Law Institute: New York University Law Center, Trustee

Carnegie Endowment for International Peace, Chairman, Board of Trustees
Freedom House, Chairman of the Board: 1954–59
Municipal Art Society, President: 1956–58
Woodrow Wilson Fellowship Foundation, Trustee
Distribution Committee of New York Community Trust, Member
Fine Arts Federation of New York, President
Council on Library Resources, Trustee
William Nelson Cromwell Foundation, Trustee

ELSEWHERE in this book, the reader will have found treatment of many of the considerations which affect the decision of whether the young lawyer should decide to practice in a small or large community. This is, of course, affected by all sorts of personal factors. The young man who has grown up in a great city, with its tendency to make almost everyone anonymous, may prefer the easier identification as an individual in a smaller city for his professional career. It is almost literally true that one can walk the length of Manhattan Island in New York without ever seeing anyone one knows, or who has the slightest idea of or interest in the walker. This is privacy in public of the extreme kind. For some it is restful; for others it is inhuman. Yet the young man who has grown up in a smaller city or in the country may choose to ignore this and seek the challenge and even the supposed glamour of a great city.

Aside from the actual professional opportunities, the dimensions of social and intellectual life differ sharply between the large and the small city, and these differences have their own appeals. In the smaller communities the extracurricular activities tend to concentrate on one's friends, the country club, outdoor activities and civic enterprises in which the young lawyer can readily play a leading role. This is not to minimize the many cultural activities which are carried on in such communities, but it is probably fair to say that they are largely run by amateurs and not professionals. In the large cities a broader spectrum of activity is at hand: the theater, music, opera, ballet, art galleries, and their usual accompaniments, conducted primarily by professionals. However, the outdoors is farther away and harder to get to, friends are physically scattered and participation in civic enterprises involves some of the competitive problems of professional life itself.

It would be unduly complicated to appraise all these values here. All one can safely say is that each year many able young men from smaller communities choose, for one reason or another, to take the leap into big-city practice, while I believe relatively few young people raised in cities seek the calmer life of the smaller communities. I have no statistics to support this, but I feel sure it is correct because all over the country I have heard that the county-seat towns are losing bright young men to the big cities. If there is a shortage of lawyers (as I and many others believe), it is most acute in the smaller communities, not the cities. I use one other casual yardstick for my view: my guess is that more than half the partners in the larger New York firms come from smaller communities, as I did myself. My impression is that this would be true of some other cities, although probably not of Philadelphia, Baltimore, San Francisco, and Chicago where the professional population seems more home-grown, for some reason not entirely clear to me.

Instead of laboring the matter further and advising about the choice (which is already pretty fully covered elsewhere in this book), I will start with the assumption that the young man has chosen to practice in a large city for some reasons which appeal to him. My task then is to explain a little about what he will encounter, what he may expect and how he should try to avoid letting the city submerge him and dry up his professional juices. I shall assume that he chose the city while he was in law school or before, that he expects to appreciate the cultural opportunities in the city, but expects to concentrate primarily on the practice rather than on municipal amenities. Thus he will not have chosen the city primarily as a place to open his own office or join with other young men in a small firm. For if that is the form the start is to take, most people would prefer to begin that particular adventure in a smaller community where getting recognized early is less difficult. And the problems of the individual lawyer or the small firm in the city are sufficiently similar to the problems in the small community so that Judge Woodbury's chapter is adequate to cover both, and I shall not treat separately the bold individual who chooses to hang out his own shingle in a big city. So, by elimination and hypothesis, we can assume that our young man will be coming to the city to work for a fairly large law firm. He will have selected that firm, or been selected by it, in the course of the rather denatured interviewing process now fashionable.

At all our principal law schools, representatives of large-city firms call during the interviewing season and talk, by appointment, with a cross section of the students interested in practicing in the cities. They sit cooped up in an office and have to sniff out each other's potentialities. The lawyer describes his firm, looks over the student's dossier (particularly his academic record) and forms his impression. The whole interview is likely to last from fifteen minutes to a half hour. Then, or thereafter, the lawyer makes an offer to those he likes and the most eligible and popular get many offers. The starting salary is usually about the same for all the firms in a city; differences develop in the rate of advancement later on and these sometimes differ widely between firms. The student finds out what he can about the various firms from faculty and friends and then makes his choice among the available offers.

This seems to me to be a pretty unsatisfactory system from the point of view of the student. He doesn't actually see the office or get a feel for its atmosphere or the people in it. Formerly, while attending such schools, the student visited the offices in nearby cities and could get that feel. Some still do, even in the larger schools, and it is still fairly universal in many schools; but it would be good, I think, if it were possible to revert to the earlier system for almost all. Of course it is a little easier on the student economically to have the employers come to him, but something of value is lost that way. The initial decision is so important, and starting with the most congenial firm is essential for the start to have every advantage, that the process should not be quite so hygienic and practical. The spirit of comradeship is one of the great joys of the profession. It is hard to know whether one feels it coming through clearly when one is under the tension of a formal interview in a law-school room.

After the interview, wherever it is held, and the decision, made on the basis of the best information which is accessible, the young lawyer approaches the beginning of his practice. About the same time he must face the bar examination. If possible, it is well to get this behind him before he starts work; otherwise he will face a constant pressure to choose between taking time to prepare for the examination and the day's chores in the office. While offices are lenient at this period, the pressures are present. In many states there is a cram course run either on a proprietary basis (like Judge Medina's course in New York, which for a generation before he went on the bench insured that thousands of us were able to pass the bar), or as a part of the routine of a law school or law institute. No one should feel too proud to take such help. Most bar examinations are pretty tough and failure leaves that hurdle to plague one's beginning years.

In many states there is a ceremony of welcome when the new lawyers are admitted. This is fine and should be adopted everywhere. Thus the young lawyer is made to feel a part of the profession at the very outset. The advantage of participating in the activities of the organized bar can be brought home to him at this time, and, from then on, the spirit of brotherhood between older and younger lawyer, between bench and bar, becomes a reality for him.

The early experiences with a large, or moderately large, firm in a city will vary somewhat; but the following is probably a fair summary of the average. With the size of the firm goes a great proliferation of specialization. Ordinarily there will be one or more partners (sometimes ten) who concentrate on some particular area of law. Among these will be general corporate law (including formation of corporations, corporate mortgages, issuance of securities, SEC registration, etc.), tax law, estate law, litigation, perhaps labor law, and others, depending on the city and the area. Thus, for example, in the Southwest, oil and gas and water law are of great importance and there are specialists in those subjects.

In the firm's hierarchy, usually each partner will have several senior associates and some juniors who work closely with him. Some of these may be general utility men in the field, who are on call to work with a number of partners. But each partner and his preferred colleagues tend to be a rather closely knit group.

Each firm has its own way of launching the new associate. Some shuttle him around the departments for a couple of years with a few months of assignment to each department. This gives broad exposure to the firm's work, but may result in some enforced boredom when he hits a department holding no interest for him. In others, he goes into a sort of pool of new talent; out of this he is assigned by someone who acts as an office manager or managing partner to do what is needed. He may do legal research in any of the departments. He may file papers or carry the bag of a litigator who needs a junior in a trial. He may help with a corporate closing where there are an infinite number of papers, or he may sometimes help to proofread the proofs of those papers. In this more hit-or-miss apprenticeship, variety supplies the interest. Gradually, under either system, the young man begins to show a flair for some particular specialty or he feels a call to one. Starting out with a general background, he, like everyone else, soon tends to be drawn to some particular specialty, and here he turns out to do his best work. Here he can see the best chance of progress and of the greatest satisfaction in his practice. If he really finds himself, he will not want to change.

As an old trial man, I look on the mysteries of corporate security work with admiration but without envy, and those who regard registration statements as more attractive than fiction regard one who loves the courtroom as mildly eccentric. Sometimes in all this process, the young man simply can't find the excitement he hoped for or the pace is too fast. Then, gradually, he may decide to go to a smaller firm or sometimes even reverse his field and go back home. Someone told me recently that the reason farm boys usually succeeded is that they know what would happen to them if they didn't. Having spent a little time on a farm as a boy, I know what they mean.

Someone may say, "I don't want to become a specialist. Can't I go with a big-city firm and be a general practitioner?" The answer is that it would be hard to do so. With specialists in every field available, one who took the time, in the complexities of today, to try to master all fields, would master only a few, and he would not be of great value to the firm which needs experts more than universal pundits. One who really prefers the joys and rewards of general practice will generally do better and be happier elsewhere.

Shortly after he starts work, the young lawyer will usually get some chance to show his mettle. He may have to deal with a problem in court on his own; occasionally the senior gets sick or is otherwise occupied and the junior must carry the burden. Or, when visiting some client, he may be called on for some extraordinary service. Or he may dazzle his senior by efficiency at a closing. Or he may write a draft of a brief of superlative quality. Then he will be watched and encouraged, first by the associates and partners, then by the clients and the judges. Out of this comes advancement, appreciation, and ultimately perhaps he will become a partner in his turn.

There is not room here to trace the whole process. The life in a large-city firm is exciting and intensely competitive in a gentlemanly sort of way. It takes great energy and effort. Sometimes hours are long and weekends have no day of rest. In a long trial the seniors and the juniors may work months before there is relief. Some trials last months or even years, although fortunately bench and bar are now finding procedural poultices to shrink the so-called "big case" to manageable size. Lawyers (and clients), however, have a way of leaving important things to the last minute. Everything is then done in a rush, under pressure and tension, and, even with the greatest care, it is a wonder that there are not more mistakes.

What rewards are there that take the place of the relatively serene pace at which the profession usually proceeds in smaller communities? First, of course, there is the rather crass notion that lawyers in large firms do well financially. Certainly this brings some able young men to the cities. And it is true that the income of a partner in a large city firm is likely to be several times the income of a partner in a small-town firm; but with taxes, such rewards have largely lost their appeal. The lower cost of living, greater leisure, and easier opportunities for participating in civic affairs in a smaller town, undoubtedly make up for any difference in income.

My impression is that it is the supposed opportunity to deal with legal problems of larger import rather than larger income, which is today the magnet drawing young lawyers to large-city practice. There is much truth in this concept. A large-city office does have a fascinating variety of problems. The corporate matters are likely to involve larger sums and tougher problems. The tax questions run the full gamut, way out into the most esoteric. The simple damage suit is rarely tried in such a firm; its cases are more likely to be crisp commercial cases or interminable antitrust matters. So, all the way along, the variety of legal problems challenges everything in a man's training, his skills and also his endurance. But it is well to remember that there may be quite as many challenging legal problems in a defense to a suit on a three-hundred-dollar note as in a one-hundred-million-dollar debenture issue. I believe the true appeal would probably be in that the large firms have a wider variety of professional challenges, because their clients are more varied, and not because of the amounts involved in any of the matters. Furthermore, where formerly one Wall Street lawyer might aspire to advise Mr. Morgan or Mr. Baker, they are more likely now to talk to office counsel and some career vice president. The notion that they will deal both with big men and big problems is one that may be more true in Texas than elsewhere.

It is fair to say that because of the nature and quality of the clientele of the larger firms, and the agreeable and professional competition between them, the lawyer's work is likely to be superlatively well done. Every possible legal question gets identified and solved. Skilled lawyers look at every alternative. The legal milk is removed from every legal cocoanut. Each adversary of similar background is a worthy foeman. The rapiers really flash in the sun; parry and thrust is expertly done. Here is the real appeal. Here professionalism is challenged to be as expert and perfect as possible. Laying aside the fact that leisure and a decorous pace—a certain reflection of the grace and charm of the Inns of Court—are ideally a part of the profession, this is where intellectual exuberance is never lacking. No lawyer who loves to chew on legal problems ever feels he can afford to get out of practice, and he rarely does.

But even a fast professional pace, and the opportunity to have a constant feast of hard and interesting problems with adequate financial reward, is not enough for most lawyers. Throughout our history, lawyers everywhere have felt a call also to serve the public. They have participated in politics so that they could help make the government function, or they have at least had a part in their community's civic affairs. Can they do this in the cities? Must they be content with their practice and then go home, tired, but fulfilled, to their beds, leaving civic affairs to bankers and others whose hours may be more civilized? If so, many young men will be disillusioned. Fortunately, the urge to serve both clients and the public interest runs very deep in the profession.

The answer to this is, I believe, that big-city lawyers have the same opportunity to serve the public interest that lawyers any-where do. Not only the opportunity, but the city lawyers seize it and they discharge it well. In both World Wars, the city law-yers, drafted like Colonel Stimson and Judge Patterson, to run the War Department, with the hundreds of others which they in turn drafted, are a lasting memorial to the dedication and ability of the metropolitan bar of the United States. But aside from these dramatic contributions in time of national peril, the day-by-day contributions are great.

The young lawyer can start at once to gain some of these satisfactions and he can have them the rest of his life. His natural field will be the local bar associations where other lawyers and judges may learn to appreciate him. Some of these associa-tions, like The Association of the Bar of the City of New York, the Philadelphia Bar Association, the Chicago Bar Association and the Los Angeles Bar Association (to mention a few) are very strong and have made a multitude of contributions to the public interest. On a slightly larger screen, he can also be active in his State Bar Association and in the American Bar Association. Through the churches, hospitals, school board, legal-aid societies, chambers of commerce, citizens unions, etc., he can find many demands and outlets for his talents. Cultural activities, too—libraries, art galleries, symphonies, amateur dramatics—all will welcome him. These activities will broaden him, make him a better and more useful lawyer, and, with good luck and the aid of a good wife and alert children, may keep him from becoming too stuffy.

In the end, he will join with his colleagues in smaller communities in remembering two great truths about the profession which deserve repeating. The first comes from Elihu Root's great speech to the Yale Law School in 1904, which goes in part:

He is a poor-spirited fellow who conceives that he has no duty but to his clients and sets before himself no object but personal success. To be a lawyer working for fees is not to be any the less a citizen whose unbought service is due to his community and his country with his best and constant effort. And the lawyer's profession demands of him something more than the ordinary public service of citizenship. He has a duty to the law. In the cause of peace and order and human rights against all injustice and wrong, he is the advocate of all men, present and to come.

And the second comes from a great friend of the United States and of mine, Lord Evershed, formerly Master of the Rolls and now a Chancery Law Lord, who said, in his 1955 speech at the University of Kansas:

. . . for the legal profession no standard of scholarship or rectitude can by any means be too high. If it is true to say (as I believe that it is) that the measure of true freedom—freedom of the mind and the spirit as well as of the person—in any country is directly proportional to the respect in which its legal profession is held by the general community, so also is it true that the future liberties of our people, the maintenance of the high standards of stability and values, are in the hands of those of our profession.

When each of us, old and young, remember the sentiments with which Mr. Justice Frankfurter so eloquently opened this volume, and some of the other declarations by the great men who have gone before us in our beloved profession, we will know that we can serve that profession well anywhere. All I want to say in conclusion is that if the call to the city is irresistible, it is clear that the law can be well served, with honor and deep excitement, there, as well as anywhere else.

11 _Shall I Practice_

IN A SMALL COMMUNITY?

BY PETER WOODBURY

CHIEF JUDGE
UNITED STATES COURT OF APPEALS, FIRST CIRCUIT
Manchester, New Hampshire

PETER WOODBURY

Born: 1899, Bedford, New Hampshire

Phillips Exeter Academy
Harvard: B.S., 1924
Columbia: Law student, 1924–5
Harvard: LL.B., 1927
University of New Hampshire: LL.D., 1960

Enlisted U. S. Infantry: March, 1918
Machine gunner: Private 1st class
Wounded, Somme: September, 1918
Discharged, Surgeon's Certificate: February, 1919

Admitted to New Hampshire Bar: 1927
Began practice in Manchester, N. H.: 1927
Selectman, Bedford: 1928–31
Justice Bedford Municipal Court: 1928–32
Associate Justice, New Hampshire Superior Court: 1932–33
Associate Justice, New Hampshire Supreme Court: 1933–41
Judge United States Court of Appeals, First Circuit: 1941–59
Chief Judge, United States Court of Appeals, First Circuit: 1959–

President New Hampshire Council on World Affairs
President, Board of Trustees of the Elliot Hospital
Trustee of Holderness School for Boys
Chairman of the Mount Washington Study Committee
President of the Board of Trustees of Currier Gallery of Art
Vice Chairman of New Hampshire Reorganization Commission
Fellow of the American Academy of Arts and Sciences

ONE WAY to answer a question is to ask another. Adopting that technique I would answer the question posed in the title of this chapter by asking: "Do you want to live in a small community?" If your answer is a clear and resounding "No!," if you are convinced in your own mind that you can live happily only in a big metropolitan center, or in a suburb and commute to one; that you can find fulfillment only in dealing with matters involving dollars expressed in seven or more digits, then you need read no further. By all means go to New York, Philadelphia, Boston, Chicago, New Orleans, Detroit, Los Angeles or some other big center of population, to live your life and seek your fortune, for you may rest assured you will not find the satisfactions that will make *your* life worth living anywhere else. On the other hand, if you are not quite sure where you want to practice, it is well worth your while to consider establishing yourself in some smaller, even much smaller, community.

First, what is a small community? Within wide limits mere population is not the criterion. While an isolated crossroads village may appeal as a pleasant place to live and bring up your family, it can hardly be expected to produce either an intellectually stimulating or a financially rewarding practice. Therefore, unless you have substantial independent means and wish to live the life of a country squire with a law practice only as a side issue, as a sort of part-time hobby, you must seek a more populous center. How populous depends upon many factors.

A relatively small city, if it is the focal point or trading center for a large surrounding rural area, particularly if it is also a county seat or better still a state capital, can provide an interesting, financially rewarding practice. If, in addition, such a community also is or is near a college or university town, it will be sure to provide plenty of intellectual stimulation outside your profession. A relatively larger community, however, in close proximity to a very much larger metropolitan center may be a horse of another color, for in such places the tendency sometimes is to rely on the neighboring metropolis not only for intellectual and cultural satisfactions but also for legal service, leaving only minor or routine matters to the local practitioners.

In choosing a place to practice, consider first the general area of the country in which you wish to live. And in doing so, unless for reasons of health, do not think only of climate. Consider local social and cultural attitudes. You can hardly expect to be happy, or perhaps even successful (Have you read Mark Twain's *Pudd'nhead Wilson?*), if you do not understand, or worse yet, if you are openly at odds with, regional customs, attitudes, and patterns of behavior. Also take your recreational interests into serious account. You can play golf almost anywhere, at least in certain seasons of the year. But if you like to hunt or fish or ride horseback, or ski or sail or swim, go to the part of the country which provides ready opportunity for your chosen pleasures. Man does not live by bread alone and satisfactory places to practice exist in every section of the country.

Coming now to the choice of a particular community, look first to the quality of the public education it affords. Naturally you want the best for your children. Moreover, no other factor more clearly reflects the cultural and political standards of a community. Good schools indicate a community which not only wants educational advantages for its children, but also one which is willing to make the effort to acquire what it wants both in the way of schools and in the way of local government generally. Thus good schools betoken an alert community of public-spirited citizens in which a young, able, energetic lawyer should quickly gain acceptance and soon come to be relied upon for advice and eventually for leadership. If you find that you have no interest in sinking your roots deep in the community in which you live and in becoming an active participant in local affairs, you are probably not cut out for a small-town practice.

Now how should you get started? Should you start out alone or join an established firm? The latter course I believe preferable, unless, perhaps, you are returning after college and law school to your home town where you and your family before you are well and favorably known. A great advantage of association with a firm is that you will quickly and easily pick up the local practice. The partners will show you the way things are done, such as how a complaint is drawn or an answer filed, or the local way of drawing and recording a deed or forming a corporation, and many other minor but far from unimportant details that the law schools cannot possibly undertake to teach. Moreover, association with an established, respected firm—in addition to giving you ready access to little tips on the way things are done, so that you will not blunder into needless minor but sometimes embarrassing mistakes of local practice and procedure—will launch you on your career; for it will be rightly assumed that a high-grade firm would not take you on unless the partners had confidence in your industry, integrity, character, and ability. But if you decide to join a firm, pick it carefully. Consider not only the kind of practice it has but also the character and personality of the partners. You can be miserable with associates you neither respect nor like, but happy, indeed, with men you look up to and enjoy.

Naturally you will begin, whether in a firm or on your own, by doing legal chores such as searching titles; collecting, or trying to collect, bills; drawing deeds, bills of sale or maybe simple wills; and if in a firm, preparing legal memoranda for the partners. But while starting at the bottom you will be learning local law and practice and what is even more important, learning early in your professional career to make decisions on your own and to take responsibility. You will perforce have to take responsibility if you start off on your own; you will also be expected to take responsibility if you join a firm, for smaller firms can hardly afford to keep a man or make him a partner if he is afraid to make decisions.

Do not be discouraged if at first the cases you handle seem trivial. Small cases can often present interesting and intriguing questions of law for you to explore. And remember that, although a case may seem trivial to you, it probably, at the moment at least, is of the first importance to your client. Furthermore, you will be gaining practical experience.

One of my early clients was a neighbor whose cart loaded with wood was struck from behind by an automobile. He told me the extent of his damages, fortunately only a matter of about twenty-five dollars, and asked me to collect. I presented the claim to the adjuster for the automobile driver's insurance company, who immediately disputed liability on the ground that my client was driving on the wrong side of the road, and then, with an air of generosity, offered me fifteen dollars in settlement. This put my dander up. I had ample testimony that the collision occurred on the right-hand side of the road, verified by a personal view of the scars left on the highway by the horse's shoes when they were violently propelled forward from behind, and the amount of my claim was fully supported by the blacksmith's bill for repairs. I insisted on collecting in full, and, after much not entirely good-natured haggling back and forth, I finally succeeded.

When I recounted my difficulty with the insurance adjuster to a senior partner of the firm for which I worked, he told me that my approach was wrong. He said that insurance adjusters by nature and training liked to haggle and moreover that they received credit with their company when they succeeded in settling claims for less than the amounts originally demanded. Therefore, he told me, the proper technique was to determine the extent of the actual loss, and then add about 50 per cent to it to give bargaining room. With this advice in mind, I approached settlement of a later claim for the wrongful death of a heifer slain by an automobile while being driven home from pasture over the road.

My client valued the heifer at ninety dollars so I presented a claim for one hundred and forty, which I thought sounded more convincing than a round one hundred and fifty. Apparently it was, for the insurance adjuster called at my office, verified the amount of the claim, and then without more ado sat down and wrote my client a check for one hundred and forty dollars. Feeling a little guilty, but not wanting to admit to the insurance adjuster that the actual amount of the claim was only ninety dollars, I took the check to the same partner and, telling him what had happened when I followed his advice, asked him what I should do now. He came up with the eminently practical suggestion, that I give my client all he had asked for and keep the balance for my fee. This solution appealed to me but, believe it or not, my client demurred. He wanted to pocket the entire proceeds of the check and pay me nothing. I got my fifty dollars but never saw the client again.

I learned another practical lesson in what I suppose would be called office management from two women of indeterminate age who came into my office. After much giggling and elbowing one another, and saying back and forth, "You tell him," "No, you tell him," one of them finally disclosed the following situation.

It seemed that they lived with their widowed mother, who was a little peculiar (more giggles), and that their neighbor's barn was built very close to her property line. The neighbor decided to paint his barn and inquired of "mother" whether she would mind if he put his ladders on her land when he painted the side of his barn near her line. Mother peremptorily refused permission, indignantly ordered the neighbor off her premises and told him under no circumstances to trespass on her land.

The neighbor departed and later suspended a staging from the roof of his barn and climbed down onto it to paint. Mother observed this maneuver but waited until her neighbor was well established swinging in the air and then, in defense of her air space, seized the garden hose and played it on him. The neighbor, naturally, to put it mildly, was displeased. Getting soaked and unable to escape, in self-defense, or perhaps in retaliation, he emptied his paint can on mother's head, and not content with that, sued her in trespass for squirting water on his barn. They showed me the copy of the writ which had been served and asked me if I would appear in their mother's defense. No lawyer likes to refuse a case. But the case could be nothing but a nuisance, and having a sudden inspiration, I told my callers that I would gladly enter my appearance for their mother and conduct her defense but first I would have to have a retainer of twenty-five dollars. They left and I never saw them again.

I am also reminded of an experience with a middle-aged lady, obviously from a farm and equally obviously highly suspicious of lawyers, who marched grimly into my office, sat down, and saying that she had been advised to consult a lawyer, put a half-dollar on the corner of my desk and told me to talk fifty cents' worth, then stop and she would tell me whether she wanted any more of my advice. I hope the advice I gave her was worth the fee.

But do not think for a moment that practice of the law outside of metropolitan centers is made up entirely or even in large part of the kind of practice described by the late Arthur Train in his entertaining stories of Tutt and Mr. Tutt. There is plenty of interesting and important legal work to be done in the smaller cities and eventually you will participate in that work, provided you are industrious and have legal ability.

You need only to start at the bottom, and you *will* start at the bottom in the courthouse as well as in your office. Almost of necessity your early experience in court will be in a minor role with a senior partner or in small cases on your own. Do not dream of making your first appearance in court as counsel in an important case and astounding the court, jury, opposing counsel and the assembled public with your poise, eloquence, and vast knowledge of the law. Important cases rarely are entrusted to a beginner, but if by chance one should come your way and you are practicing alone, you would be well advised to associate yourself with some senior member of the local bar rich in trial experience. You will learn much from such an association, which you will inevitably have if you join a firm, and you will find that you have much to learn from skilled senior members of the bar before you can try a case even passably well.

The way to learn is by carrying the bag for a senior and later by trying small cases alone, such as suing or defending in small claims litigation or defending a client charged in police court with a minor traffic offense. If you like trying cases, however, and have capacity in that important but often sadly neglected phase of the profession, you may confidently expect that in a small community you will relatively soon graduate to trying cases of importance. Then, if you do well, you can enjoy the deep satisfaction that comes from the knowledge of difficult litigation conducted with skill.

But can you make a living practicing law in a small community? Can you make enough to live in reasonable comfort and provide the sort of education and inheritance you want for your children? The answer is: "Yes, of course you can. Witness the tens of thousands of lawyers who are making a very comfortable living indeed out of their practices in small, some even in rural, communities." But do not for one moment think that a good legal education is enough to carry you in a small community, or that you can make a comfortable living without working. You will find plenty of competition from well-trained men of first-rate legal ability, who simply do not choose to live and work in a big metropolitan center.

Thus you must expect to work and work hard to get started. And I mean work at your profession, not at making social contacts. By all means join the local country club if you like to play golf, but do not for a moment think you are going to build a successful practice on the golf links. You will very naturally meet men prominent in the business and social life of your community at the local country club or similar organization. But do not think that legal counsel are chosen just on the basis of a social contact or a golf score. To be sure a friend may give you a small case to try you out. Thus social contacts may provide an opening. But whether you make the most of the opportunity afforded will depend upon your legal competence, and the place to develop legal competence is in your office or in the courthouse, not in the locker room or worse yet the bar of a country club. So play all the golf you want to on holidays or weekends, but not during office hours unless you want success on the links more than success in your legal practice.

This does not mean that you should confine yourself to your profession to the exclusion of everything else. Participate in politics if that appeals to you, but remember that you cannot simultaneously practice law and politics full time, so do not let politics absorb too much of your attention if your goal is a career at the bar. By all means, however, participate in politics part time or in a minor way if you wish. There is always need for able men of character and integrity in local political office, and you can serve your local community well in politics. Moreover, you can reasonably expect to render such service earlier in life in a small community than in a big one—young men in big metropolitan offices have little time to spare from their work—and in a small community you are more likely to become generally known earlier in life.

Also if so inclined, participate in local civic or charitable organizations such as PTA, your church or local hospital. Such organizations are always looking for active, energetic young men and women and if you are cut out for a small-city practice, you will enjoy working with and for people, and will find working for civic, charitable or educational organizations congenial. Furthermore, taking an active interest in political, civic, or charitable affairs will bring you to the favorable attention of your community as a young man with ideas and a serious purpose in life destined to succeed at the bar. If you participate in such activities only for advertising purposes, however, rest assured that your ruse will soon be discovered. Do your best in these activities, as well as in your practice, or you will be marked down as lazy, lacking in ability or as one who does not attend to his responsibilities. News travels fast in small communities.

Now what kind of a practice can you expect to have in a small community? You can, of course, engage in a general practice doing any and every kind of legal work that comes along, from settling estates and preparing tax returns to trying cases at *nisi prius* or on appeal. Some lawyers still have such practices and find them very pleasant and satisfactory indeed. But for a great many years the members of the bar in the United States have tended to become either "trial lawyers" or "office lawyers," either barristers or solicitors, in English terminology. Thus it is likely that you will choose, or perhaps drift into, one category or the other. And in this age of legal proliferation in the race to keep up with our ever more complex society, further specialization, particularly in the "office" category, is far from unusual even in the smaller community.

If you have an interest and think you have talent for trying cases, do not look down upon a trial practice as beneath you or shy away from it because of the hard work involved. There is plenty of room at the trial bar for able men skilled in the art of trying cases, and you can perform notable service in the courtroom not only to your clients but also to the courts. Badly tried cases waste uncounted and uncountable hours, days, weeks, months and, in the long run, years of judicial time at great expense to the public. I could expand upon this subject fervently and at length.

There is now some specialization in the trial practice even in the smaller communities. The defense of persons charged with crime is a definite specialty of its own, and one in desperate need of more dedicated men of character and ability. Unfortunately it appeals to only a few. There is also a growing tendency to specialize in the trial of civil cases, not merely as to subject matter but also as to the side on which one appears. There are today lawyers at the trial bar who are recognized as plaintiffs' lawyers, or as defendants' lawyers, and in consequence usually appear on one side or the other. But in general the trial practice is not yet very highly specialized outside the big metropolitan centers.

If you have no flare for trying cases and an office practice appeals to you, you will find ample room in the smaller communities for practice in that field and for some specialization in it. There is now wide demand for the services of lawyers skilled in tax matters, and demand for lawyers skilled in corporation law and finance, or labor law, or in the settling of estates, or in drawing trusts and in many other specific fields. In the smaller communities you probably cannot practice exclusively in any one special field or subdivision of an office practice. But you can practice in fields that are allied, such as trusts, taxes, and settling estates.

Perhaps you do not now know what aspect of the law will appeal to you. That is not uncommon. Indeed, usually one does not know at the outset how his major legal interest may develop; whether he will want a general practice or want to specialize in office work, or trial work, or want to specialize in some narrow legal field. But time will tell. The chances are that, before you have been in practice very long, you will more or less naturally gravitate into the kind of practice that interests you most, which almost certainly will be the kind of practice best suited to your abilities. One does best that which one enjoys most, so let your inclination shape your career.

Your natural inclinations can also lead you out of the practice of law to law teaching or to judicial office. Also a law practice can lead to a career outside the law altogether. It leads very easily to politics, for that is a logical career for one with legal training, and many of our greatest statesmen have started at the bar, many at the bar of a small community. This country will ever be grateful for the services of men like Thomas Jefferson and Abraham Lincoln, to name but two of the many thousand members of the bar who have served, and are now serving, so well in national, state, and local government.

A small-community practice as well as a big-city practice can also lead to a career in business. Nowadays business is always in need of legal advice of one sort or another and a lawyer with business skills and acumen is not infrequently invited to join the larger corporations, not merely as a house counsel but in the higher echelons of corporate management such as a director and chief legal counsel or even in a purely executive capacity such as a vice president or president. Moreover, if your major interest proves to be finance, a banking career often beckons.

In short, the practice of law, even in a relatively small community, can develop in many different ways and lead in many different directions. How it may develop or where it may lead will depend upon you, your natural inclinations, your character, your industry, and your ability. It will be a dreary cul-de-sac only if you make it so.

To summarize all this, analyze yourself as best you can. Try to decide what you want out of your life at the bar. As a starting point, try to decide whether, by and large, you are primarily interested in legal issues or in people, and whether you get such a thrill out of handling cases involving large sums of money that anything else seems trivial. Decide, too, whether your goal in life is a big income, for if you want an annual income in six figures and think you are one of those rare people who have the personality and ability to rise to the very top of your profession in a big metropolitan center, by all means go to one and try your wings. Also, even though you do not aspire to the pinnacle but still crave the bustle and activity of a big city, wanting to rub elbows with the great in law, finance, or business—or if, caring little for personal contacts, you want to spend your life digging deeper and deeper into some one narrow legal specialty to the complete exclusion of every other branch of the law—then go to a metropolis. Keep this in mind, however. Many men once committed to practice in a big city, but finding the life distasteful, discover that it is difficult to uproot themselves and their families and take the financial risk of starting all over again in a smaller one. The opposite of this has been and still seems to be easier— a lawyer proving himself a success in a small community and then moving on, if he likes, to a larger one.

But if you do not care for life in or near a big city or do not want the pressure of big-city practice, if a comfortable competence is all that you aspire to, and, especially, if you like dealing with people as individuals rather than dealing with matters—that is, if you prefer dealing directly with men and women in all walks of life, coming to know them and their problems at first hand and helping them in person, even though their problems at times may seem slight to you—if this is true of you, then you are cut out for practice in a small community, for there you will find the deep satisfaction of rendering personal service that will make your life at the bar worth while.

12 *The Lawyer*

IN GOVERNMENT

BY JOHN K. CARLOCK
FISCAL ASSISTANT SECRETARY
UNITED STATES DEPARTMENT OF THE TREASURY
Washington, D.C.

JOHN K. CARLOCK

Born: 1912, Globe, Arizona

Phoenix Junior College 1930–31, 1934–35
University of Arizona: LL.B., 1941

U. S. Coast Guard: 1942–45

Worked on various Arizona ranches; U. S. Indian Service, Fort Apache;
  Inspiration Consolidated Copper Company: 1931–34, 1935–38
Temporary Ranger, Grand Canyon National Park: 1939, 1940 (summers)
Student librarian, University of Arizona: 1939–41

Admitted Arizona Bar: 1941
Appointed Law-Clerk-Trainee, Office of General Council, Treasury Department: 1941
Attorney in Office of General Counsel, Treasury Department: 1945–48
Special Assistant to General Counsel: 1948–49
Assistant General Counsel: 1949–52
Senior Assistant General Counsel: 1952–62
Fiscal Assistant Secretary of the Treasury: 1962–

RECENTLY a form letter came to me from a bar-association group studying the problem of retaining lawyers in the government service. Their question: Why had I stayed so long in government? At first the question struck me as odd. You do not ask a lawyer why he has stayed so long in any other practice; you assume that since he went into it in the first place, that is what he wanted to do. But after I had thought about the question for a while, I came to see that it was really not odd at all. For lawyers in great numbers do not seem to be interested in the career possibilities of government service.

Yet, while career service may not be a common goal, we are very accustomed to seeing young law-school graduates coming to the various government agencies and seeking experience. They know that more and more the government is touching the lives of everyone, and they believe vaguely that a few years' experience will enable them, when later they go into practice, to deal with the problems that their clients will have with government. A great many of these young applicants are frank enough, or naïve enough, to say that they are seeking a job for a year or two because they think it will be valuable to them in their careers in private practice.

At the same time we are used to seeing established lawyers, successful in private practice and who now are looking for other challenges, come into the government seeking the prestige and satisfaction of certain important jobs—jobs in the Little Cabinet, for instance, or as agency heads or chief law officers.

But the lawyers who by free and affirmative choice make government their life's work, beginning upon graduation from law school and progressing through the grades, leaving only upon retirement, or upon advancement beyond the limits of career service, cannot be counted in great numbers.

The bar group asked another question: Was I satisfied that my choice was wise? For a flickering moment the thought crossed my mind that the two questions answered each other. If I had not thought my choice was wise, would I have stayed so long? Since I had stayed so long, must I not have thought my choice was wise? As is often the case, however, the impulse toward an aphorism resulted in oversimplification. No one can be objective enough and wise enough in self-analysis to know exactly why he did what he has done as a career; much less can anyone articulate all the reasons that inclined him to do what he proposed to do. The factors are not vegetables that can be weighed in a balance, but a person has a way of deciding these things for himself remarkably well, call it reasoning or intuition or what you will. Sometimes he knows himself what he wants better than he can explain objectively, but then again there is always the possibility that deep within his psyche can be found reasons that he will not avow even to his own conscious mind. Of all the imponderables that go into making his choice, which turns the scales?

Actually, I stayed so long in the government because I could not get a better job. I will leave it to each reader to decide for himself what that statement signifies. What I told the bar group was that for me, given my temperament and my own personal set of illusions and ideals, I am satisfied that my choice was wise. Subjectively it was wise, and that is all that counts.

It is a truism that nothing ever stays the same. Of course it can't. For one thing, the old days, paradoxically recalled with pleasure rather than relief that they are no more, were always the hardest. When I was a kid hanging around ranches, the cowboys always told it that way, and I still believe in both sides of the paradox. Being a last-year law student today is not the same as being a last-year law student in the spring of 1941, but in this case I cannot swear that the old days were harder.

I am trying to convey (perhaps to explain for myself) some of the reasons why I became a government lawyer and there was, it seems to me, one external factor affecting my outlook when I approached the end of law school that is not present today. That was the Great Depression of the 'thirties. I hope I am objective when I say that jobs were not quite as easy to come by then as they are now; it was certainly not a matter then of looking over the field and deciding what you liked. There were no law firms clamoring for my services as I approached graduation, and the prospects of existing while I built up a practice myself, after having already experienced ten years of Depression living, seemed bleak in comparison to an immediate and regular income.

At the same time, the Depression itself contributed to a great growth in government, and to an increasing recognition that government has not only its negative role as a regulator, but, more importantly, an affirmative role in fostering the welfare of its citizens. This and the concomitant increase in government's importance in everyone's daily life seemed, at least in my mind, to be dignifying the role of the career lawyer in government. The government, therefore, seemed to be attracting the better legal talent and the eleemosynary view of government employment, that had long been a part of American political thought, was disappearing. I no longer visualized the government employee as a clerk with a green eyeshade and black sleeve covers, but as an important and respected functionary working in the common cause of improving the human condition. To some extent the government tends to have a less volatile income scale than other legal opportunities, so that in bad times it affords relatively better starting salaries than private opportunities, although in good times it tends to run behind them. Thus in the Depression days, with government expanding because of the Depression at the same time that other opportunities were contracting for the same reason, the government afforded one of the better prospects for a law-school graduate.

I had always liked the public-law aspects of my law-school courses—constitutional law, administrative law, taxation, and so on—but my interest quickened when I learned, early in the spring of 1941, that an alumnus of the law school, well into a successful career in Treasury, had invited applications from prospective graduates. I began to get used to the idea of going to Washington, and, when the bar exam was over, I left the next day to investigate the invitation. I immediately liked the whole atmosphere of the Treasury, from the columned halls and quiet dignity of the building itself to the air of calm confidence I felt surrounding it. Such are the things on which decisions appear to turn. It took no soul searching to decide to take the job that was offered to me.

As I told the bar group that sent me the questionnaire, I am sure that for me this was a wise decision. I can see now that during my first year I did not really understand all the activity, and hardly knew what it was about, but I never regretted my choice. My job was to analyze assets in this country and to determine whether they should be frozen because they were subject to Axis use, either directly subject to that use or because the owners were under Axis pressure. I do not believe I ever fully appreciated the importance of this second reason for our control, and at times I would become disheartened when I thought that we were tying up the assets of innocent human beings. Contrarily, at times the suspicion would cross my mind that the whole operation was dealing only with abstractions. There is no doubt, however, that the public interest was served—my work was used by higher authority with critical perception—and, fortunately for my career, the sort of introspection out of which these irrationalities came never lasted long enough to interfere with what I had been assigned to do. And I was never bored: Washington was an exciting place for me then, as, indeed, it is now.

After about a year I went into the Coast Guard, and, a year later, was assigned to the legal division. This was a stroke of sheerest good fortune, because there I worked with a staff of experienced and highly talented lawyers, attracted by the war effort, and I had the opportunity for informal association with them that contributed more to my development than would have been possible under more normal circumstances. I learned a lot about public law from that exceptional group, and if any of them should read these lines, they will find admitted for the first time the important part they played in shaping my thinking and my aims.

At the end of the war there was a universal desire among servicemen to abjure governmental employment in any form, and I thought that I shared the desire. I thought that I wanted to go back to my home, sink my roots there and become a part of the community, establishing a practice and devoting myself to extricating my neighbors from the difficulties they got themselves into. To that end I used my terminal leave for an on-the-spot survey, interviewing lawyers and other repositories of local influence. I think that that convinced me. The wishing, inspired by distance, had done its old familiar job of making the grass look greener; but when I got close enough to the scene, I could see that private practice did not hold for me what public law does. With some relief at having rid myself of questions and doubts, I returned to the Treasury, and there I have been ever since.

A friend of mine, a brilliant and articulate fellow, who has made a highly successful business of explaining things for people better than they can explain them themselves, always says that he finds it hard to tell people what he does, largely because he doesn't know himself. I often feel that way, too; I guess it is a feeling many of us have in common. I remember a *New Yorker* cover of a little old lady painting in a gallery before a gigantic oil teeming with magnificently bearded satyrs and well-upholstered nymphs. The little old lady, peering myopically at her canvas, was copying one tiny corner of the painting in which there was nothing but one lone bird. Sometimes I feel that I am like the little old lady, that all I can see is a small corner of the painting.

One device we use in the Treasury for explaining our job is to describe our client's business. This has the advantage of producing prodigious figures. We say that our client collects almost one hundred billion in taxes ever year, manages a debt of almost three hundred billion, manufactures three billion coins and twenty-eight billion pieces of such things as currency and stamps every year, and has law-enforcement duties that would supply TV script material into eternity. All this is true, but by itself it falls a bit short of explaining what the lawyers in the Treasury do.

I have noticed that a new General Counsel, the chief law officer in the Treasury, can tend to feel disheartened when he spends all morning working out the wording of a simple letter to a Congressional committee, important at the moment but relatively minor in the larger scheme, only to learn at lunch that there was a ten-billion-dollar offering of securities on which he was not consulted. However, he fails to remember that some earlier General Counsel would, of course, have spent hours on any doubtful aspect of just such offerings; and the new General Counsel will find, soon enough, that he has other colossal problems with which to wrestle.

Later, I will say more on this subject—that it is not the job of the lawyers to run an agency; it is their job to concentrate on the areas of conflict, to prepare the way for management—but now I would like to point out that any lawyer's personal experience in the government will provide illustrations of the kind of momentary discouragement that my mythical new General Counsel encountered. I remember, after I had been in the Treasury for five or six years and had worked closely with an official responsible for several general areas of activity, I mentioned to him one day that in that whole time I had never worked on a problem of the Bureau of Engraving and Printing. All those billions of pieces of currency and stamps were not producing a single legal problem. Out of his greater experience, he suggested that I not become restive—a problem would come up, he predicted. It so happened that a very short time afterward, the Bureau of Engraving and Printing instituted a new program which was fought in every form and in every forum that the ingenuity of its opponents could devise. It was attacked administratively, it was fought legislatively, and it was litigated. The Executive Branch, the Congress, and the courts were its battlegrounds, and there was all the grist that any lawyer could need for his mill.

But something more specific about the legal organization may be called for. The Treasury Department has what they call in Washington, for some reason I have never fully understood, an integrated legal division. It means that all of the lawyers in the department are responsible professionally to the General Counsel, even though they may be administratively attached to one of the operating bureaus. The heads of the various operating units may be the clients, but the General Counsel is the senior partner. There are over seven hundred lawyers on the staff, all but about thirty of whom are assigned to the operating bureaus: the Internal Revenue Service, the Bureau of Customs, the Bureau of the Public Debt, the United States Coast Guard, the Bureau of Narcotics, the Office of the Comptroller of the Currency, the Office of Defense Lending, and the Foreign Assets Control. Heading the legal staff attached to each bureau is a chief counsel, who reports to the General Counsel through one of four Assistant General Counsels. The Chief Counsel for the Internal Revenue Service, heading by far the largest part of the staff, is one of the Assistant General Counsels. There is also a Tax Legislative Counsel, who reports directly to the General Counsel. The titles of the positions provide a clue to the functions with which each staff works: it does not take guesswork to know that if you are in the Bureau of Customs, you will deal with importation of merchandise. But no cataloguing of an agency's activities can convey much of a feeling for what the lawyers really do. Perhaps something on how the lawyers are useful to their agency will, after all, best suggest what they do.

Almost every government lawyer becomes at one time or another the world's greatest living authority on some particular provision of law. That this is true should not be cause for surprise. Agencies are charged with the administration of particular laws; they derive authority from particular laws; they are limited by particular laws. Someone in each agency applies these laws or construes them more than anyone else, and it is always, of course, a lawyer who most consciously wrestles with the areas of doubt. However, no one lawyer can be an authority on all these areas or on all laws affecting the agency. A private practitioner once asked me what a particular law, that came within the Treasury's province, was supposed to mean. I told him that I had never had occasion to be concerned with this particular law or to think about it. I was amused when he seemed surprised that my general experience with Treasury laws had not developed in me an instinct, denied to outside lawyers, for parsing the complicated prose of all of them.

Knowing more than any other human being on earth about a particular law is only a tool. It does not make a man the best lawyer, any more than the best saw makes the best carpenter or the best club makes the best golfer. It is an accomplishment of sorts, but a very minor one, an accomplishment not to be vaunted with pride any more than owning the best saw or the best club. One needs only to reflect on the fleeting nature of the accomplishment to realize this: if you do not deal with the statute for a few months and somebody else does, then he becomes the world's greatest authority.

This knowledge about the law does have a certain usefulness, to be sure. It speeds up the counseling process and is of great assistance to any lawyer, from the highest to the lowest, in a government agency. The sheer volume of problems in any agency would delay decision-making, actually slowing it almost to a halt, if every problem had to be approached from the beginning. Yet without people who know where the statutes are, and how they have been construed before, each problem would necessarily have to be approached in this way. However, as important as this knowledge is, as useful as it is, let me make it clear that the knowing of certain specific facts is not the one essential token, the single distinguishing countersign, that attests a good lawyer.

In a government agency, there is generally someone who knows more about any given provision of law, with which that agency deals, than the chief law officer himself knows. Certainly this is true in agencies like the Treasury that are concerned with thousands of provisions of statutory law. It is an inexorable fact that the man who forms the peak of a pyramid cannot specialize in the same manner as those who form its great bulk and base. Just so, the chief law officer of a government agency does not have to know more about the laws of the agency than members of the staff know. To be effective, however, he must have the attributes that are the distinguishing mark of a good lawyer.

In the Treasury Department the title of the chief law officer, fixed by statute, is General Counsel and this title suggests the key, in the best and most simple terms, I think, to the abilities that are the mark of the good government lawyer. It is not, as I have said, his role to run an agency, but to counsel the people who do run it.

Suppose you reflect on the word "counsel." As you do, you will realize, I am sure, that *counsel* can never be fulfilled merely by exploiting legal technicalities. The essence of the lawyer's craftsmanship, in both public and private law, lies not in technicalities but rather in a variety of skills, and, of course, in judgment. It lies, for example, in practical, inventive, persuasive, skills in getting things done. There must, of course, be effectiveness in finding the correct rule of law; but there must also be effectiveness in getting done whatever needs to be done, in whatever field it is needed. This craftsmanship lies in skills for conceiving actions, for co-ordinating the efforts necessary for their accomplishment, and for utilizing the results. Most important of all, it lies in judgment—judgment in selecting desired results, judgment in selecting the means to obtain them. This is the art of the profession, and this is the craftsmanship of which lawyers can be proud. These are the abilities that a good lawyer has to offer, and there is no place in which he can reveal, more quickly and more surely, the extent to which he has them, than in the intricate business of government.

Early in my career in government, I had the personal experience of seeing the distinguishing marks of the good lawyer manifest themselves graphically. I had worked hard on a problem, one I felt was important. I had worked out the law, but I was assailed by doubts of many kinds, and I had only a few minutes to explain all this to my boss as we walked down the corridor to a group meeting, outlining all that I could of the problem after my days of research and reflection. Troubled by my own doubts and misgivings, it seemed certain to me that my boss, after such a meager briefing, would not be able to handle the meeting. But it did not turn out that way at all, because this lawyer knew his trade. Knowing it, he could take the few coherent facts I had conveyed to him and present a thesis so irresistible that I could hardly recognize the pale reflection of it in my own mind.

He did not need to know the law until I told it to him, because a lawyer's judgment told him where he wanted to come out and a lawyer's skill told him how to get there. Judgment told him when to talk and when to keep quiet, what to emphasize and what to de-emphasize, when to agree on a small point to win a big one, when to press and when to withdraw, which technicalities were important and which ones were not. By a lawyer's skills, he worked out the result and persuaded others to accept it. That example of the essence of the craft of the lawyer impressed me. I have seen it many times since, and I am sure that every junior lawyer has seen it, certainly all of those who market their wares in a complex of institutional relationships like the government.

We have to have a government, so the old joke says, because there are some things we can't blame on our wives. In a democracy it is natural that the government should provide this safety valve for letting off steam. Use of the government as a whipping boy has long been accepted in the American conscience, just as the parasitic view of government employment has prompted overtones in our humor.

For some years I was inordinately sensitive to these barbs. I took all attacks on the government personally, and all jibes at the charity of government employment seriously, and I was indignant that they should be spoken. I assumed, perhaps guiltily, that people who attacked the government, because they subscribed to a political philosophy different from the philosophy prevailing when I went into government, did not approve of my choice of a career. I had a friend who knew he could always annoy me by mentioning that now that I had my feet in the trough, no one would ever see me back in Arizona. After some twenty years in government, I can see these things in a more detached and philosophic light. I no longer regard it as my duty to defend every action the government takes; in fact, I realize that it would be morally dishonest to try to do it. And I no longer feel obliged to defend my honor for every passing slight on government employment. Some people can understand these things instinctively; they can respond to humor and brush off anything that is otherwise motivated. I had to learn a harder way, through the process of getting older. It is much better to learn the first way.

A part of these comments on government, humorous and otherwise, is owing to the fact that it is possible, in our system, for conflict to exist between those who are in career service and those who are political appointees. Fortunately, so it seems to me, this conflict does not exist to any really important degree. What little there is, I believe, is more within the mind than in actuality. I remember one time, after a change in administration, I was sent to talk to a ranking lawyer in another agency about a program that the Treasury believed was desirable. We in Treasury had no doubts about our legal authority, and I was surprised when the other agency's lawyer, despite our efforts to persuade, disagreed. Later, at a meeting attended by a number of both career men and political people, I reported the state of negotiations to one of our new officials, a very thoughtful and intelligent man, but one with strong views on the differences between the parties. He looked at me for a moment, and then said, "Is he a hold-over from the last administration?" The question was so ludicrous, so obviously unreasonable, that everyone in the room, including the man who had asked it, burst out laughing. I know that there has been conflict between career men and political appointees in government; but I think that such conflict is the exception, and I believe there has been almost none of it in Treasury. I am quite certain there has been none in the legal division.

I have found it almost unbelievable how little the changes in administrations affect the exercise of a Treasury lawyer's functions, how little they involve his philosophic principles. Old programs give way and new programs are begun, of course; but this happens every day, with, or without, changes in the administration. For the lawyer, the government has programs, the Treasury has programs, and it is the lawyer's privilege to share in constructing them; but, by and large, they come and go, so far as the lawyer's role is concerned, without significant identification with any political philosophy.

However, one thing is sure, regardless of what changes are taking place: no lawyer in government should attempt to insulate himself from the possibility of involvement by withdrawing into the seclusion of his technical specialty. Perhaps the private practitioner can function successfully as an autonomous unit, but in government there is no possible way of dividing functions so that they are really self-contained. If government lawyers want to be effective participants in the administrative scheme, they have no choice but to relinquish the safety of their technical specialty. In government, just as much as in business, the executives are interested in results, not means; they are interested in accomplishments, not techniques. And this drive for results is not a practice of the officials at the top only, a determination of the top lawyer only; instead, it is generated and regenerated in every operating unit down the line. The process makes sharp demands upon each lawyer, but it also gives each his opportunity, providing the single greatest privilege in being a government lawyer, the privilege of feeling the life that runs through the agency and being an active part of it.

A few years ago I sat with a panel of lawyers, discussing the role of the lawyer in government. At the meeting the thesis was postulated that an agency lawyer had some inherent and compelling responsibility, superior even to that of the agency head, to determine whether various courses of action can or cannot be undertaken. The theory seemed to be that the lawyer, by virtue of having taken the oath as a member of the bar, had acquired some duty—divine, sovereign, or constitutional, I am not quite sure which—to be the final arbiter of right and wrong. I cannot quite agree with this philosophy, though I have found it widely and earnestly held. Certainly it is the agency lawyer's duty to make his views felt by the agency head; for without that, his counseling becomes a cipher. Certainly he must have ideals, for technique without ideals is dangerous. But I do not believe that the ritual of becoming a member of the bar invests a government lawyer with a power of life and death over the agency he serves. The agency head takes his own oath of office, and he is also subject to the inscrutable forces of public opinion. In carrying out his responsibility to decide policy, the agency head looks to his lawyer's counseling as one of his strongest supports; but the lawyer's counsel can never usurp the decision which must be made by the responsible head of the agency.

If an agency lawyer feels strongly enough that he does not want to be associated with a given program, he can, of course, always resign. There is a well-known story of a high Treasury official, long before my time in the Treasury, who resigned because he did not agree that authority existed for a course of action the Secretary had decided was best in the national interest. The official no doubt had high moral incentives, but I look back at that episode as a lesson for the lawyer who would believe that the welfare of mankind turns on the acceptance of his legal view; because, from the vantage point of time, that legal issue now looks like a quibble.

No lawyer is wise enough to decide that his concept of legal principle can never give way to the course of action a responsible administrator, charged with a legal duty and clothed with a Constitutional responsibility, thinks is wise. If the lawyer's skills as a counselor cannot convince the administrator that he is heading down a dangerous course, then how can he be sure that his judgment as a lawyer is infallible? Any government lawyer who thinks his legal conclusion has some divine significance would do well to remember Lincoln's answer: "Are all the laws but one to go unexecuted, and the government itself to go to pieces lest that one be violated?" Lincoln's instincts were sounder than those of some of his professional legal advisers. Let the agency lawyer who stakes his reputation on disagreeing beware: time and history have a way of vindicating the rightness of actions responsible officers have found necessary.

In a government agency, a lawyer's art is utilized in a great variety of ways, and his special influence generally goes far beyond the range of duties ordinarily reported in official descriptions of his job. In the formative stage of policy, for example, the lawyers within an agency may disagree sharply, both with administrators and among themselves. Their very training as lawyers incline them to advocacy, and until policy is fixed each will argue his own views. To some extent this internal controversy, impossible to describe or to evaluate, is essential to the construction of beneficial policy, and the earnestness with which lawyers develop their own points of view is certainly an asset to the agency. But it should be recognized that the zest of government lawyering comes from being a part of a common enterprise, from assuming a place in an organization bound together by a common mission, from being in the main stream of the agency's activities. The great bulk of government lawyers know this deeply and surely, and that is why our system of changing political administrations need cause no concern for the loyalty of the career lawyer.

Many of the higher executive positions in government are held by lawyers, and legal training is generally recognized as one of the better preparations for these positions. I once heard a Secretary of the Treasury say that, since he was not a lawyer, he thought that the Under Secretary, the number two man in the department, should be a lawyer. Indeed, in the last fifteen years three of the five Secretaries of the Treasury have been lawyers. For an even better percentage, four of the six Under Secretaries have been lawyers. Eight of the fourteen Assistant Secretaries have been lawyers, and, narrowing this down to the Treasury's one nonspecialized position of Assistant Secretary, seven out of seven have been lawyers.

Appointments to all these positions are made by the President, after confirmation by the Senate. For this reason we use a simple catch phrase to describe them: we call them "political appointments." Because of the method of the appointment, these officials, after having been associated with one administration at a high level, ordinarily can be expected to be replaced when there is a change of administration.

There is another side to this coin: it is unusual for a person already in government service to receive a political appointment. In this respect, therefore, a career in government becomes a handicap. Presumably the reason that a career employee seldom reaches an appointed position is that he has adapted himself to changes of administration, working under one and then another, and this militates against his selection for political jobs. It might be noted that in the British system offices are regarded as political only at the top Cabinet level. The career service in this system extends up through the Under Secretary level; but in our government the line, traditionally, has been drawn further down the career scale.

In the Treasury Department there has been a General Counsel only since 1934, but since that time there have been eleven of them. It goes without saying that they all have been lawyers, but I can add that they all have been good lawyers, respected by other officials and by their own staff; hence lawyers one could be proud and happy to work under and with. I feel sure of this because I, while Assistant General Counsel, worked for nine of the eleven, and I know the kind of men they have been. There has been the widest differences in their personalities, the greatest range of talents, but each has had qualities of skill and judgment that make the good lawyer. Any lawyer who is a good lawyer, because of these qualities, will be a good government lawyer.

The General Counsel of the Treasury is appointed by the President after Senate confirmation, and his job, therefore, is regarded as political. Sometime ago I was surprised when my father mentioned that he supposed I would never want to be a General Counsel of the Treasury, because then my tenure would be insecure. For the first time it occurred to me that if my own father thought this, then so might others—even those charged with making recommendations for the appointment of a General Counsel. I took pains to make sure that any such beliefs, if they existed, were not perpetuated. Of course, any agency lawyer worth his salt wants to be the chief law officer of his agency. Like a Supreme Court judgeship it is not, as Mr. Justice Brandeis once said, something that anyone turns down.

But, as I have already told you, it is very difficult to break through the barrier between career service and a political appointment. It is something of a paradox that a man who starts at the bottom in the government can hardly hope to work up to the top legal job of his agency. The position is not foreclosed to him, of course, but for him to achieve it is unlikely. Fortunately, however, it is true that the career horizon in government is broadening, and, perhaps before long, our system will become more like the British system.

Whatever a lawyer's future may be, whatever his career horizon, there is a real attraction for any lawyer in public service, an attraction that can justify itself under an objective analysis. It is the privilege of having a client with a public interest: which is to say, a client with *selfless* interests. An enduring satisfaction can come to a government lawyer, not because of any possible altruism of his own in choosing his career, but because, day in and day out, he is engaged in promoting the general benefit of the body politic, rather than the interests of any group or individual, no matter how deserving those private interests may be.

There is a consciousness now—in private law no less than in government—that the object of the law is to serve right and justice. Lawyers know that the great mass of people feel this, and they have learned, I am convinced, that their responsibilities are clear and fixed. For the lawyer in government service, there can never be a question of his responsibility: in public administration, he must, without hesitancy, put the public interest first. This is the responsibility, and the privilege, of any lawyer who devotes himself to public service.

13 *The*

WOMAN LAWYER

BY FLORENCE M. KELLEY

ADMINISTRATIVE JUDGE
FAMILY COURT OF THE STATE OF NEW YORK
New York, New York

FLORENCE M. KELLEY

Born: 1912, New York, New York

Baldwin School
Smith College: B.A., 1934
Yale Law School: LL.B., 1937
Smith College: LL.D., 1960

Hull House, Chicago: 1933 (summer)
Rhode Island State Labor Department: 1935, 1936 (summers)
Assistant District Attorney, New York County (Appointed by Thomas E. Dewey): 1938–42
Appointed by Frank Hogan: 1942
Associate in Simpson Thacher and Bartlett: 1942–47
Attorney-in-Charge Criminal Branch Legal Aid Society: 1947–60
Presiding Justice, Domestic Relations Court: 1960–61
Appointed Administrative Judge in New York City of state-wide Family Court: 1961

Governor's Committee to Review Parole System in New York State: 1957–59
New York Joint Legislative Committee to Study Narcotics: 1956–58
U. S. Delegate to Congress at New Delhi, International Commission of Jurists: 1959
Advisory Council of Judges, National Council on Crime and Delinquency
New York City Commission for the Foster Care of Children
National Council of Juvenile Court Judges
Treasurer, New York State Association of Children's Court Judges
American Law Institute: Criminal Law Advisory Committee for drafting Model Penal Code
Trustee League School for Emotionally Disturbed Children
Director, Florence Crittenton League, Barrett House

Reginald Heber Smith Award, National Legal Aid and Defender Association: 1961
Huntington-Manning Medal from Youth Consultation Service: 1962

IN LOOKING BACK to the period of time before I graduated from college in the spring of 1934, it is impossible to be sure now what the compelling reasons were then for my willingness or eagerness to attend law school. After over twenty-five years of full enjoyment of the legal profession it is easy to think that I was smart enough back then, or perceptive enough, to want to undertake law training. I am fearful that the intervening years, which have been such gratifying ones, now serve to color what the true picture was in my senior year, 1933–34, at Smith College. I am convinced that I am in no position to tell a girl in her junior or senior year in college why she should want to go to law school and pursue a legal career. But the possibilities in the legal profession for a female law-school graduate who has somehow lived through passing her bar exams are so numerous and varied, and the opportunities for a gratifying life at law so wonderful, that I enjoy looking upon them.

I admit to being entirely mystified by the motivating forces acting upon college students which impel them toward one pursuit rather than any one of the myriad other pursuits. The possibility that any of these motivating forces are amenable to change, influence, or guidance by an external force, fascinates me. In my own case, I have no way of knowing how much I was influenced to attend law school by the fact that in my senior year in college I studied constitutional law under a young and handsome professor who himself had very much wanted to attend law school but had not been in a position to do so. This, it must be understood, was a constitutional-law class that dealt very little with law. This was a course primarily concerned with historical chronology of legal decisions and legislation in the field of constitutional law. I found the subject fascinating. I also found the professor fascinating. And it is true that he asked whether or not I had ever considered studying law.

On a certain day after the seminar period he showed me an application blank for the Yale Law School. At the same time there were numbers of my friends in their senior year at men's colleges who were enthusiastically seeking entrance to various law schools. Perhaps I should not overlook the fact that I was coming to the end of four years in a woman's college. It is true that on week ends our campus took on somewhat the aspect of a co-educational institution, but during the week days it was certainly a preponderantly female world.

It may be that my wish to enter the legal field was born even before my senior year in college. My family consisted of an extremely lovable and feminine mother, a strong father—a lawyer—and two brothers, one two years older than I and the other two years younger. Ours was an extremely male-geared family. I liked the male world that I saw and wanted to be allowed to share in it, not competitively but simply to be allowed to be there. It may very well have been that law school, particularly Yale Law School, seemed to me the male world and, therefore, very alluring. I wanted to study law in this wonderful male world. My father was a graduate of Harvard Law School. My older brother was, at the time, a student there. In my particular Kelley male world I might well have preferred the even more male world of the Harvard Law School, but had been told that women students were not admitted because the law school did not have the toilet facilities to make the admission of women possible.

Whether or not it ever entered my mind when I chose to go to law school that I might eventually practice law is a matter that it is impossible for me now to determine. After I had been in law school somewhat over two weeks I had become completely won and enthralled by law as a subject of study. Mind you, the male world of the law school had somewhat given way to the wealth of the subject of law. The glittering Phi Beta Kappa keys on manly watch chains ceased to intimidate me. The fact that in every classroom I had been surrounded by a solid ring of vacant seats became a fact of no concern to me whatsoever. Never before had I had the stimulation of mind and the satisfaction of discovery that I experienced in my introduction to the study of law. So strong was, and is, my feeling about the law that my emotional attachment to the Yale Law School and each and every one of my classmates in the Yale Class of 1937 has grown stronger with every year.

Old Blackacre had really got me. Every case I was asked to study seemed more fascinating and intriguing than any puzzle or mystery story. The concept of building present case law from past experience, reflected in judicial decision, appealed to me in every way. How exciting for me was the study of law as a moving, living pattern for human action and behavior, cast in terms of the needs and acceptances of society and the community. How revealing of human nature was the study of law, dramatizing, in the unfolding of a case in decision or briefs, the behavior and activities of the plaintiff and respondent as well as other parties in interest which ultimately formed the basis of the litigation.

Not the least pleasure was the intellectual discipline of the study of the law. What higher goal could there be than to weigh and evaluate fairly and objectively? What other study can there be which offers as its field the universally interesting rules by which all of us must live? If you should ask me why this training in law should be appealing to women, I would answer, "Why should it not be appealing to everyone?" A student who is fascinated by the subject matter of the study of law will not be troubled about the incidental fact that she is a female student. Such matters as "female aggression," "beating men at their own game," the advisability of assuming severe masculine garb, and all similar matters simply do not occur to the woman student who has discovered for herself the wonderful world of the law.

By nothing I have said do I mean to leave what would be a very false impression, that the law schools are eagerly enlisting female applicants. Nothing could be further from the truth. Few top-grade law schools allowed women students before World War II. Those that did carefully limited the number of such students in proportion to the total number of law students. During World War II, when so many of the young men who would have been applying for admission to law school were otherwise occupied, many law schools increased the proportionate number of female students in order to fill their classes. This evidently was not a totally unsatisfactory move. After World War II the number of female law students was never again reduced to the figure that it had been prior to the war.

In law schools where a "legal aptitude" test is given I have no doubt at all that the fact that an applicant is a woman is "taken into consideration." I do not believe for a minute that this policy is anything but realistic. After graduation from law school, a woman lawyer is going to have a more difficult time in finding a legal position than her male ex-classmate who received the very same grades. In my senior year, when members of my class were seeking future jobs in New York City, I understood that there was a limited number of firms who were willing to interview female law students at all. This seemed eminently fair to me. As a matter of fact the firms which were unwilling to state frankly that they had no intention whatsoever of hiring a woman lawyer, but instead proceeded to make elaborate appointments with them, were the ones I thought were unfair. I assumed that it was a great waste of time for the busy partners who interviewed the women students. Then, too, why were they not willing to recognize the fact that a law student on Christmas or spring vacation has a limited time in which to find a job?

Speaking now of the spring of 1937, in which the echoes of a recent depression were still heard, I quickly exhausted the list of those law firms which Yale Law School advised me might possibly be willing to employ a woman lawyer. So I tried another plan and I found that I could visit more law firms and be turned down more often in one day by going to a large downtown building and entering every law office on every floor, whether I had ever heard of the particular law firm or not. In this imaginative way I would say that in almost record time I had been turned down by every large and small law firm in the City of New York in the downtown area. Well, I had been warned it was a man's world and I had taken my chances.

My only moment of real chagrin occurred when I learned from an ex-classmate of mine that he had been accepted by a firm in which I had been told by a partner that should my marks be higher than those of a male classmate, I would be offered a job. Perhaps that partner really did not know that everyone in my class knew perfectly well what the marks of everyone else were. My marks were a great deal higher than those of my lucky and happy classmate. This, I thought, was dirty pool, not that I should be excluded from the wonderful male world of law, but that the rules of exclusion should be set forth to me in a way which was not followed.

But women do get jobs in the legal profession. Many more do now than in that long-ago spring of 1937. It is true that neither law firms nor public agencies are yet sending representatives to the law schools to seek to interest women students in a legal position; but many women in law have made excellent records and in recognition of those records many doors of opportunity have opened, an opportunity to be a lawyer, not a woman lawyer but a lawyer.

There is no room in the field of law for the woman who wishes to be extended every gracious gesture that is her due in her contact with men in her social life, while at the same time insisting upon absolute fairness and equality in her professional life. She may, by being an able and devoted lawyer, earn a position of respect in the practice of law. As a lawyer she will never be able to command or demand special treatment because she is a woman, and at the same time win recognition as a good practitioner. Every time a woman lawyer indulges in "vagaries," "the misery," "sick headaches," or other wonderful vague female physical ailments in order to make it impossible for her to accept the unpopular assignment, she is making it a great deal harder for every woman who wishes to practice law in a man's world. And every time a woman lawyer takes the assignments as they come, does her share of the dirty work, asks no quarter, practices law to the best of her ability, she will enjoy the practice of the law in the male world on a satisfying basis for herself. I fear I made a great many enemies when I was asked to address a women's bar group recently and told the members that I was convinced they should spend less time worrying about how unfairly they were treated because they were women, and spend more time in trying to develop themselves as capable practitioners of the law.

Realistically, of course, women lawyers are sometimes treated if not unfairly, then certainly differently than their male counterparts. Obviously, any intelligent woman contemplating a career at law must expect this and deal with it. I have a few sharp little memories of my own. But I am getting ahead of my own story.

I finally did get a legal job and a wonderful one. This opportunity came at a time when I had already accepted employment as a research assistant to a former law-school professor of mine who had undertaken to write an article on the law for *Fortune* magazine. Some time before I had gratefully accepted this job, I had been interviewed in the office of the District Attorney for New York County. Now, having committed myself as a research assistant, I was advised that my application at the district attorney's office had been approved for the position of legal investigator. I found myself in a real quandary.

January, 1938, had seen Thomas E. Dewey move from the office of Special Prosecutor to the elective office of District Attorney for New York County. These were the days of the "Racket Buster" Dewey. These were the days when the citizens of New York had demonstrated their eagerness for forceful law enforcement by giving Mr. Dewey the nomination for district attorney by three parties. Mr. Dewey had electrified the City as Special Prosecutor by his vigor, high ideals, and ability to bring into public service, joining him in his fight against organized crime, recent graduates of the best law schools of the country. These were the young lawyers who in other years would have sought employment in downtown corporation law firms. These young lawyers had little resemblance to the general run of lawyer who entered the criminal law field, either as defense lawyer or as prosecutor. They had great dreams of a city freed from organized crime, and, by the same token, many of them were unfamiliar with the city in its entirety and few of them, in their naïveté, even knew the name of their district leader. The prospect of working in such an office seemed too good to be true. But, as I say, I had already accepted another job.

On my own initiative I do not believe I could have brought myself to tell my former law professor that I wished to be freed from my commitment to him in order to accept a more enticing job. But our class of 1937 at Yale Law had been a very close one and I had briefly conferred with two or three of my friends in that class, ruefully telling them that I must refuse the job at the district attorney's office. We were all wont to inform one another of any vacancy we might learn of in any law office or government agency dealing with law, and before I officially refused the position I wanted my friends to pass on the word that there would be an opening at the district attorney's office. Instead, they passed on the word to my law professor and he, a kind and understanding person, telephoned me within an hour to release me from my undertaking with him and to congratulate me on the opportunity that had been offered me.

How very stirring the job at the district attorney's office proved to be! Most of us on the staff had lived a great part of our lives in the City of New York, but now we were to see a side of New York that was entirely new to us. Many of us had led somewhat sheltered lives. Our only picture of the city's underworld, viewed through movies and stories, seemed an exaggerated and distorted one. Actually, we were to learn that this picture understated the real conditions. After announcement of my appointment to Mr. Dewey's staff appeared in the city press I received countless threatening letters, most of them anonymous. This seemed to me the final stamp of guarantee of a truly thrilling job. My mother and father, with whom I was living at the time, reacted to these letters but not quite in the same way that I had.

During the ensuing years I pursued the practice of law in a setting of detectives, secret investigations, witnesses produced from protective custody, handcuffs, endless interrogations, Q and A's signed and unsigned, confidential police information, and all the trappings of the grim hunt for legal proof against the organized marauders of our city's society.

I was to learn with a great deal of shock and consternation that one of the forces that will always be the hardest for a prosecutor to deal with is the strong urge of the private citizen to fight free of ever being personally involved in the prosecution of crime. From my earliest days in school I had been given some kind of concept of the private citizen's duty to his community and to the maintenance of an orderly life for that community. A citizen's duty I had been taught involved more than observance of the law; it involved whatever activity was necessary to guarantee law observance in a community in which to live and raise a family. Now I was to learn that many of our outstanding and seemingly upright citizens would much prefer to pay tribute to the rackets than assume the role of a complaining witness against those rackets. It was all very well that a prosecutor's office was eager to bring the racketeer to the bar of criminal justice, but without a complaining witness how could this be done? In all fairness to the citizen, it should be remembered that these were days of violent reprisals.

A man who was victimized by the rackets had a very hard choice to make. Would he fight back against the racket through the law-enforcement agency, hoping that somehow he and his wife and children would be protected? Even if he did this, testifying as a complaining witness, the prosecuting office could not assure him that the persons against whom he testified would be convicted and, if convicted, removed from society.

One man who was persuaded to testify against organized crime found tragically that, having assumed all the risks that this entailed, the defendants against whom he testified were convicted, but the conviction was reversed by an appellate court. The case was tried finally three times. During this dragging, protracted period of trial, conviction, reversal, retrial, second conviction, another reversal, another retrial and conviction, his wife died violently. It became necessary to hide his two small daughters in a convent upstate. He was allowed during the lengthy preparation for the trial to visit with these two girls only when they were brought to an office in the district attorney's building by some extremely courageous nuns. The witness himself assumed the guise of an engineer on the custodial staff of the building. How well I remember these Saturday morning visits, the sweet-faced nuns, the small, timid children, the man whose past associations and present role placed him in mortal danger every minute of the day. Now if you think this sounds like a movie you vaguely remember having seen some time ago, you are right. An associate of mine in the district attorney's office used this as the basis for a movie which enjoyed wide circulation.

One of my most interesting experiences during these days was a chance acquaintanceship made actually in the district attorney's office. A bright young lawyer, who had acted as counsel for one of the top members of the rackets, was married to a very beautiful red-haired show girl of whom he was extremely fond. The lawyer had agreed to turn state's evidence against the racketeer, and, for his own safety, he was being held in protective custody. In order to keep him firm in his resolve to testify for the state, he was allowed to see his wife when he was brought in for interrogation.

These meetings between the lawyer and his wife were very carefully planned. He would be secretly produced in the office of one of the assistant district attorneys who was busily preparing the case and his wife would, by chance, be sitting in the waiting room of my office which was two doors away. At some time, the lawyer would be led past my waiting room under heavy guard and he would be able to speak to her briefly.

Now, on many of these occasions, the wife would spend hour after hour waiting for this "chance" brief meeting. She would often bring with her a close friend, another show girl; as a matter of fact, one of the world's greatest strip-teasers. These two gorgeous ladies would sit endlessly smoking cigarettes and gossiping a few feet from the open door of my office. I suppose it was inevitable that they, with their beautiful furs and magnificent jewels, would find me an object of real curiosity. I evidently intrigued them as much as they intrigued me. I have the fondest memories of our conversations, which were invariably friendly but lacking entirely in any basis of mutual understanding.

First of all, out of the sheer kindliness of their hearts they offered to send me to their hairdresser, beautician, tailor, dressmaker, furrier, jeweler, and masseuse at reduced rates. They questioned me pointedly about my salary, which I think truly at that time would more accurately be described as wages and then, of course, looked fittingly embarrassed and sad at the answer. No two ladies ever worked harder and more sincerely to improve my prospects in life. Their good advice as to how I should pursue my future, how I could catch a husband or a "friend," I still cherish.

I tried in every way I knew to show my appreciation; but the friendlier I tried to be, the harder they struggled to give me the benefits of their knowledge of the world of men and of money, and of how a female should go about separating one from the other to the female's best advantage. I hope that in some small measure these two birds of paradise did realize the admiration and affection the drab sparrow felt for them.

At the end of the trial we separated, the red-haired beauty to accompany her husband to a small obscure town in the West to open a soft drink stand and hope for anonymity; the strip-tease star to rise to even greater heights; and I to continue practicing law. Shortly after the news of my marriage appeared in the papers, I received a telephone call at three o'clock in the morning. It was a long-distance call. "Well, kid! You finally made it. All the best of good luck, kid. Good-bye!" The voice was husky, charming, slightly boozy. It was the last time I was to hear the voice of my erstwhile, exotic red-haired friend.

The fact that the staff of the district attorney's office was concerned, for the most part, with the trial of cases in the courtroom gave to the practice of the law there a unique aspect. Even in the litigation departments of downtown law firms a recent graduate from law school cannot really expect to find himself or herself a court lawyer, civil or criminal. The excitement and the drama of the courtroom are almost indescribable. I had not been on the staff of the district attorney's office long before I was assigned to a trial court.

It is true that the cases I presented on behalf of the People of the County of New York were misdemeanors, lesser crimes; but to me the excitement of such a trial was no less than the trial of the most serious felony. The real difference lies in the fact that in New York City a misdemeanor is tried by a bench of three judges who act as both judge and jury, whereas a felony case is heard by a judge and a jury. Nothing will be gained by discussing the relative merits, so far as the prosecuting attorney is concerned, of presenting his case to judges without a jury, or to a judge and a jury. This is a subject which can be discussed at any time when a member of the staff of one prosecuting attorney meets a member of the staff of another prosecuting attorney.

I could not have enjoyed my pursuit of the law any more than I did in the four and a half years that I served first as a criminal investigator, and then as an Assistant District Attorney, for New York County. Then came World War II. The downtown law firms had a very serious decision to make. Their young men were volunteering or were being drafted. The senior partners needed to decide whether they would go to the library and look up the law points which they required or whether they were willing now to employ female lawyers—a tough decision, indeed. I would say that they chose correctly. They chose to employ lady lawyers.

One of the law firms that I had wanted very much to be employed by telephoned and asked me to come in for an interview. I could not have been more surprised when I learned that they had kept my name on file and that they had taken the trouble to find out where I was working. I hastened to assure them that I was wonderfully happy where I was. I was urged to come for an interview in any case. Now, just as at law school I had fallen in love with law, so in the district attorney's office I had fallen particularly in love with the practice of criminal law, with all its aspects of vigorous prosecutions, protection of the community, and protection of the innocent against false charges. On the other hand, as my father so fairly stated, I could not possibly prefer the practice of criminal law to the practice of civil law if I had never pursued the practice of civil law. I was curious, too, to know what would take place at the interview. My curiosity won, as it so often does.

The interview was very simple. Did I want a job with the firm? For many reasons, of course, I did not. I was happy where I was. The practice of criminal law is for the most part divorced from research in a law library. I had great doubts that after four and a half years of criminal practice I would be able to do acceptable legal research. But there was a senior partner in this particular firm whom I had long admired and respected. When he looked me in the eye and said that after many, many years of existence the firm had decided to employ its first woman lawyer and he very much hoped that I would be that first woman lawyer, I knew that I would enjoy the association, fearful of it as I was.

The firm as a whole was extremely kind to me and considerate. Those of the young male lawyers who were left, obviously saw me as no possible threat. However, this move to hire a female lawyer had not been a unanimous decision on the part of the partners. One large, impressive, and full-throated partner had protested and never ceased to protest. Some of my young male associates had taken a great deal of pleasure in telling me that this one partner was irreconcilably opposed to the firm's employment of a woman.

He marched into my small cubicle one day and in resounding tones said, "I am Mr. So-and-So. How do you do? You stay down at your end of the hall and I will stay at my end of the hall. In this way everything will work out very well." Then he departed. I trembled slightly and tried to convince myself that the whole thing had never really happened. Sometime later, through an intermediary, he had me sent, representing one of the firm's clients, to the Municipal Court to defend an action in which there was no defense. Having successfully withstood being bodily ejected from the court, I returned to the office and reported to the intermediary. He seemed somewhat flustered. Later, I was to learn that the partner had high hopes that my experience in the courtroom would somehow convince me to go home and stay home.

I really did enjoy my years of association with this large firm. I was fortunate enough to have the opportunity to work, in a very minor capacity, a good deal of the time with the partner whom I considered then, and still do consider, one of the outstanding litigation lawyers of the country. This opportunity has been one of the high points of my life at law. This same partner, as it happened, was elected President of the Legal Aid Society.

The Attorney-in-Charge of the Criminal Branch of the Legal Aid Society was assuming the job of Attorney-in-Chief, on the sudden and shocking demise of the man who had held the position so honorably for so many years. This left the position of Attorney-in-Charge of the Criminal Branch vacant. I was asked if I would consider taking it.

It so happens that the Legal Aid Society was and is a highly respected charitable organization operating a unique legal service in New York City. It was started many years ago by members of the bar. Its Board of Directors consists of some of the most outstanding legal practitioners in the city. This is a board that meets regularly and carefully considers every aspect of the operation of the Society. Membership on the board is eagerly sought and regularly yields up presidents of the Association of the Bar of the City of New York.

The Legal Aid Society provides legal representation to those persons who need it and are unable financially to provide it for themselves. The Criminal Branch of the Society asks no fees for the services of its staff to represent persons who cannot afford the fee of a private criminal attorney, even one who is not very competent. The work of the staff of the Criminal Branch is greatly augmented by prominent, private practitioners who volunteer to accept cases when called upon.

I wanted that job as Attorney-in-Charge more than any other job I had ever thought of. Now that I had had some practice in the civil field, I realized that I did, indeed, prefer the criminal field. As a matter of fact, during the next thirteen years of my life I was to enjoy the most gratifying law practice that anyone can conceive of, but getting the job was not very easy. The president of the Legal Aid Society was willing to offer me the position, but there was a certain amount of resistance from within the Board of the Society and this was resistance because I was a woman. I do not think the president convinced the opposition so much as the opposition was willing to allow him his choice of the person to fill the position. The battle did not end there.

After I had been duly installed as Attorney-in-Charge of the Criminal Branch, one of the judges presiding over one of the courts in which I would be appearing advised the Legal Aid Society that he would never again assign a case to the Society as long as the head of the Criminal Branch was a woman. Then began a strange and harrowing interlude in my life. Every day, after this judge had adjourned court at the end of the court day, he would send for me. For anywhere from one to three hours he would then explain to me his position, which was that his opposition to me was not personal, but on the valid ground that a woman should not be the head of a legal operation in the criminal field. It meant nothing to him that as an Assistant District Attorney I had appeared in his court, and he had not seemed to notice particularly that I was a woman in any way that bothered him. Over and over he told me that a man charged with crime who was represented by a woman, who was then convicted and sentenced to prison, would feel very much that he had not had a fair shake so far as criminal jurisprudence is concerned.

It was the practice of the Legal Aid Society in its Criminal Branch that all cases were assigned in the name of the Attorney-in-Charge of that branch. Cases handled by staff members, other than the head of the Criminal Branch, all were listed on the calendar under the name of the head of the branch. My late-every-afternoon friend, the judge, would not countenance having defendants assigned to the Legal Aid Society in the name of a woman. However, the president and the board of the Society were loyal and staunch, and I continued to represent clients assigned to the Society in all of the criminal courts, except in the court of the protesting judge where I was never assigned a case. I did, however, represent many Legal Aid clients that had been assigned to the Society in a preliminary Magistrate's Court and then had arrived, by action of the Grand Jury, before this particular judge. He did not go so far as to relieve me of those assignments made by other judges.

This painful situation continued for some weeks. Every day I had business in his court and every day there appeared in his court defendants who did not have an attorney, either because the attorney had stepped out of the case or because the money for a legal fee was not forthcoming. The judge would assign the defendants without counsel to some lawyer sitting in the courtroom, but never to me.

Then one day a horrible example of humanity was brought before this court to be arraigned. The defendant was small, grimy, whining, defiant, and had only one shoe. When he was asked if he had a lawyer, he said that he did not. When he was asked if he could afford to retain counsel, he replied that he could not. When he was asked if he would like the court to assign counsel to represent him, he said in an unmistakably clear voice, "I want Miss Kelley to be assigned to my case." The judge turned purple.

To this day I am convinced he believes that I put the defendant up to it. I had never seen the defendant before in my life.

The judge then proceeded to persuade the defendant that he would be ably represented by some other attorney that the judge would select. The defendant would have none of it. He whined, he sniveled, and remained obdurate: "I want Miss Kelley." The judge, very grudgingly, assigned me to represent the defendant. I meekly accepted the assignment and my grimy client was marched off triumphantly by two large court attendants to the detention room outside the court.

The next day the judge made an extremely gracious speech in which he withdrew his formal protest against my acting as the Attorney-in-Charge of the Criminal Branch. The battle had been ended by one small, grubby individual who might be the defendant under a criminal charge, but who still felt that he had some rights and insisted on them. I wish I could tell you that I defended this client so ably that he was acquitted. That is not the case. He pleaded guilty to a minor charge and was sent to prison for a short term.

During the ensuing years I was to represent him on numerous occasions. He always was brought in on a minor matter never involving violence. He had chosen a life of petty crime and was not successful at it. But he knew loyalty. He would have no lawyer except Miss Kelley. As a matter of fact he even refused to speak to my staff associates. He never held against me the sentences which I was unable to protect him from receiving.

When the time came for me to leave my position as Attorney-in-Charge of the Criminal Branch of the Legal Aid Society, I was confronted with the hardest decision that I have ever had to make. It was hard because I thoroughly believe in the principle of legal aid as a necessary implementation of the concept of equal justice for all. It was hard because I had the greatest respect and affection for each and every member of the Board of Directors of the Society. It was hard because I liked the clients that we represented. It was hard, too, because for thirteen years I had been in a position of hiring staff who had the same interest that I did in the work of the Society. Over those years I had been fortunate in being able to put together a staff that differed in color, sex, size, shape, political affiliation and religious bent, whose one common factor was a strong belief that a person charged with crime was entitled to be represented, and well represented, and if he could not afford to hire counsel, he should be given counsel free of charge for his defense.

When I first went to work for the Legal Aid Society the Criminal Branch handled between 7,000 to 8,000 cases a year. The last year that I worked for the Society the Criminal Branch handled over 35,000 cases. More than that, during those years an Appeals Bureau was developed which accepted cases not alone arising from the ones handled by the Legal Aid staff in the trial court, but even cases which had been tried by other attorneys and where the defendant no longer had the means to retain counsel after the trial. How could I leave?

However, the Presiding Justice of the Domestic Relations Court of the City of New York was required, by action of law, to retire at the end of 1959 because of age. The Domestic Relations Court is divided into two parts, a Children's Court Division and a Family Court Division. The families and the children seeking the help of this Court suffer from many of the same problems that my clients at the Legal Aid Society sought to resolve.

The three major religious faiths are represented on this Court. It was a courageous act on the part of the Mayor to offer me the position of Presiding Justice in that, despite my name, I am a Quaker and married to a man of the Jewish faith. As I look back over the happy years that I have spent in the field of law, it appears to me that unconsciously I have been seeking a position where I might put to use my legal training in finding some kind of help for those who are least in a position to find it for themselves. The Domestic Relations Court of the City of New York is probably the final answer.

Law is a profession of discipline. The training for it is an exacting one, but this training will enable a person to serve legal clients in their time of greatest need and concern. The training makes a lawyer a participant in the whole system of justice of this country, a defender of the liberties of the country as a whole, and of the individual. In this wonderful field, a woman lawyer will find a wonderful life.

14

The Lawyer Becomes

A JUDGE

BY WALTER V. SCHAEFER

JUSTICE
SUPREME COURT OF ILLINOIS
Chicago, Illinois

WALTER V. SCHAEFER

Born: 1904, Grand Rapids, Michigan

Hyde Park High School—Chicago
University of Chicago: PH.B., 1926
J.D., 1928

Admitted to Illinois Bar: 1928
Statutory draftsman, Legislative Reference Bureau, Springfield, Illinois:
1928–29
With firm of Tolman, Sexton & Candler, Chicago: 1929–34
Litigation Attorney, Agricultural Adjustment Administration, Washington:
1934–35
Legal Department, Reconstruction Finance Corporation, Chicago: 1935–37
Assistant Corporation Counsel, City of Chicago: 1937–40
Professor of Law, Northwestern University: 1940–51
Commissioner Chicago Housing Authority: 1940–46
Referee in Bankruptcy, United States District Court: 1942–43
Chairman, Illinois Commission to Study State Government: 1949–51
Justice, Illinois Supreme Court: 1951–

Ernst Freund Lecturer
   University of Chicago: 1955
Oliver Wendell Holmes Lecturer
   Harvard University: 1956

Co-editor: Illinois Civil Practice, Act, Annotated, 1934

YESTERDAY you were a lawyer, and today you are a judge. You walk the same streets that you have walked for years as a lawyer, and you see the same people. The slight shift in direction that takes you to the courthouse instead of to your old office is hardly noticeable. You know yourself, and you know that your knowledge of the law is no greater today than it was yesterday, and that you are no wiser. Yet there have been subtle changes in the attitude of other people toward you, the kind that you may first sense when some lawyer unconsciously touches his hat as he greets you. There have been more important changes, too, although you may not be aware of them at once—changes in your attitude toward the law and toward your own role in it.

While there are about 280,000 lawyers in this country, there are only about 8,200 judges. Each of the 8,200 has gone through the transition from lawyer to judge, for with us, as with England and all other common law countries, no one becomes a judge who is not first a lawyer. Unlike other legal systems, ours affords no special training for judicial office. In some continental legal systems, the choice between a career as a lawyer or a career as a judge is made at the outset, and different educational programs are pursued. In those systems, once the choice is made the practical possibility of transferring from one career to the other is almost nonexistent. The continental judge will have had long training as a judicial apprentice, but he will never have appeared on the other side of the bench as an advocate.

No one in this country becomes a judge just because he wants to. Federal judges are appointed, and they have life tenure. Most of the 8,200 are state court judges, and their method of selection varies from state to state. They are appointed in a few states. In a very few they are still chosen by the state legislature. But in the main, state court judges are elected, for terms that vary from twenty-one years, in the case of the highest court of Pennsylvania, to six years for the highest courts of several other states. There are comparable variations in the length of terms of trial-court judges.

None of the existing methods of selecting judges is wholly satisfactory. In an appointive system, the caliber of the judiciary will depend upon the caliber and the concern of the President or Governor who makes the appointment, and under an elective system the initial selection of a judge, or his retention in office, may depend much more upon the popularity of his party's candidates for national office than upon his own individual merit. The organized bar has long advocated a method of selection designed to enhance the likelihood that only the most competent men will be selected for judicial office. The basic thought is that those lawyers best qualified for judicial service should be selected by a nominating commission of citizens and lawyers, charged only with responsibility for selecting the ablest men, and that appointments should then be made only from among the men so selected. The trend is in this direction, and in the direction of longer terms and greater security of tenure.

I think it is fair to say that politics has entered, to varying extents, into the selection of each of the country's 8,200 judges. But the term "politics" is a generic one and its overtones have the widest range, all the way from the wholesome notion that "what is good government is good politics" down to considerations that are quite sordid. There is also a similar range, perhaps even to its full extent, in the selection of judges. It is true, of course, that one man may be selected for judicial office because he is sincerely felt to be the man who is best qualified for the position. It is likewise true that another man may be selected for reasons that have no relevance to his ability to render satisfactory judicial service.

In considering a man for this service, most people would probably concede that it is desirable for him to have shown an active interest in public affairs, and have had some experience with the operation of government. This kind of experience is relevant to qualification for judicial office, but of course it is not determinative. Lord Goddard, formerly Lord Chief Justice of England, remarked that a man's prominence and his participation in politics could be valuable assets, "but it is judicial and not political capacity which ought to be the deciding factor."

Whether determinative or not, it would seem that holding public office in the United States is a favorable prelude to a judgeship. About 80 to 85 per cent of all judges in this country have served either in public law offices or have been elected to public office as prosecutors, members of the legislature, or officials of local governments before they became judges.

In my opinion, it is true that in any judicial system the quality of the judge depends much more upon the quality and spirit of the bar, and upon tradition and the expectations of the community, than upon the formal method by which judges are selected. I think, for example, of one state in which judges are elected at the time of the general November election when national political offices are filled, and serve only for short terms. It would be hard to devise a system of selection less likely to produce and retain top-quality judges; but in this state that I have in mind the tradition of electing good judges and retaining them in office is so strong that both political parties take account of it, taking care that their varying political fortunes do not substantially influence the selection or retention of judges.

Apart from the common denominator of their training as lawyers, it is difficult to sketch very accurately a composite profile of the 8,200 judges. Every effort at comprehensive characterization that may be made can be contradicted by specific instances of variation from the norm. But if the impossibility of complete accuracy is recognized, an attempt can be made.

In this country our judges are not young men. A sampling of their biographical sketches suggests that the average age at which lawyers become judges is about forty-seven to forty-eight years. It runs somewhat higher for judges of reviewing courts.

Most judges not only have held public office, or served in

some legislative or governmental position, but at some time in their careers they have also engaged in the private practice of the law.

The 8,200 judges serve in many different courts. The federal government maintains a system of federal courts, and each of the states has its own judicial system. The distribution of jurisdiction between state and federal courts is a subject too complex for discussion here, and nothing in the nature of the work of a judge, which is what we are concerned with, turns upon that distribution.

The basic judicial structure is the same in the federal system and the state-court systems. Each has at the apex a reviewing court of last resort, typically called a Supreme Court, and at the base a trial court of general original jurisdiction. In the federal system and in thirteen of the larger states, there are intermediate appellate courts whose function is to review the judgment of the trial courts, and whose judgments in turn are subject to review by the Supreme Court, usually in its discretion.

In addition, there are sometimes specialized courts, of limited jurisdiction, that deal with such matters as federal taxes and patents in the federal system, and the probate of the estates of deceased persons, family problems, or matters pertaining to juveniles in the state systems.

Whether a judge sits on the bench of a trial court or of a reviewing court, his primary function is the same—the decision of litigated disputes. By no means do all disputes reach the stage of litigation; far more are disposed of by settlement than ever reach the courts, but the influence of the law and the work of the judges affects the resolution of all disputes. Even those that do not result in the filing of a lawsuit are disposed of in the light of what the anticipated decision of a court would be in the event of litigation.

There are, however, differences that should be noted between the work of a trial judge and the work of a judge of a reviewing court. The trial judge is responsible for the conduct of the proceedings leading up to the trial, and for the trial itself. He may be called upon to analyze the statements of position, called "pleadings," which are filed by each of the parties, to determine whether the facts asserted, if true, are legally sufficient to establish a right to judicial relief, or a defense to the asserted right. If they are insufficient, he decides the case by ruling as a matter of law for the appropriate party. But if the rights of the parties turn upon the resolution of disputed facts, a trial is necessary, and he decides the case at the conclusion of the trial.

A trial is ordinarily an attempt to reconstruct a past occurrence through the testimony of witnesses. The trial judge comes directly into contact with the litigants and the witnesses, and with the heat and drama of the trial. The version of the actual occurrence that he hears is a diluted one, of course, because it comes to him through the words of others, but it is as close to the raw facts as anyone comes. Although the dramatics of an actual trial seldom attain the intensity that seems to be the norm for the theater and television, there is no absence of drama. Indeed, there has been much professional effort in recent years to reduce some of the dramatic potential in order to make the trial a more accurate instrument for ascertaining the truth.

Judges of a reviewing court have the same responsibility for decision, but they operate in a different atmosphere and with different materials. They do not see the litigants or the witnesses. I have known able trial judges who have asked to be relieved of such an assignment because they were unhappy in the impersonal atmosphere. The concern of reviewing courts is with errors that are said to have occurred, either in the steps that led up to the trial or in the trial itself, and they reach their decisions on the basis of a written record of what took place in the trial court, supplemented by the oral and written arguments of counsel.

As soon as the lawyer becomes a judge, he becomes conscious that a new element has come into his life—an unceasing, inexorable demand for decision. In the words of the spiritual, for the judge "there's no hiding place down there." On a reviewing court just as on a trial court, the present case must be disposed of so that the next one can come on for decision. Our entire procedural law is designed to bring narrowly focused issues of law and fact before the courts for decision. And our system leaves little room for equivocation; in the reviewing court as in the trial court, decision must, ordinarily, go wholly for one party or wholly for the other.

The judge does not choose the cases that he must decide. He has nothing to do with their selection. They are churned up out of real life by the legal system, and they involve deeply felt interests of real life litigants. They may present typical patterns to the judge, or they may not. Whether the issue as it comes to the judge is familiar, or lies entirely beyond his experience, makes no difference so far as his responsibility is concerned. Neither doubt nor misgiving excuses decision.

Upon whatever court he sits, moreover, the judge must assume that his decision will be final. The trial judge knows that only a minute percentage of his judgments are appealed, and so his responsibility for an ultimate decision cannot often be discounted by the possibility that the case will go on to a final determination by another court. And for the judge of a court of last resort, finality is inescapable. It is true that courts of review are multijudge courts, but for the conscientious judge each decision of the court is his own, and the participation of his colleagues does not lessen his sense of individual responsibility.

Responsibility for an ultimate decision forces upon the new judge an instinct for objectivity. Over the door at the rear of our courtroom in Springfield, facing the bench, is inscribed the admonition, "*Audi Alteram Partem*," which means, "Hear the other side." Probably no one but the members of the court ever notice that inscription. The room is so designed that it is dominated by the bench of judges, but those words dominate the judges. They reflect the attitude that the new judge quickly acquires—an instinct that makes him discount, and even mentally counter, the argument of the advocate for each side even as it is being made. The most objective lawyers are the best lawyers, but always they are advocates. The judge's "open mind" is not, of course, an empty vessel into which content is poured by lawyers. Rather it is an active mind, trained in the art of advocacy, that weighs the arguments as they are advanced, but consciously strives to keep judgment suspended until the case is fully heard.

Almost as soon as the new judge senses his responsibility for decision, he encounters a new sense of loneliness, felt most deeply in those cases where the current of his doubt runs strongest. That loneliness, so often felt by the responsible judge, is recognized only by the most perceptive lawyers, and not at all by the public. It is not loneliness in a general social sense, for judicial office need not and does not profoundly affect a judge's social life. Perhaps it is a product of the judge's sense of fallibility. As Cardozo said, "A brief experience upon the bench was enough to reveal to me all sorts of cracks and crevices and loopholes in my own opinions when picked up a few months after delivery and reread with due contrition." (He added, more happily, "The persuasion that one's own infallibility is a myth leads by easy stages and with somewhat greater satisfaction to a refusal to ascribe infallibility to others.")

Perhaps, too, the judge's loneliness is an inevitable concomitant of power, and the responsibility for its exercise. There is no question as to judicial power. The judge's decision can determine whether a man lives, goes to his death, or to the penitentiary, and for how long; it can determine the course of events in matters of major industrial and commercial consequence, and it can change the custody of a child, and so alter the course of several lives. Judge Henry J. Friendly, a leading lawyer recently appointed to an important appellate court, mentioned as one of the two most striking aspects of his transition from lawyer to judge, "the enormous change in the effect of the simple act of signing his name. He does something he has done thousands of times without any great consequences attaching to it; then, suddenly, '. . . the whole power of the state will be put forth, if necessary,' to carry out his will."

Despite the responsibility they bear and the power they exercise, judges are not particularly well paid. They are able to educate their children, and provide modestly for them, but even in the federal courts and the courts of those states where judicial salaries run highest, a judge's salary is much less than the earnings of the leading lawyers. Yet it is a truism that almost every lawyer wants to be a judge. Seldom do you hear of a lawyer who has refused either an appointment to judicial office, or the opportunity to become a candidate for a major judicial office if there is a fair chance of election. And when, most infrequently, a judge resigns his office to resume the practice of law, it is front-page news. Yet judge's work, well done, is hard work. The explanation may lie in Mr. Justice Holmes's observation that "the prize of the General is not a bigger tent, but command."

Judicial office is not viewed in the same light throughout the world. I have heard Continental lawyers speak of this country and other common-law countries as nations of "judge worshipers," and I remember my surprise when it was explained to me, as I was briefed with two other lawyers for lectures in a foreign country, that I would be presented as a former lawyer and professor of law, rather than a judge, so that the stature of the American group would not be depreciated.

Many factors account for this difference in attitude toward judicial office. The common-law tradition of judicial independence is a long one, going back to Coke's defiance of James I in 1616. Moreover, as De Tocqueville noted long ago in his "Democracy in America," in the United States almost every question sooner or later becomes a legal question. "In no country," Mr. Justice Frankfurter has pointed out, "is the incidence of law as pervasive as it is with us." The unique power that our judges have—to set aside as unconstitutional those statutes that contravene the provisions of our state and federal constitutions—gives our judiciary an authority far beyond that recognized in most other countries.

In addition, the judges in a common-law system, and especially the judges of reviewing courts, are themselves responsible for the development of a large part of the body of law that they administer. In our system the written opinion of a reviewing court not only disposes of the case at hand; it also becomes a precedent for the decision of future cases. Judge Friendly described this aspect of his new work in these terms: "More enduringly impressive to the lawyer-turned-appellate-judge are the reverberations of his judgments beyond their immediate context. The decisions of our judges—and this is where they differ from the arbitrator, the jury, and, to a considerable extent, from their counterparts under other legal systems—not only determine the case for the litigants, but help, in greater or less degree, to 'make law' for thousands of others."

The details of the operation of the common-law process, and its controls, are too complex to be fully explained here. What is presently important is that the common-law system places upon our judges the necessity of constant reappraisal of the results yielded by old rulings, measured against present day ideals and aspirations. The backbone of legal education in this country is not a study of the laws enacted by legislative bodies. It is rather a study of the opinions of the courts and the common-law process. From his first days in law school, the lawyer has been conscious of the importance of the role of the judge in the development of our law.

Because our law is so pervasive, the judge comes into close contact with almost every aspect of the life of his time. Yesterday it was necessary to decide what to do with a juvenile delinquent; today's case concerns the rate structure of a public utility, and next week's will involve difficult problems in corporate structure and relationships. In a society that seems to tend more and more toward narrower and narrower specialization, the judge remains an outstanding generalist. He need not, of course, encompass the full range of knowledge of the engineer, the accountant or the medical specialist, but he must, upon occasion, impinge upon their fields of learning.

The attractiveness of a judicial career to any man depends on what that man wants out of life. If his objective is great wealth, or if he wants to avoid responsibility and to escape involvement in the affairs of his time, he should not become a judge. If he is unduly sensitive to criticism, he should not become a judge, for judicial decisions are subject to criticism in forums that range from the tavern across the street from the courthouse, through the newspapers, and on to the law reviews and legal treatises. On the other hand, a judicial career offers an opportunity for meaningful service to objectives that transcend self-interest. Judges are not a sentimental group, and they do not speak of their work in terms of service to an ideal. Perhaps in this they are not exceptional, for few of us talk very freely about those matters of faith or philosophy that are the mainsprings of our conduct. The expression that judges use about their work is the homely one that I have heard so often: "If I didn't get paid for doing this, I'd pay for the chance to do it."

One might suppose that all the problems had been settled by the countless judgments that have been rendered over the centuries. Yet it is commonplace among judges that it is the unexpected that always happens. Tomorrow always brings its own set of new problems, and the law must be reshaped to meet them. It must be so in a world of change. There have been great judges in the past and there are great judges among us today. By no means do all of the great judges achieve wide acclaim. For many of them the outward recognition that they receive is the respect, the admiration and the affection of their fellow lawyers, and even that is more frequently felt than expressed. Their inner satisfaction, which they do not articulate even to themselves, comes from devotion of their best efforts of mind and heart to the service of the ideal, unattainable perhaps, but still inspiring, of universal justice for all men.

15

One Lawyer's

LIFE

BY HARRISON TWEED
New York, New York

HARRISON TWEED

Born: 1885, New York, New York

Browning School, New York City
St. Mark's School, Southborough, Mass.
Harvard: A.B., 1907
Harvard: LL.B., 1910
Syracuse: LL.D., 1954
Harvard: LL.D., 1958

Private, US Army (Officers Training Camp): 1918

Admitted to New York City Bar 1911
Associate, Byrne & Cutcheon 1910; Partner, Byrne, Cutcheon & Taylor and
successor firms, 1916–31; Partner, Milbank, Tweed, Hadley & McCloy
and predecessor firms: 1931–

President, The Legal Aid Society, New York, New York, 1936–45, now
Director; President, National Legal Aid Association, 1949–55, now Director; President, The American Law Institute, 1947–1961; Chairman of
its Council, 1961–; Chairman of the Joint Committee on Continuing
Legal Education of American Law Institute and American Bar Association, 1947–; Chairman, New York State Temporary Commission on the
Courts, 1953–58.

President, Sarah Lawrence College 1959–60, Trustee: 1940–54, 1960—;
Trustee, The Cooper Union: 1951 to date; Overseer, Harvard College:
1950–56.

Author: "The Legal Aid Society–New York City 1876–1951" (1954);
"Lifetime and Testamentary Estate Planning" (with William Parsons)
(1949-rev. to 1959); various legal articles and addresses, including The
Gasper G. Bacon Lectures at Boston University (1950); The Cardozo
Lecture at New York City Bar Assn., 1955; The Tyrrell Williams
Memorial Lecture at Washington University School of Law, St. Louis,
Mo., 1960.

I HAVE BEEN practicing law for fifty years. But I am not sure that that entitles me to give young people advice or even information about the law as a profession. I say this because the profession offers a great many different varieties of work, and a lawyer must choose between them according to his particular preferences based on inclination and justification. Obviously, I can give very little *information* about any sort of professional life except that which I have lived, and cannot give any sort of *advice* to unknown readers. So I can really do little more than give you the story of what I have done and heard and seen and let you draw your own conclusions and make your own decisions. Even with these caveats, I worry that something I say may be exaggerated or underestimated or misunderstood to such an extent that a reader who has pretty definitely determined to go to law school decides not to, and then lives to regret it; or another reader decides to study law and that turns out to have been a great mistake. But perhaps I am taking *myself* too seriously, which is all wrong, since what I am trying to do is to persuade you *not* to take me too seriously.

I would be less timid about what I am about to say if I were talking or writing to a young friend, or even an acquaintance of whom I had seen enough to appraise his personal characteristics and qualities because they largely determine what advice he should receive. In the same breath that I say this, I will add that in the ultimate success a man achieves, it does not make very much difference what he starts out to do. If he has the stuff of which successful men are made, which very definitely includes a willingness to work hard, the sort of work he first undertakes will make very little difference in the long pull.

This, of course, is even more true when a young man is weighing the varieties of professional life that the practice of law offers. Probably there is some line along which any individual lawyer will move fastest and go furthest but, granted the inherent ability, it is by no means essential that he start along that line. These things are said upon the assumption—and it is not one which can be safely made in all cases—that a man will be quick to realize that he has made the wrong choice and be willing to admit his error and change to some other business or profession, or to some other branch of the business or profession in which he is engaged.

At this point, and quite illogically and inconsistently, I have an irresistible impulse to quote my favorite Aesop fable:

A Miller and his Son were driving their Ass to a neighboring fair to sell him. They had not gone far when they met with a troop of girls returning from the town, talking and laughing. "Look there!" cried one of them, "did you ever see such fools, to be trudging along the road on foot, when they might be riding!" The old Man, hearing this, quietly bade his Son get on the Ass, and walked along merrily by the side of him. Presently they came up to a group of old men in earnest debate. "There!" said one of them, "it proves what I was a-saying. What respect is shown to old age in these days? Do you see that idle young rogue riding, while his old father has to walk? . . . Get down, you scapegrace! and let the old Man rest his weary limbs." Upon this the Father made his Son dismount, and got up himself. In this manner they had not proceeded far when they met a company of women and children. "Why, you lazy old fellow!" cried several tongues at once, "how can you ride upon the beast, while that poor little lad there can hardly keep pace by the side of you?" The good-natured Miller stood corrected, and immediately took up his Son behind him. They had now almost reached the town. "Pray, honest friend," said a townsman, "is that Ass your own?" "Yes," said the old Man. "O! One would not have thought so," said the other, "by the way you load him. Why, you two fellows are better able to carry the poor beast than he you!" "Anything to please you," said the old Man; "we can but try." So, alighting with his Son, they tied the Ass's legs together, and by the help of a pole endeavoured to carry him on their shoulders over a bridge that led to the town. This was so entertaining a sight that the people ran out in crowds to laugh at it; till the Ass, not liking the noise or his situation, kicked asunder the cords that bound him, and, tumbling off the pole, fell into the river. Upon this the old Man, vexed and ashamed, made the best of his way home again—convinced that by endeavouring to please everybody he had pleased nobody, and lost his Ass in the bargain.

The foregoing, as I have said, has no relevance to anything I am saying, but it may perhaps suggest the number of differences of opinion which a lawyer will encounter on his journey through life and will imply that if he tries to reconcile all of them he may well follow the ass to the bottom of the river. But there is another side to this picture. Differences of opinion not only make horse racing but also make life interesting and stimulating. While it is not advisable to try to agree with everyone, neither is it advisable to violently disagree with too many people and particularly with too many clients. It is a mistake to think that one's own opinion represents perfection and is the only permissible one. There is almost always room for some compromise or adaptation, and, in many situations, one of the most important qualifications of the lawyer is to be able to work things out satisfactorily to two or more people who have different preconceptions.

I did not learn this until I had had a couple of experiences which pretty well demonstrated that I ought not to be so sure that my way was the one and only right way to get the job done. I remember one instance when the client and I had reached an impasse and I so reported to one of my partners. He promptly took the matter over and, by using a somewhat different approach and one which I would have disapproved, managed to work things out to everyone's satisfaction in no time at all. This is a very different thing from compromising on a matter of principle or accepting something less than the objective. It is merely an example of the validity of the old saying that "there is more than one way to skin a cat."

I don't think that there is any single convincing and conclusive basis on which a man should decide to become a lawyer. The

nearest to it that I can come is what I believe to be the fact, that
the decision can be revoked without much damage. This suggestion carries further my thought that no decision is irrevocable
and stems from my belief that a law-school course is of great
value, whatever sort of life follows it. This was my father's conviction and he had reached it when he graduated from law school
in 1870. Fathers and sons do not always agree about this sort of
thing, but my opinion today is the same as his was in that long
ago.

It is my opinion that a man who finds himself unqualified or
indisposed to commence practice after graduating from law
school, or to continue after having started, has not greatly im-
periled his ultimate success. I have a pretty good piece of evidence to offer in support of this opinion. A few years ago I
checked up on what had happened to the hundred young men
who in the preceding ten years had entered one of the best law
firms in New York City (not mine). I found that ten had become
partners and that, with one exception, the ninety had made excellent connections in law, business, or public service. The one
exception had gone into the movies where he was a failure. A
couple of years later I discovered that he had been elected governor of a neighboring state and he has since gone on to a very
worth-while public career.

It would be interesting to have the facts as to why each of the
250,000 lawyers in the country decided to go to law school and
then to enter practice. But there are no such statistics and I doubt
whether, even to a limited extent, the facts are ascertainable. I
once said that in most cases the mental process is one of elimination of other possibilities rather than an affirmative selection of
the law, and I added:

If a man has no great acquisitiveness but wants to live comfortably,
have children, educate them and make some provision for his widow;
has no definite artistic or literary flair; is not facile in mathematics or
things scientific but has an interest in the intellectual, and perhaps
particularly in argument, analysis and logical presentation, orally or in
writing; wants to be free to take a position on public questions and to
play a part in the affairs of the community in which he lives and, per-

haps above all, has confidence in his physical and mental ability to work hard enough and do good enough work to survive in keen competition—then the law seems to offer him the best chance for happiness.

That statement was based on the impression which I had obtained from knowing a good many lawyers and the further impression that the precise reason for studying law was somewhat different in almost every individual case.

I would not like to say that my years at the bar demonstrate either the validity or the invalidity of the implication that that statement describes the sort of man who *ought to* take up law. I am pretty sure, however, that my own decision to go into practice was pursuant to substantially that line of thinking. I say "go into practice" because the fact is that the reasons why I went to law school had no real connection with my later decision to go on and become a lawyer.

The first discussion I ever had about the legal profession was with a cousin three years older than I—when I was ten. He was already determined to be a lawyer and was expatiating on the subject. I, in my abysmal ignorance, said, "All that a lawyer does is to lie for whoever pays him." And this notwithstanding that both my father and my favorite uncle were lawyers and men of the highest standards.

It is one of the tragedies of today that a great many youngsters, and quite a few adults, have somewhat the same point of view. This is because people know that judicial proceedings are conducted on an adversary basis with the lawyer on each side trying to persuade the court of the soundness of his case. To the uninitiated it is logical to assume that each lawyer tries to misrepresent the facts and pervert the truth. They do not know that the highest duty of the lawyer is to refrain from misleading the court. He must press his client's case to the best of his ability within the ethical limitation that there must be no misrepresentation of facts or of law. Our adversary system whereby a judicial determination is reached by a judge or jury after hearing testimony and argument on both sides is not perfect but, so far as I know, it is the best system that has ever been devised. Certainly the lawyers who participate are not "paid to lie." On the contrary, the price of a lie is disbarment.

I went to law school for two reasons. One of them was that my father wanted me to go, and in those days sons generally did what their fathers wanted. The other was that I welcomed three more summer vacations. But when I got to law school, I found that I enjoyed the work just as much as the vacations and I did enough of it to get good marks.

I look back on my three years at the Harvard Law School as much as on any years of my life. It was the first time that I had done any real studying and the group of us who lived together all worked very hard. Nevertheless, none of us felt the sort of strain that apparently many students in law school stagger under today. Life was simple and few decisions had to be made. We got up early in the morning and went to bed when we felt like it. I remember nostalgically my habit of throwing my clothes on a chair before I fell into bed and jumping into exactly the same clothes when I got up in the morning and hurrying to breakfast without going through much in the way of ablution. Only the week end interrupted this routine.

No one who owes as much as I do to the Harvard Law School should fail to say a little more about it. I will borrow the words of the late Learned Hand, which are inscribed on a tablet there:

I carried away the impress of a band of devoted scholars; patient, considerate, courteous and kindly, whom nothing could daunt and nothing could bribe. The memory of those men has been with me ever since. Again and again they have helped me when the labor seemed heavy, the task seemed trivial, and the confusion seemed indecipherable. From them I learned that it is as craftsmen that we get our satisfactions and our pay. In the universe of truth they lived by the sword; they asked no quarter of absolutes and they gave none.

I treasure memories of three of those who taught me there. To get to know such men was an education in itself and so strong were their personalities and characteristics that even as students in a class of over a hundred we did get to know them. One was Samuel Williston, still alive at the age of one hundred, who, on a question of law which he had answered conclusively to his own satisfaction years before, could make us believe that he was in doubt and was seeking the answer from the class that very day. Another, of a very different type, was Edward H. (always known as "Bull") Warren, who could have been the outstanding corporation lawyer at any bar, but who preferred to teach. I still recall his instructions and his admonitions and have tried for fifty-five years to follow the advice he gave us at our first class: "Keep your minds and your bowels open."

Finally, there was Dean James Barr Ames, perhaps the most learned of them all and certainly the greatest gentleman. During one lecture in Trusts, which was his specialty, he asked me question after question, to each of which I replied promptly and with great confidence. Afterwards, one of my brilliant classmates, undistinguished for tact, said to me, "Well, Ames certainly made a fool of you this morning." He had done it so gently that I had been proud rather than ashamed of my performance. Not long ago, I happened to pick up "Bull" Warren's *Spartan Education* and, in the chapter on Dean Ames, found this:

He was invariably courteous and altogether the gentleman. He had a patience that was stupidity proof.

That seems all too pertinent to my story.

I am lucky to know many of today's successors to that faculty, and, even in my weather-beaten eyes, they measure well up to the standard set by the great teachers of 1910. In many other schools of law, but not in all, there are the same dedicated and inspiring leaders of legal thought.

It seems to me that one way to determine one's qualifications for the legal profession is to study in college those subjects which fall in the same general intellectual area as law. This, I believe, is not the common opinion, but it is mine. Perhaps I exaggerate it because of my own personal experience. In my senior year of college I elected a course which had as its textbook *Scott's Cases on*

International Law. It interested and stimulated me and yielded one of my few good marks. When my father suggested that I go to law school, my concurrence was aided by this first wetting of my feet. Just what other subjects come into this category, I will leave to the professors to say.

Another test of aptitude to which anyone contemplating the profession can subject himself is to read a little of what such legal philosophers as Holmes and Cardozo have written. There is a more recent book by Charles P. Curtis, *It's Your Law,* which is a particular favorite of mine. The extent to which the reader is interested in these writings is a forecast of how favorably he will react, first, to the study and then to the practice of law.

One night, during my third year in the Law School, my father said to me, "Well, Harry, I have arranged for you to go into one of the best law offices in New York," mentioning the name. I had heard of it as the office which drove its young men night and day harder than any other office in New York, except one. And I was not sure that that was where I wanted to go. But I said nothing either by way of question, criticism or thanks. The next day I decided to be reconciled to what seemed to be a finality of fate, and this may have been the beginning of my fatalism because my association with that firm turned out to be a very happy one.

I arrived in the office early in September, 1910. The details of the next decade are not worth going into for readers of today or of the future. We worked long hours, but for many of us our development as lawyers was much slower than for young lawyers today. There was a great deal of looking up of law on questions which did not seem to us to have any relevance at all, but we were well disciplined and didn't talk back. My favorite story of that office includes a colloquy between my particular boss, James Byrne, and me. He assigned me a question of law to look up on a Friday afternoon, insisting that I have a memorandum ready for him by ten o'clock on Monday.

At that hour my memorandum was still in the hands of the stenographers. Mr. Byrne demanded to know why it was not ready and I humbly pleaded that I had not had time to finish it. He glared at me and asked, "What time did you go home on

Friday night?" I replied, "Three o'clock in the morning." "What time did you go home Saturday night?" I told him that I had quit at two o'clock in the morning. Then came the final "What time did you go home Sunday night?" And I had to confess that I had done so at eleven o'clock; whereupon he pounded the desk and said: "Don't tell me that you didn't have time to finish that memorandum. Tell me the truth—that you wanted to go home early Sunday night."

I am confident that James Byrne had more influence on my work and my attitude toward it and life in general than anyone else except my father. In writing about him in 1932, I said:

Young men learned much more than law from Mr. Byrne. They learned a supreme devotion to the interests of clients and a sort of optimistic fatalism—a philosophy of life that if you work and live hard and faithfully, all will come well in the end.

No one could possibly have taught me as well as Mr. Byrne did that an essential of the good lawyer is that he visualize all the possibilities and particularly those that might make trouble. He had the imagination of a child alone in the dark and when he had time he could think up the most dreadful of possibilities. There was a Thanksgiving Day when this happened and I got no turkey until very late in the evening. Mr. Byrne had represented the executors of William M. Rice, under whose will the Rice Institute in Houston was established. Rice's valet, Jones, had murdered the old gentleman, while his lawyer friend Patrick had forged a will in his own favor. The will was rejected for probate, Patrick was convicted as an accessory and sentenced to life imprisonment. On the Thanksgiving Day in question, the governor pardoned Patrick.

Mr. Byrne was certain that Patrick would start some sort of litigation. I was instructed to learn all about the case and to be prepared to discuss the situation with Captain Baker of Houston, counsel for the Rice Institute, if he should turn up in Mr. Byrne's absence. This involved the examination of forty tin boxes of files and, notwithstanding a conscientious study of them, I was much worried. Many times Captain Baker appeared in the still watches of a restless night and finally he arrived in person on a hot summer day when Mr. Byrne was in Maine. Captain Baker came in and lit a cigar. He was not as terrifying as he had seemed in the darkness. He sat down on a chair and crossed his legs. "Well, Tweed, I understand you know all about this case. What do you think Patrick is going to do?" Fearing that it was the last thing that Mr. Byrne would want me to say, I answered, "Captain Baker, I don't think Patrick will ever try to do anything." He said, "Neither do I," and departed. The fact is that Patrick never did do anything. But it was the duty of the good lawyer to be ready for the worst.

I do not think that today young lawyers spend as many hours on office work, or are subjected to as rigorous discipline, as we were. But the beginner still gets a pretty severe initiation and responds good-naturedly and with an understanding that it is all for his own good. This is true in the 1960s, notwithstanding that the conditions which confront a lawyer during his first few years of practice are very different from those which prevailed fifty years ago. Then almost all of us lived in the city or within easy subway transportation and we did not marry until our late twenties. Today most of the lawyers who come into my office direct from law school, or after one year's apprenticeship to a judge, are married and a great many of them commute to distances which involve from an hour to an hour and a half of travel each way.

The young lawyer of today has also the problem that he has jobs to do at home as well as in the office. This applies even to the bachelors who live at home, because their parents do not pamper them and domestic servants are rare. All of this makes long hours in the office or a library more inconvenient than used to be the case, but nonetheless necessary if the lawyer wants to get ahead.

It is impossible to present a picture of the average lawyer's average day. There is no average lawyer and no lawyer has an average day. As a try at it, I give you this: eight hours to sleep, three hours to eat, presumably with conversation and newspaper reading, two hours to and from the office. That makes thirteen hours and leaves eleven: eight of these are for work—most, but not all of it, remunerative office or court work. The other three are for optional and differing activities. There would be considerable variance in the number of hours I have allocated to work. The variances would be of two kinds: First, more hours during periods of pressure, although not many fewer when the pressure is off. Second, more hours during the early years of practice because then there is not only work to be done but education to be acquired, and I want to emphasize the importance of giving time to that. The three hours I have called "optional" would be just that—a matter of personal choice in the light of particular existing circumstances and varying from time to time.

This imaginary and illusory schedule covers five days of the week. I will not offer any schedule for the forty-eight week-end hours. I think it is true, however, that there are very few lawyers who do not give somewhere between five and ten of those hours to work. But it may well be less intensive and include professional reading, social relations with clients and fellow lawyers, and things of that sort. Week ends, like the evening and night hours, offer an opportunity to catch up on whatever needs attention, and there is almost always something to catch up on.

It may or may not have some relevance here, but once, in the course of a lecture entitled "The Continuing Education of the Complete Lawyer," I was rash enough to try to define that ideal as:

. . . One who gives a considerable part of his time and energy wholeheartedly to advising and representing clients and doing it with a broader viewpoint than the mere self-interest of the clients, and who gives the rest of his time and energy, and is not limited by any union rules, to the sort of work in the public interest for which he is particularly qualified.

Thus, for completeness, a desire to go outside the limits of pure practice is the first step. The next is willingness to learn through study or through doing. In most cases this leads to active service in the spirit of both usefulness in the world and enjoyment of life. At that point the lawyer has become complete so far as my definition is concerned. He may be more or less successful competitively in number of clients, amount of income, extent of influence or importance of position. Progression towards completeness as a lawyer is not a rat race. Securing clients, business, big fees, high salary or important public offices is not the test. The completeness of the lawyer is to be judged less on the basis of what he does than on the basis of what he is.

Resuming after this considerable digression, the years of my life at the bar, and picking up at the end of the first decade, which was approximately the end of the First World War, gets us to the 'twenties and the era of prohibition, prosperity and irresponsibility.

About 1920 the firm, of which I had become a partner in 1916, broke into two pieces. The break-up of the firm left me with a group of lawyers quite different from that with which I had started. For the first time the problem of "getting business" raised its ugly head—because its head is ugly to anyone who is not a "good business getter." And I am not. If you should ask me what makes a good business getter, I would not be able to give you a very enlightening answer. The generally accepted theory is that he is a man whose family has social and financial standing in the community, so that people will be prejudiced in his favor. It is frequently said that the large law firms seek that sort of a man when he is in law school. Obviously, the theory does not apply when a law-school graduate goes to work in some city other than the locality in which his family lives. But, entirely apart from that, and while, of course, such standing is no obstacle to the young lawyer, I have seen the theory work rather seldom. And I have seen many a lawyer attract important and profitable business to his firm or to himself although he had no such connections.

So far as the personal qualities which make a lawyer successful in securing clients and cases, I would say that a liking for trying to do it is perhaps the most important. People like to do the things that they do well, and they do well the things they like to do; whereas people, and perhaps lawyers particularly, who try to act parts for which they are not temperamentally qualified generally give a poor performance. I do not want to hold out a lack of liking for this sort of thing as an excuse for not doing it; every lawyer owes it to himself and to his firm, if he is in one, to make reasonable efforts to develop his and its clientele. Furthermore, many a lawyer who originally approached the problem with reluctance has discovered that he is pretty good at it after all.

Perhaps I should add that, in my prejudiced opinion, one of the advantages of working for, or being a member of, a comparatively large firm is the lack of pressure to produce business. In an established firm, and in most cases that means ten or more partners, it is less important to bring in business than to keep existing clients by doing their work supremely well and promptly. I am not here referring only to the distinctly non-business-getting type of lawyer, who has come to be known as a technician in a narrow specialty but is nonetheless a valuable partner; I am referring to the general run of partners. The percentage of substantial business-getters in a firm is usually not more than one in five. The others do the work of the office and retain and increase its clientele as a result of satisfied clients.

I was rescued from my unhappy association by an offer to join another firm as a partner. This was luck, pure and unrefined, acting through the person of a college and law-school classmate who thought well of me as a working lawyer. I don't want to be overmodest. I would not have been sought by this firm if I had not previously established a reputation for hard and competent work. But the fact is that all through that first ten-year period I had worked to the satisfaction of partners, associates, and clients, and yet at the end I found myself in an unsatisfactory position through no fault of my own. That is why I refuse to belittle the significance of luck and why I emphasize the need to be prepared for the run of bad luck—lost cases and lost clients—which comes to every lawyer. He must not let it discourage him and he must remember that it is like the tide which rises and falls and which, given time, will turn. In justifying my thesis, and particularly my analogy, I quote from the nautical classic Eldridge's *Tide and Pilot Book,* now in its eighty-seventh year:

It will be well to remember that tides do not flow steadily until high water, as is generally supposed, but rise by waves or swells, always making three waves or swells, before reaching the highest point or high water. In other words, the tide begins to rise steadily until it reaches about one-third of its usual height, when it stands still for a short time, and then ebbs or recedes slightly; it then begins to flow again until it has reached about two-thirds of its height, when it stands still and recedes as before; after this it flows until high water. . . . I speak of this particularly because I have observed in many cases where vessels were ashore, or instances wherein high water was of the utmost importance, that the captain or those interested abandoned their labors or hope when, if they had waited and held on an hour or so longer, their object would have been accomplished.

The association I formed in 1921 has continued to 1961, aided and amplified by a couple of so-called mergers whereby the firm grew in numbers and in volume of business. At the beginning, most of the partners were between thirty-five and forty years old and I remember the leader of the group saying to me one night, "If we are going to keep the important business the firm has had, we must not only be good lawyers—we must work like the devil."

I think we all recognized the challenge and individually and collectively did our best to meet it. It was inevitable that the eight partners should specialize—many of us had already done so—and we did. Only one of us—and it wasn't I—was so competent as to be truly an all-around lawyer. A rough approximation would be that in the large firms in New York City there is on an average only one partner every ten years who can be said to qualify as able to handle clients and problems in more than a very few areas. In any event, and with that exception, each of us worked harder and harder in his particular branch of law and practice and became more and more expert in it. There was no other way to keep the numerous and diverse clients satisfied. The matter of specialization presents a difficult question. There are still those who believe that the law is a "seamless web" and that any lawyer is qualified to deal with any problem contained within it, but I think such lawyers are in a distinct minority and certainly they are diminishing in number.

Most lawyers now recognize the necessity for specializing within some branch of the law. At the same time most of them believe that the lawyer newly admitted to the bar should postpone the choice of the particular subject in which he will specialize for at least a year or two and perhaps longer. I accept the fundamental necessity of specialization with one reservation, and that is that every lawyer should get some experience in litigation —perhaps not in the actual trial of cases, but in the handling of appeals, and in observation of what goes on in the trial courts. Otherwise, he cannot appraise with any accuracy the probable outcome of the trial of a given question of fact or law, and that is essential in counseling clients.

Just at the end of the 1920 decade our acknowledged senior, who was nevertheless no older—forty-five—than the rest of us, left to go into banking. Soon after, two other firms—one smaller, the other of equal size—separately merged with us. In the case of this second merger, there was a considerable controversy in the fixing of percentages of earnings. This stimulates a comment. Only on this and one other occasion have I ever been involved in any altercation concerning the division of earnings among the partners. On the first occasion a senior partner, who was as superbly equipped and experienced as any I have ever known, was the cause of the difficulty. He was the only lawyer with whom I have been associated who practiced law for the money in it. If anyone should ask me what that means, I would be hard put to give him an adequate answer.

In my mind the difference between the lawyer who practices for the money in it, and the lawyer who does not, lies less in how he acts than in how he thinks. Every lawyer must be willing to compete not only with outside lawyers but also with those in his firm, in the sense that he must try to be a better lawyer and to do better work. But to carry the competitive spirit into the matter of dollars and cents stirs up the reaction of a similar absorption by partners and associates. Worse than that, excessive interest in figuring one's own, and the other fellow's financial rewards, is utterly inconsistent with the team play which is so essential to the success of any law firm, large or small, and inevitably eliminates the fun which the joint venture ought to bring. Indeed, I would risk the guess that most lawyers who are really acquisitive prefer to practice law alone, if not in the beginning at least after a while. And probably they are right.

After joining my present firm in 1921 I continued in the same work groove into which I had already fallen, more by happenstance than by choice or dictation. But the years have demonstrated that it was the sort of work which I could do best and enjoy most. This was largely the drafting of wills and trust agreements, administering of estates, advising in connection with such matters and writing briefs in litigation arising out of them and some others also.

This sort of practice presents not only many problems of law and of draftsmanship, but also of psychology and of the professional responsibility of the lawyer in advising a testator or settlor. Often it is difficult to know what attitude the lawyer should take in leading or restraining a client in disposing of his property. The question here is similar to that which is presented when the lawyer in court, who must press his client's rights to the utmost, at the same time must recognize his obligation not to mislead the court. However, I am not writing a treatise on ethics, so enough of that.

One important and protracted bit of litigation in the 1930's was that involving the Estate of Colonel Edward H. R. Green, the son of the fabulous Hetty Green. There were not only nice questions of law but a trial of the facts to meet the claim that an antenuptial agreement had been procured by fraud. There was also involved the domicile question par excellence. Four states —Texas, Florida, New York and Massachusetts—claimed inheritance taxes on the ground of the decedent's domicile there at his death. Very ingeniously one of the lawyers—not me—suggested that the claims of all four states could be disposed of in an original proceeding commenced in the Supreme Court of the United States on the ground that this constituted a controversy between the states. Texas was quick to bring such a suit and testimony was taken by a Master, who traveled around with an army of lawyers to each of the claimant states. In the end, Massachusetts triumphed.

Throughout this litigation we represented a corporate and an individual executor who, unlike most executors, left the conduct of the legal matters entirely to the lawyers. This was a unique and enjoyable experience because, generally speaking, clients create complications. It has often been said that this would be a very pleasant world if it were not for the people in it and many an harassed lawyer has thought that the practice of law would be more fun if it were not for the clients—necessary though they are. So when, once in a lifetime, the ideal is realized, the lucky lawyer should be very grateful. Such a situation and such a litigation gives the young lawyers, who are working with their seniors, a unique opportunity to observe how the work is done as well as to participate in it. This collaboration between the initiatee and the old-timer is one of the pleasantest parts of the practice of law. Formerly I used to expatiate on this from the point of view of the junior, but now I appreciate the enjoyment of the older collaborator.

In 1920, my senior partner, together with Charles Evans Hughes, had represented the recipient of stock dividends in a tax case which went to the Supreme Court of the United States— *Macomber v. Eisner.* The Court held that the ordinary stock dividend was not a distribution of earnings so as to be taxable as income under the Sixteenth Amendment to the Constitution. Later we represented taxpayers in other cases involving corporate distributions which were not strictly stock dividends, such as the distribution by some of the Standard Oil Companies of the stock of the pipeline companies which they had organized. In these we were unsuccessful, but that did little to diminish the zest of the contest or the joy of briefing difficult questions of law. And the clients were well prepared mentally and financially to pay the taxes.

Another series of cases in which the office was involved in the 1920's concerned the Federal Estate Tax and the constitutionality and scope of State Inheritance Taxes in various parts of the country. In some of them there was involved also the question of domicile. These presented interesting and clean-cut questions of law. Very large sums of money were involved but in such situations the worry for the lawyer is often less than in cases involving small sums which actually mean a great deal more to the litigants.

During these years I had the privilege of working with and against those giants at the bar—Charles Evans Hughes and John W. Davis. The former was the most convincing lawyer I have ever listened to in court or in conference. He had a force and vitality which were almost irresistible. Even at the peak of his career at the bar, in 1920, when he had more clients than most lawyers, he never shirked work or delegated it to juniors; he always knew as much about the details of the case as anyone working on it.

John W. Davis' success was due to a personal persuasiveness, a clarity of language and a unique ability to make the problem seem simple, and his side of it obvious. Sometimes, listening to him argue a case, I wondered whether the Court appreciated that there was any question for it to decide. I remember one argument, however, in which his calm was shattered when ex-Governor Nathan Miller, arguing on the other side with his usual meat-axe approach, implied uncomplimentary things about Mr. Davis' client. Thereupon Mr. Davis let loose to the great dismay of Governor Miller and the huge enjoyment of the Court, on which the Governor had sat some years before.

Another great lawyer was George Wharton Pepper of Philadelphia. He was not only both forceful and persuasive in court but, on any sort of an occasion, he spoke more interestingly and amusingly than any one I can think of. As president, and later as chairman, of the American Law Institute, he kept his audiences of serious-minded lawyers laughing continuously and indefinitely.

Somewhere along the way I formed a close friendship with Judge Learned Hand, although he was fifteen years my senior. His unique contributions as a philosopher, jurist, and defender of the rights of man, both legal and human, are common knowledge. I want to speak only of what he gave me as a friend. It was not limited to example and advice; he gave me spiritual and intellectual support so strong that sometimes it seemed as though his broad shoulders were actually carrying me along. In addition, he was the very best of companions and, when aroused, his profanity was something to treasure.

Judge Cardozo was the greatest judge on the New York Court of Appeals in this century and we were all saddened when he went to Washington. Personally a shy and sensitive soul, he was unsurpassed in legal logic and the use of the English language. I will add a personal recollection. I was to argue before him a case involving a question on which some years before he had written an opinion which, unless a very fine distinction were recognized, would be conclusive against us. We all agreed we could win only if, as we put it, Judge Cardozo was willing to take back some of the things he had said by way of dictum in the earlier case. The other side was very sure that he would not do it. On the argument, I had hardly stated the facts when the Judge saw the point and began helping me to make the distinction, which permitted a decision in our favor.

I have been writing about what I call the strict practice of law and that is the biggest part of the lives of most lawyers. But it isn't the whole of their lives. In the first place, this strict practice of law is very much broader than that phrase would suggest. The preparation of a case, the writing of a brief, the giving of advice, all call for preparation which goes far beyond the mere reading of decisions and textbooks. Professional articles, the briefs of counsel in other cases, the history and philosophy of law so far as applicable for or against the question involved, must be consulted. Often knowledge of other disciplines—medical, economic, or what not—must be acquired. Most important of all, there must be many hours of constructive and creative thinking. At a guess, two-thirds of what a lawyer puts on paper—long hand, typewritten or printed—goes into the wastepaper basket after further consideration. And the preparation of a case for trial requires infinite imagination and patience in assembling facts, ascertaining the sources of proof of them, laying them down beside the established legal principles and rules, and welding the whole into a unit which will carry conviction. The pay-off is the final argument when the lawyer faces the court or jury and knows that, whatever the decision may be, he has done his very best.

Even so, most lawyers want an even broader life. It has been well said that "a good lawyer cannot help being something more than a technician. By training and experience he possesses certain qualifications which create a demand for his services in diversified fields, some of them quite remote from practice. Generally speaking, a man does not choose the bar as a career unless he has the inherent ability and willingness to be useful in wider fields of endeavor."

I am convinced that what leads the lawyer to give of his talents, beyond what has been called "client serving," to some form of work of value to the community is a search for variety and a spirit of adventure more than it is a sense of duty or a desire to perform professional or public obligations. To put it in another way, the impulse does not come from the conscience of lawyers as much as from their common sense. It is not a compulsion to do good in the interest of others, but rather to live one's own life to the full. Justice Oliver Wendell Holmes once said that "The rule of joy and the law of duty seem to me all one"; and again, "Life is an end in itself, and the only question as to whether it is worth living is whether you have enough of it."

Probably it should be said here that it is easier for lawyers, as compared with those in other professions, or in business or banking, to give their time and energy, beyond their primary money-making duties, to participate in the solution of community, national or even international problems. I say this not because I think the lawyer is a nobler work of God than other men, but because the fact is that, to a large extent, he is his own master. Subject only to the demands of his clients, who are not entitled to twenty-four hours of his time and all his energy, he can do what he pleases. And, by inclination and habit, he serves others—not himself or the source of his pay check. It is also true that neither his clients nor his partners will object, because they are happy to see him improve his standing in the community.

The lawyer who seeks opportunities for this fuller life will have no difficulty in finding them. Here I speak from experience. It is logical that there should be a demand for the help of lawyers in a variety of activities because they are peculiarly qualified to be helpful. I would like to add that the opportunities which I have accepted have given me just as much enjoyment as my office and court work for clients—if not more.

My first venture furnishes an example. It did not take me very far beyond ordinary legal work, but it was in an area where lawyers should work, both because they will enjoy it and also because they will discharge a professional responsibility. This was in 1930, twenty years after my admission to the bar. The objective of the project was the improvement of the law and my job was to assist Professor Austin W. Scott of the Harvard Law School in preparing the American Law Institute's Restatement of Trusts. More or less contemporaneously, I wrote:

I enjoyed this excursion into the academic atmosphere, where you can hold an opinion to the utmost without risking anybody's money and can feel that perhaps you are doing something constructive. It has been my only digression from the rut, which has always been deep and narrow, sometimes rough but never, I hope, muddy.

This brought me in contact with some of the best legal minds among practicing lawyers and law professors. And I found them far from stuffy fellows. I still participate in the work of The American Law Institute as well as of the bar association. My only regret is that I postponed these activities as long as I did. It is very easy for a lawyer to engage in somewhat similar and equally interesting work earlier in his professional life. Frequently the opportunity will come because the lawyer has shown an interest in bar-association activities. The doors of bar associations are open to every lawyer in good standing and particularly to younger ones, for whom the dues are nominal. Bar-association activities differ in many ways from what the lawyer does in practice, but most of all perhaps in the extent to which there is a working together among members of a small committee or a participation in the deliberations of a large group. Here a lawyer learns, on the one hand, to co-operate and collaborate and, on the other hand, to stand up and dissent when he wants to. And, let there be no misunderstanding about it, the activities are not all ponderous or even serious. In my experience, the camaraderie and fun to be had in the American Law Institute or a bar association are greater than can be found in most social clubs. The community of interest and the similarity in line of thought make for friendship and good fellowship.

Another extracurricular activity which brings me great satisfaction is participation in legal-aid work. I have done this for years, partly because the work of assuring to the indigent the right to receive as nearly as possible the same quality of legal advice or representation in court, particularly in the Criminal Courts, that a rich man can obtain is one of the primary obligations of the legal profession. But largely I do it because participation has enabled me to learn a lot and to make many friends.

Another example of the sort of opportunity open to lawyers for broader experience and additional contacts is membership on educational, charitable and religious boards or other groups. It might seem that a lawyer has nothing special to offer in activities so remote from the law and the practice of it. That is not so. What the lawyer has learned in law school and in a very few years in practice will often constitute a substantial contribution in solving the problems which arise in such areas.

Even if he contributes nothing more than a sense of orderliness and an ability to organize thought and to pose the right questions, the lawyer will have pulled his weight in the boat. Mr. Justice Frankfurter tells us that the outstanding value of the legal mind is its ability to define the relevant. This can certainly be very helpful in many of the discussions, to say nothing of the altercations, which arise on a board of trustees of an eleemosynary organization. To turn to the other side of the coin, the lawyer learns from his laymen associates, makes friends with many of them, and converts some of them into clients.

My interest in educational matters began when I was in college and would have led me into teaching had not my father intervened and convinced me that I would not enjoy a life of poverty. It continued through trusteeships and overseerships and, finally, landed me as president for one year of a women's college. It was a unique and delightful experience. And while I have no illusions that I contributed anything to the educational philosophy of the college, I think that I did manage to bring to the faculty an organization and an understanding of democratic procedures which no one but a lawyer could have done.

In a lull in the demands on my time, Governor Dewey asked me, in 1953, to be Chairman of the New York State Temporary Commission on the Courts. He told me that this would take about two afternoons a week for six months or a year. In fact, it continuously consumed more than one-third of my waking time for five years. The fundamental objective was the improvement of the administration of justice in the State of New York. We did pretty well when we secured the establishment of a Judicial Conference within two years but, despite our best efforts to draft a constitutional amendment which would really accomplish something, and at the same time be accepted by the politicians, we failed. The legislature rejected our final proposal and abolished the Commission at the end of its 1958 session. The Judicial Conference picked up the ball and drafted a constitutional amendment which was approved by the voters in 1961. This is a source of gratification to all concerned, notwithstanding that the amendment is a much-watered-down version of what everyone wanted except the politicians.

I won't try to draw any moral or give any advice, but I suppose this constitutes another example of the saying that "Politics is the art of the possible." At any rate, I enjoyed the experience, which was of the sort to which every lawyer should be exposed.

During the last twenty years I have devoted less and less time to financially remunerative work. Concurrently, the number of hours I spend in other activities has increased so that the combined figure is not very far below that of twenty years ago or the theoretical daily schedule which I outlined earlier. But, even so, the total number of hours each week is much less than it used to be in the days of my greatest professional activity. This is largely because my working day no longer extends beyond nine o'clock in the evening. Night work is a sport for the young and I have had to give it up along with skiing and yachting. And, as sports, I put all three of them on the same high level. The thrill that comes at two o'clock in the morning when a difficult brief is finished or an accord between counsel is reached is as great as that at the bottom of a snow slope or the dropping of anchor at sunset in a strange harbor.

Very few readers will be interested in what a lawyer admitted to the bar in 1911 is doing now, so I will abbreviate my valedictory. I know some lawyers in my age bracket who continue to confine themselves to the same sort of practice in which they have engaged for fifty years and who continue to enjoy it just as as much as ever. My guess is that in the future there will be fewer of them, partly because the custom of early retirement—compulsory or semi-compulsory—will become more prevalent and partly because there is developing not only a strong demand by youth that it be served, but also a preference by clients that they be served by youth. The earlier the age at which a lawyer's practice comes to an end, the longer the period thereafter during which he is going to need broad interests to give him a satisfying life. For my own part, I am convinced that I would not be as happy in this eighth decade of my life if it had not included outside activities and contacts in which there is still a demand for my services and which keep me busy. I believe that the same thing is, or in the future will be, true of most lawyers.

I was asked to tell my story and I have done it. I hope that what I have written will be helpful to some young people. I have been glad to do my best and, as always, that has meant time and sweat—but no blood or tears. I am proud of my profession and anxious that it be understood, and particularly that it be understood by young people who stand on the threshold of their life's work and must choose what it is to be.

16

A Letter to My Son—

ON HIS BEGINNING LAW PRACTICE

BY HERMAN PHLEGER

San Francisco, California

HERMAN PHLEGER

Born: 1890, Sacramento, California

Public Schools, Sacramento
University of California: B.S., 1912
Harvard Law School: 1913–14
Mills College: LL.D., 1935
University of California: LL.D., 1957

Lieutenant, United States Navy: 1917–18

Admitted to California Bar: 1914
Partner: Brobeck, Phleger & Harrison, San Francisco

Legal Adviser Department of State: 1953–57
U. S. Delegation Inter-American Conference, Caracas: 1954
Indo-China and Chinese Conference: 1954
Summit Conference and Foreign Ministers Conference, Geneva: 1955
Suez Conference, London: 1956
Bermuda Conference: 1957
A United States Member Permanent Court of Arbitration Under The Hague
　Treaties
U. S. Representative Thirteenth Session United Nations General Assembly:
　1958
Chairman, U. S. Delegation to Antartic Conference, Washington: 1959
General Advisory Comm. U. S. Arms Control and Disarmament Agency
Associate Director Legal Division Office of Military Government (Ger-
　many): 1945

Director: Wells Fargo Bank
　Union Oil Company
　Fibreboard Products, Inc.
　Moore Dry Dock Company
　Matson Navigation Company
Trustee: Stanford University
　Children's Hospital
　William G. Irwin Charity Foundation
Fellow American Bar Association
American Society International Law
International Law Society

THE LEGAL ADVISER
DEPARTMENT OF STATE
WASHINGTON *

February 14, 1953

Dear Atherton

Congratulations on your admission to the bar! I am sorry I could not be there to witness the swearing-in ceremony. It marks an important milestone in your life—you have completed with success several years of preparation for entry into your chosen profession—now you start your life work.

I know you will find much satisfaction in the practice of the law—it is a calling that will have as its greatest reward the knowledge that you have lived up to the high ideals of the profession. I know you are familiar with the Canons of Ethics of the American Bar Association, but I suggest that you read them again and at least once every year for they furnish a true guide to what is right and what is wrong.

Be courteous, friendly and deferential to the court, but don't be servile. Particularly be friendly and helpful to your fellow lawyers for you will find them to be good friends and generous in their estimate of your ability and character when they are asked, as they frequently will be, about you.

Never underestimate the ability of your opponent or deprecate his motives or ethics. Rarely if ever does a lawyer feel that he is proceeding other than on the highest plane. On the other hand, don't be afraid of your opponent or his case.

Don't underestimate your own case or your own client. If you work hard enough on your case and master it, you will attain a strength and power that will permit you to present it at its best. The court, not you, is the one who determines the ultimate right

* This letter to his son was written by Mr. Phleger about a decade ago, when he was serving as The Legal Adviser in the Department of State. While the letter is dated, the ideas and the beliefs are not.

of your client's cause, and the court, as well as your client, is entitled to have it presented in the best possible way. On the other hand, never let your client persuade you, or permit your enthusiasm to lead you, to present a case other than fairly or honestly. Don't criticize or deprecate your client, but help him secure his just rights.

Don't talk about your clients' affairs to anyone. Don't have conflicting interests, no matter if you believe they will not affect you —for they unconsciously will.

Don't think about your fee, but about how well you must do the work—the fee will take care of itself. Clients' estimates of the worth of their attorney's services are invariably generous if they know how much time and effort has been devoted to their affairs.

Never browbeat a witness or be cruel to a person who has made a mistake. Be firm, but fair—resourceful, but not "smart"—responsible and reliable, rather than brilliant.

I envy you all the fun and joy you have before you. Make each day count, so that when you are through you can look back on a lifetime of service to others—well and faithfully performed. Good Luck to you!